Designing Powerful Training

Designing Powerful Training

The Sequential-Iterative Model

Michael Milano

with

Diane Ullius

Illustrations by

Ed Trenn

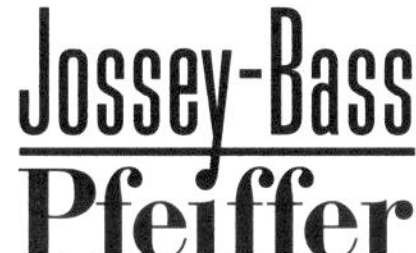

San Francisco

ISBN: 0-7879-0966-1
Library of Congress Catalog Card Number 97-49624

Library of Congress Cataloging-in-Publication Data
Milano, Michael
Designing powerful training : the sequential-iterative model / Michael Milano with Diane Ullius
p. cm.
Includes bibliographical references (p. 331) and index.
ISBN 0-7879-0966-1
1. Instructional systems–Design. 2. Training. 3. Adult learning. I. Ullius, Diane. II. Title
LB1028.38.M55 1998
371.3–dc21 97-49624

Printed in the United States of America

Published by

JOSSEY-BASS/PFEIFFER
A Wiley Company
350 Sansome St.
San Francisco, CA 94104-1342
415.433.1740; Fax 415.433.0499
800.274.4434; Fax 800.569.0443

www.pfeiffer.com

Acquiring Editor: Larry Alexander
Director of Development: Kathleen Dolan Davies
Developmental Editor: Susan Rachmeler
Senior Production Editor: Dawn Kilgore
Interior Design: Joseph Piliero
Cover Design: Richard Adelson

Printing 10 9 8 7 6 5

This book is printed on acid-free, recycled stock that meets or exceeds the minimum GPO and EPA requirements for recycled paper.

Contents

Preface

Welcome to *Designing Powerful Training: The Sequential-Iterative Model,* a step-by-step guide to help you design training programs for adult learners. This book will answer the question "What do I do to go from identified training needs to a completed design for a training event?" As you use this book, you will find yourself engaged in a process that is both systematic and fluid, both creative and disciplined. Whether you are a beginner or an experienced practitioner, a subject-matter expert or a training specialist with a wide range of general knowledge, you will find that *Designing Powerful Training* answers the questions you face in the real world. If you are a classroom trainer, *Designing Powerful Training* will give you a framework for assessing and tailoring any existing training program. If you are a manager of designers, this book will provide the five key components against which you can measure the effectiveness of the training design processes you oversee: goals and objectives, key topics, training flow, training materials, and evaluation tools.

WHAT THIS BOOK IS

Designing Powerful Training is a tool to help you design training events that are

- *Effective:* Accomplish specific objectives, which are relevant to participants' success.
- *Efficient:* Meet the objectives without wasting time or energy.
- *Engaging:* Attract and involve learners and incorporate their experience into the training.

Moreover, *Designing Powerful Training* will teach you how to design training that meets the varied needs of adult learners; that supports an organization's strategic imperative for the training department to be a partner in the business; and that smoothly involves the other people who may collaborate in the design and delivery of training. Beyond all that, *Designing Powerful Training* will teach you to use a design process that builds upon your own strengths and helps you to balance your limitations, so that all of your training designs will be better and more complete.

The Sequential-Iterative Model

Designing Powerful Training accomplishes these objectives by means of a method that we call the SIM (rhymes with Kim)—the Sequential-Iterative Model for Training Design. Yes, the words are a mouthful, but they express exactly what is vital about the design process.

Design is *sequential:* after you and the organization have determined that what you are facing is a training need (and not a need that would be better addressed through some other intervention), you follow a logical, step-by-step sequence. But design, as its name implies, is not purely logical or sequential; it is also creative, artistic, and fluid. The SIM recognizes that fact by building in an *iterative* process: with the SIM, you will be guided to go back at certain stages and reconsider the work of earlier stages—and not to feel bad about doing so, because the iteration is an integral part of the process.

This book reflects our experience designing trainer-facilitated learning events. Over the years, our workshop participants have demonstrated through their work that the SIM is effective with a variety of training delivery platforms. We believe that it will work well for you, regardless of the platforms for which your training is designed.

Where It Came From

The SIM—and, in truth, this whole book—came out of years of designing training, teaching workshops on training design, and coaching designers. Clients and participants regularly asked for a design process that they could use back on the job—a process that they could apply to any subject matter, to any length of session. That is what this is. Workshops called "STAR Designer," developed by Murphy & Milano, Inc., and taught all over the United States, are where the SIM grew up. The version of the SIM that you will encounter in this book is one that has been tested and refined through eight years of teaching design in the Training Specialist Certificate Program at Georgetown University—plus many more years of teaching design and coaching designers in a variety of large and small organizations, including the Library of Congress and MCI Telecommunications. Participants in "The STAR Designer" workshops, in fact, have provided many of the real-life examples that you will find sprinkled through the book.

WHAT IT IS NOT

Although *Designing Powerful Training* firmly situates training design in the overall context of the training process, it maintains a tight focus on design itself. The book does not attempt to provide a detailed guide on conducting a full-scale needs assessment, nor does it address every aspect of preparing evaluation tools. This is not primarily a book about integrating the training function into the organizational structure or about building and reinforcing the support of line managers. It is not a book about marketing training or about building presentation skills. This is a book about *design*.

HOW TO USE THIS BOOK

Designing Powerful Training is divided into two parts. The first, "The Foundations of Powerful Training," lays the groundwork for designing training. In this part you will find our assessment of what makes for powerful training (Chapter One); an overview of the SIM and how it relates to powerful training (Chapter Two); principles of adult learning (Chapter Three); the many roles of the training designer (Chapter Four); and how needs assessment relates to the training process overall and to training design in particular (Chapter Five).

The second part, "Using the SIM," is focused on applying the Sequential-Iterative Model. You will move through the stages of the design process with the SIM (Chapters Six through Eleven). Each chapter gives some background on the topic, then lays out that stage of the SIM, step by step; at the end of each chapter you will find a question-and-answer section. In Chapter Twelve, you will read about how to create the kind of introductory activities, transitions, and summaries that, used in conjunction with the SIM, can really make your training designs shine.

The Running Example

Starting with Chapter Five ("Needs Assessment") and continuing throughout the chapters on using the SIM, each chapter is followed by a segment of the Running Example—an extended case study about a fictitious company. The Running Example uses and illustrates every single step of the SIM design process. Depending on your own learning style, you may choose to read each chapter all the way through and then turn to the Running Example, or you may prefer to consult the Running Example as you read about each individual step of the SIM. Perhaps you will even refer to the Running Example only for the steps or stages of the SIM that may be new to you. The choice is yours.

Meeting Your Needs

Designing Powerful Training will be useful to you regardless of your role in training design. Depending on your own situation, of course, you may find some sections especially applicable.

If you are new to designing training events, you will probably want to read the first part of the book, "The Foundations of Powerful Training," very carefully. It will give you the background you will need for the second part, "Using the SIM." Once you get there, you can follow the SIM step-by-step, using the many examples to help you along the way. You may find the Running Example especially useful to illustrate the SIM design process. We urge you to follow the SIM rigorously the first several times you use it in designing training. After the model is ingrained, you can safely begin to tailor it for your personal use, considering the specific needs of your organization and assessing honestly the steps that come naturally to you and the ones that do not.

If you are an experienced designer, you may want to skim the first part of the book—although probably you will be intrigued with Chapter Four's presentation of the balancing acts that you perform every day in your design role and Chapter Five's discussion of converting needs assessment data into design requirements. Then work your way through the SIM in the second part. Consider how it is similar to or different from other design approaches you may have been using, and give it a chance to work for you. Using the SIM will help you design more powerful training by helping you to systematize the process and to identify your own personal strengths and trouble spots.

If you are a manager of training designers, you can consider the five stages of the SIM as "deliverables" that will help you to guide and monitor the design process. The first section of the book will provide a context-rich overview of the principles that undergird solid training, which will help you to mentor designers and evaluate their work.

Whatever your role in the world of preparing training events for adult learners, *Designing Powerful Training* will help you perform excellently. Are you ready?

ACKNOWLEDGMENTS

We want to thank the special people who helped us to create this book. We have received encouragement, suggestions, support, and good wishes from innumerable friends and colleagues. Chief among them are, of course, the members of the stellar team at Murphy & Milano, Inc.—Lisa Sottosanti Doyle, Sheryl Kelm, Fiona Kydd, Peter Murphy, Barry Strong, and Nancy Maloney Williams—who have offered essential advice, multiple consultations to clarify points in the book, and lots of love and good humor.

In a category by herself is Barbara Daly, who introduced us to each other and who taught the SIM in its early stages and helped us to refine it.

Rhonda Buckner has cheerfully provided selfless service throughout the process, supporting us each step of the way. Mama Milano has regularly asked, "Now what is this book about?"—a question that has been invaluable in helping us maintain focus. Ed Trenn has shared his wonderful artistic talents to create most of the illustrations in this book, and the star designer character has won a place in all of our hearts. Mimi Banta was our first reader, back when there were just a few chapters of the book; her advice helped us to establish a style and format that we hope will work for readers. Elaine English, our attorney and friend, has offered her practical and supportive counsel throughout this process. Lynn Page Whittaker, Carolyn Mulford, and other colleagues in the Women's National Book Association guided us to Elaine and helped us define our collaboration. Beverly and Mark Griffin graciously offered their lakeside retreat as a writer's haven. At Jossey-Bass/Pfeiffer, we are indebted to Josh Blatter, Kathleen Dolan Davies, Dave Horne, Susan Rachmeler, and Rebecca Taff for their perspective, suggestions, and sage advice.

We are especially grateful to our colleagues in Georgetown University's Professional Development Programs—particularly Frank Ball, Bill Doherty, Bonnie Kramer, Jack Levy, Peg Long, Geri McArdle, Karan Powell, Bonnie Tyler, Chris Wahl, and Ann Williams—who have worked with us over the years, shared their questions and wisdom about design, and encouraged us to "write the book." At Georgetown and elsewhere, our participants in "The STAR Designer" workshops have asked questions to help us clarify, shared practical applications for our design process, and given us many metaphors and images to bring life to the process. In addition, we want to thank the many clients who have formed partnerships with us to design training that would meet their organizations' needs. Their feedback and their use of the SIM have helped us further refine our design process.

And of course we want to thank each other. Writing a book brings to the surface every skill, limitation, quirk, and frustration that lodges within a person. We have worked diligently to perfect one another's work and produce a book that will engage a variety of readers. Throughout the process we have rejoiced in the one constant—that working together has been a delight, both personally and professionally. We are a good team. We thank each other for listening, for negotiating, for putting forth from our hearts and souls, and then for letting go of what we have each created to see what can and did come from the collaboration.

April 1998

Michael Milano
Alexandria, Virginia

Diane Ullius
Arlington, Virginia

Part One

The Foundations of Powerful Training

1 Powerful Training

When you walk into a training session, you can tell right away if things are going well. The room is filled with energy. Visual cues to the key learnings are posted: charts, models, drawings. People are really listening to one another. Differing opinions are being shared and valued. There is a true sense of dialogue and shared experience. Eduard C. Lindeman, in his 1926 classic, *The Meaning of Adult Education*, states: "In an adult class the student's experience counts for as much as the teacher's knowledge. Both are exchangeable at par. Indeed, in some of the best adult classes it is sometimes difficult to discover who is learning most, the teacher or the students" (quoted in Knowles, 1990, p. 31).

One of our friends talks about things "humming." Of course, the humming is due largely to the facilitation skills of the trainer: the way she greets participants, asks them questions, responds to their questions, listens to their judgments, fears, and concerns, and treats them with respect.

However, design also plays a critical role in powerful training. No matter how skilled the trainer, without a strong design she will have a hard time creating a learning environment that hums.

THE THREE E'S

If you asked us what makes training powerful, we would say: "Powerful training is effective, efficient, and engaging."

Effective

Training is effective if it accomplishes its objectives *and* if those objectives are relevant to the participants' needs. Effective training provides a foundation that enables participants to perform the behaviors described in the objectives for the training, which in turn should relate directly to desired performance on the job or in life.

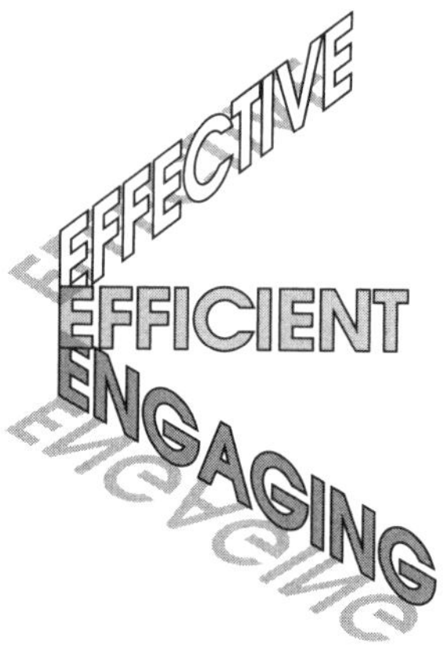

Efficient

Efficient training makes good use of participants' time and energies, maximizing the relationship between training time on the one hand and comprehension and retention on the other. The content and learning activities make the best use of time by directly supporting the learning objectives. The content and activities are as straightforward and uncomplicated as possible, so that the learners' energy is not drained unnecessarily.

Engaging

Engaging training grabs the learners and brings them directly into the learning process. The training supports them in interacting with the trainer, with one another, and with the content. It draws forth the wealth of related experience about the topic and about learning that the participants bring to the learning experience, and it uses this experience to help them acquire, analyze, and evaluate new learning.

THE THREE E'S OF POWERFUL TRAINING

- *Effective:* Accomplishes specific objectives relevant to participants' success.
- *Efficient:* Meets those objectives without wasting time or energy.
- *Engaging:* Attracts and involves learners and incorporates their experiences into the learning.

EDUCATION VERSUS TRAINING

Notice that we focus first on effectiveness—specific performance outcomes. Really understanding this focus involves understanding some of the differences between education and training. The words are often used interchangeably and, in practice, education and training are bound so closely that they often overlap. However, there are conceptual and practical differences that are significant for the training designer.

One way to look at the differences is to view education as a process of building a knowledge base and the skills for further developing that knowledge base; education often focuses on conceptual or historical knowledge. Training, in contrast, focuses more on building the specific areas of knowledge, skills, or attitudes that directly influence a person's ability to perform a job, execute a task, or solve a problem. Education focuses on *learning about;* training focuses on *learning how.* The aim of training is new or enhanced skills. The content provides essential knowledge so that participants are able to perform specific tasks.

Education about taxes, for example, might include legal seminars, workshops in the history of taxation, or discussions about taxation systems in other cultures. Training about taxes would be more likely to focus on skills—how to plan for taxes, how to calculate taxes, how to complete the appropriate tax forms. Compared with education, training is generally more immediate, skills-oriented, and focused on application.

DESIGN GUIDELINES

On the basis of our experience with designing training and with training and coaching designers, we have come to believe that—regardless of the content of the training—there are certain guidelines to be followed in order to produce training that is effective, efficient, and engaging. We have detailed these guidelines on the following pages. They form the basis of all the practices and tools in the rest of this book.

DESIGN GUIDELINES

To create powerful training, designers need to follow these guidelines. Powerful training

- Is driven by objectives.
- Focuses on application.
- Fits the characteristics of the adult learner.
- Balances the diverse realities of multiple learners.
- Places minimum reliance on the lecture-process approach.
- Avoids having to correct for the "right" response.
- Includes appropriate evaluation points.

Objective-Driven

In a powerful training design, the relationship between the training objectives and the application of those objectives is clear and explicit. It is equally clear that the training itself will provide the framework for successfully meeting the training objectives. For example, if the training objective is "by the end of the training, participants will be able to demonstrate their ability to service an ATM machine," the relevance of the skill should be obvious to everyone concerned, and it should be equally obvious that the content and learning activities in the training do provide a framework for servicing an ATM.

Powerful training, then, springs from performance-based objectives, which form the basis of the contract between the designer and/or trainer and the client and the contract between the trainer and the learners. They are the outcomes against which all decisions about design and presentation are evaluated.

Application-Focused

To arrive at objectives that can drive powerful training, the designer begins by focusing on application rather than on content or knowledge for its own sake. This focus highlights another subtle difference between educational design and training design. Educational design generally begins with the content itself: "What do we know about X?" and "How do we teach it?" Training design, in contrast, begins by focusing on application: "What is the desired performance?" and "In order to achieve that performance, what does a person need to know and be able to do?" Out of these questions can come objectives that are tied to successful performance.

In training design, we usually find answers to these questions through needs assessment. Our aim is to determine the gap between what people are currently able to do and what they need to be able to do—the desired performance. Through a close connection with a realistic needs assessment, efficient training maintains its tight focus on application. (For more on needs assessment, see Chapter Five.)

Fits the Adult Learner

Powerful training addresses the characteristics of adult learners. After all, participants are the immediate clients for any training design. If the design does not fit their needs, how can it enable them to meet objectives? Powerful training design capitalizes on the characteristics of the adult learner, and it meets the needs of a variety of learning styles and preferences. (See Chapter Three for an overview of the principles of adult learning and learning styles.)

Balances Diverse Realities

Powerful training designs engage participants by walking a fine line between responding to the common needs of the particular group and embracing the diversity of those present. The design must engage the learners by addressing what the group has in common (for example, they all are supervisors or managers who must write and deliver performance appraisals), while also bringing in the richness of the perspectives in the group. It must take into account the differences of personal experience related to such factors as gender, race, ethnicity, religious background, age, physical and mental abilities, language proficiency, sexual orientation, marital status, social and economic background, and career history.

Minimizes Lecture-Process Approach

An unwritten Lecture-Process Law seems to pervade most training designs. It says, "Training people is easy. First you give them information, then you plan an activity during which they process what you've told them." In most training designs, the application of this law takes the form of a lecture followed by some activity in which participants analyze or apply the information in the lecture.

It is not always a bad model for design, but it's not usually engaging or efficient. It is overused and has some serious limitations in terms of comprehension and retention. This model is pervasive for many reasons—some of them good ones. When participants know very little about a subject, they may need information to enable them to perform a skill; for example, if a new policy is being introduced in an organization, people need to know the content of the policy before they can consider its application.

However, the major reason this design model is so common is precisely that it is so common. In other words, we have all been exposed to it so many times that it is a norm most designers fail to question. We invite you to question it. In truth, adults do not always have to be told about something before they can learn about it; often, they can discover what they already know *before* they receive new information. A powerful training design includes a variety of approaches to learning. Activities can be used to create a need to know as well as to assess what learners already know; activities can help participants to gain and share information in ways other than being told.

Avoids Correcting for "Right" Responses

In too many training sessions, an individual or a small group reports out to the large group, only to be corrected by the trainer so that all participants have the "right" response. How engaging is that? How well does it honor the needs and experience of adult learners? If the trainer is good, of course, she is working hard to balance the self-esteem of the small group or the individual with the responsibility for conveying accurate information. Sometimes this situation is unavoidable, and skilled trainers can handle it with grace. Yet there are many steps the designer can take to minimize its likelihood. Powerful design decreases the possibility that the trainer will have to intervene with the "right" responses.

Includes Evaluation Points

Another common approach to design involves putting all the evaluation at the end of the training—whether that evaluation focuses on participants' demonstration of skills and competencies or on their satisfaction with the training event. In either case, it's too late by then. If the trainer and the participants find out at the end of the training that participants cannot perform the behaviors described in the objectives, it's too late to do anything about it. Also, if the trainer discovers just minutes before the end of the training (or, worse, afterward) that participants are dissatisfied, she has lost the chance to make adjustments.

Adult learning is a two-way process—a reality that is, in Lindeman's words, "reflected by shared authority" (quoted in Knowles, 1990, p. 31). Sharing authority means enabling both the trainer and the participants to evaluate success and make adjustments in the learning, while it is happening, in order to achieve success.

Powerful designs offer tools that let the trainer and the participants measure success *during* the training event. They include activities that allow the learners to test their progress toward the stated objectives and to provide feedback for the instructor and the learner in ways that help both parties determine where to focus for further development. Of course, sometimes it is impossible to demonstrate the final competency described in the objectives until very close to the end of the training. But even in such cases, the designer can take responsibility, identifying and describing the enabling skills and knowledge that will be required to perform the final competency, and then designing activities and tools with which participants can evaluate their mastery of these enablers on the way to performing the desired behavior described in the objectives.

DON'T FORGET FUN

Unfortunately, many adults have come to expect that learning has to involve pain—from unnecessarily hard work, embarrassment at not knowing the correct answer, fear of being humiliated, or anxiety over doing things right. This expectation is so pervasive that people often are astonished when they are learning *and* having a good time.

In the most powerful training, enjoyment of learning becomes the norm. The "no pain, no gain" theory does not apply to training. Granted, there are topics that just are not fun; but design that is effective, efficient, and engaging will make the act of learning fun—or at least as painless as possible—whatever the topic.

During one of our workshops for training designers, a participant described his long educational experience and how it had taught him to avoid thinking creatively. He had clearly heard the message that he was expected to deliver the "right answer," which was determined by the instructor. Realizing that the task of training design requires creativity, he had approached our workshop with fear and anxiety. By the second day, however, he reported that the workshop was making it possible for him to believe that he could design.

How did it happen? First, we had made an explicit contract in that workshop to "play" with ideas, to create a lab in which errors and mistakes were valued, even desired, as integral parts of the learning and in which the challenge was to try new things. This environment was enhanced by some fun activities; by crazy hats available whenever someone felt a need for a boost in creativity, energy, or enjoyment; by magic wands to assist in the process of designing creative training activities; by music; and more. The playfulness and fun that we had purposefully built into the design worked for this participant. He came expecting to suffer and to find out that he could not access the creativity needed to be a designer. He left saying that it still wasn't going to be easy for him to design, but that he felt confident he could use the tools in the workshop to help him. Mostly, through his participation in the workshop, he felt encouraged that he could rediscover his own internal creativity.

The playfulness of the workshop was no accident: it was a requirement of the design. We realize that the workshop's content and skills are demanding and intense, that they evoke fear in some people. From years of experience, we also realize that unless we can help people to relax, they will have a very hard time with the kinds of brainstorming and creativity it takes to develop good training designs. The fun built into that workshop is there to enable the learning.

ASSESSING TRAINING DESIGNS

In this book, you will learn to use the Sequential-Iterative Model for Training Design (the SIM—rhymes with Kim). With the SIM, you will be able to design training that is effective, efficient, and engaging. You will also be able to use the SIM to review an existing design for any kind of training. As a designer, you know that you cannot just wait until the day of the learning event to see whether the training is powerful. You must be able to assess a design quickly. The elements to look for in such an assessment are the same as the five key elements of the SIM. Here they are, in checklist form:

Goals and Objectives

______ Do the training goals and objectives clearly relate the training to the desired performance back on the job or in participants' lives?
______ Are the objectives realistic, and do they avoid making grandiose, unmeetable promises?

Key Topics

______ Does all of the content support the objectives?
______ Is it comprehensive enough without going into unnecessary detail?
______ Is it accurate and up-to-date?
______ Is the level of the content appropriate for the learners?

Training Flow

______ Is there sufficient variety in learning activities and training methods?
______ Do the methods included in the design support the training goals and objectives?
______ Does the sequence seem reasonable—with most elements leading clearly to the ones that follow?
______ Does the design provide options where appropriate?
______ Are a variety of learning styles engaged and satisfied by the combination of methods?
______ Are the time estimates reasonable?

Materials

______ Do the participant materials support the objectives?
______ Are they appropriate for the intended learners and easy to use?
______ Is there enough detail in the trainer's materials to enable a trainer to manage the learning activities so that the objectives can be met?
______ Is there a stated purpose for each learning activity?
______ Do the audiovisual materials fit the objectives and the learners?
______ Are they realistic for the conditions under which the training will be delivered?

Evaluation Tools

______ Are there opportunities during the training for participants and instructors to assess progress toward objectives?
______ Are there tools that measure the behavioral outcomes of the training?

A FEW LAST WORDS

So what is it that makes training powerful? At its best, training is transformational. It makes a difference in individuals' performance and in the success of organizations. Powerful training does not just present information; it helps people use that information to make their lives better. It gives participants a chance to examine and practice and interact. It builds on what participants already know, and it uses the experience and strengths of the group rather than depending solely on the knowledge and energy of the trainer. Powerful training, as we have said, is effective, efficient, and engaging.

Science and Art

Creating training is a big responsibility and a marvelous opportunity, part science and part art. There's a kind of alchemy involved, but it's not magic and it's not a secret. As you learn to use the SIM, you will become more and more able to design training that makes the most of your strengths and those of your participants. Your training will hum. It will be training that makes participants walk out of the room saying, "Hey, that was really powerful!"

Designing powerful training with the SIM is what this book is all about. Now that you have read about powerful training, you are ready to be introduced to the SIM.

2 An Overview of the SIM

The SIM is the Sequential-Iterative Model for Training Design, a process that will help you—no matter what your area of expertise, regardless of how much or little you have done this work—to design powerful training events for adult learners.

The *Sequential-Iterative Model?* Admittedly it's a mouthful, but the words are potent. The SIM process is *sequential:* it lays out a sequence of stages in a certain order. However, design is much more than just moving from one stage to another. It is an exciting and messy process. Therefore, the SIM is also *iterative;* no matter how well you design, you will continually be moving back and forth among the design stages.

The SIM's five stages will help you progress from identified training needs to a training event. The SIM (rhymes with Kim) comes into play only after the needs assessment is complete, and it ends before the trainer steps into the classroom; thus the SIM does not teach you how to conduct a needs assessment, nor does it directly address after-the-event evaluation. The SIM is all about design. Using the SIM, you will be able to design powerful learning events that are effective, efficient, and engaging.

Although it is a design process that incorporates specific stages, the SIM is not just a how-to. Because good training design is part science and part art, the SIM actively encourages creativity. The stages in the process are there to support you; as you use the SIM, you will find yourself moving back and forth between your intuitive, conceptual mode and your structured, pragmatic mode. The balance is necessary, and it is purposely built into the SIM. If, on the one hand, a design process emphasizes structure over fluidity, the training is dry and predictable. Fluidity without structure, on the other hand, yields little more than entertainment. To design great training, you need structure and fluidity, analysis and intuition, science and art. That is what the SIM is about.

Another critical component of the SIM is client involvement and feedback at every stage. Granted, there are occasions when the designer works pretty much alone, but they are the exception rather than the rule. The SIM encourages as much client participation as possible. It requires that the products of each stage receive feedback from the client—and perhaps from potential trainees. No one has time to waste—especially designers who are asked to produce good training designs on short notice. Whether you are an internal designer or an external consultant, there is a cost associated with your work. You are wasting time and money if you develop training materials or plan training methods before your client has agreed to the objectives or ratified your choice of topics. With the stages of the SIM, you will be reminded of the many opportunities to involve your client.

However, even when there is no direct client or when a full-scale needs assessment is impossible—for example, when you are designing an open-enrollment workshop—the SIM will help you.

THE SIM: WHY DESIGN THIS WAY?

On the first morning of our design workshop, "The STAR Designer," before we begin teaching the SIM, we ask people to describe the process they have been using for design. They say that they conduct a needs assessment to clarify the training needs and then define objectives. That sounds great. Around the afternoon of the second day, however, when everyone has become comfortable, invariably the truth is revealed: most people acknowledge that they often conduct their content research first, then think about how to teach the content. That process gives them an outline, and after they like the outline, they define objectives for the training. Many designers know that there must be a better way to design but admit to falling into this routine because they are always under time pressure and because they have yet to find another approach that is efficient and reliable. That is where the SIM comes in.

The SIM will give you a structured approach to designing training in five stages. If you follow rigorously the steps described in each stage, you will get what you need so that you can move on to the next stage in the sequence.

Remember, however, that the SIM is iterative. It is not about doing the stage "right" the first time. Do not assume that if you do a great job on one stage of the design process, you are finished with that stage. On the contrary, doing design right always involves going back, because each stage of design helps you become more clear about where you are going. For example, often there is no way to know for sure if your proposed objectives are realistic until you flesh out your design enough to see how long the learning activities will really take. Similarly, when designing a participant worksheet, you might have a powerful insight into a way to refine a method you had previously selected; so you will go back and make the change.

Even if you do design "right" the first time, it is still a messy process, and that fact is very difficult for people who like closure and neatness throughout the process. If "messy" is a difficult concept for you, try thinking of design as "fluid"—continually moving back and forth between stages. That is what we mean when we say that the design process is iterative.

ONE DESIGNER'S CONFESSION

In my early years as a designer, I thought first about the content I was going to teach, then how I would teach it (methods), then materials, and finally objectives. In a way it was a sure-fire system: The objectives always matched the training, because they came last.

I don't think my early design was bad, but it was lacking in three critical areas:

- The design was more aligned with the subject matter than with the specific needs of the participants or the organization.
- My outline reflected my own learning style but did not necessarily address the diverse styles of adult learners.
- The process was inefficient because it did not give me clear criteria on which to select content and methods.

If I'd had the SIM at the beginning of my career, I would have saved time. More important, my good designs could have been great designs.

THE STAGES OF THE SIM

In Part Two of this book, "Using the SIM," you will learn why and how to implement the stages of the Sequential-Iterative Model for Training Design, and you will find out what you will have at the completion of each stage—your "product." Each chapter also includes a question-and-answer section that addresses the real-life challenges that training designers face every day. Finally, after each chapter you will find a segment of the Running Example—an extended case study that illustrates all the stages and steps of the SIM.

The SIM includes five key design stages. Each one provides a foundation for those that follow.

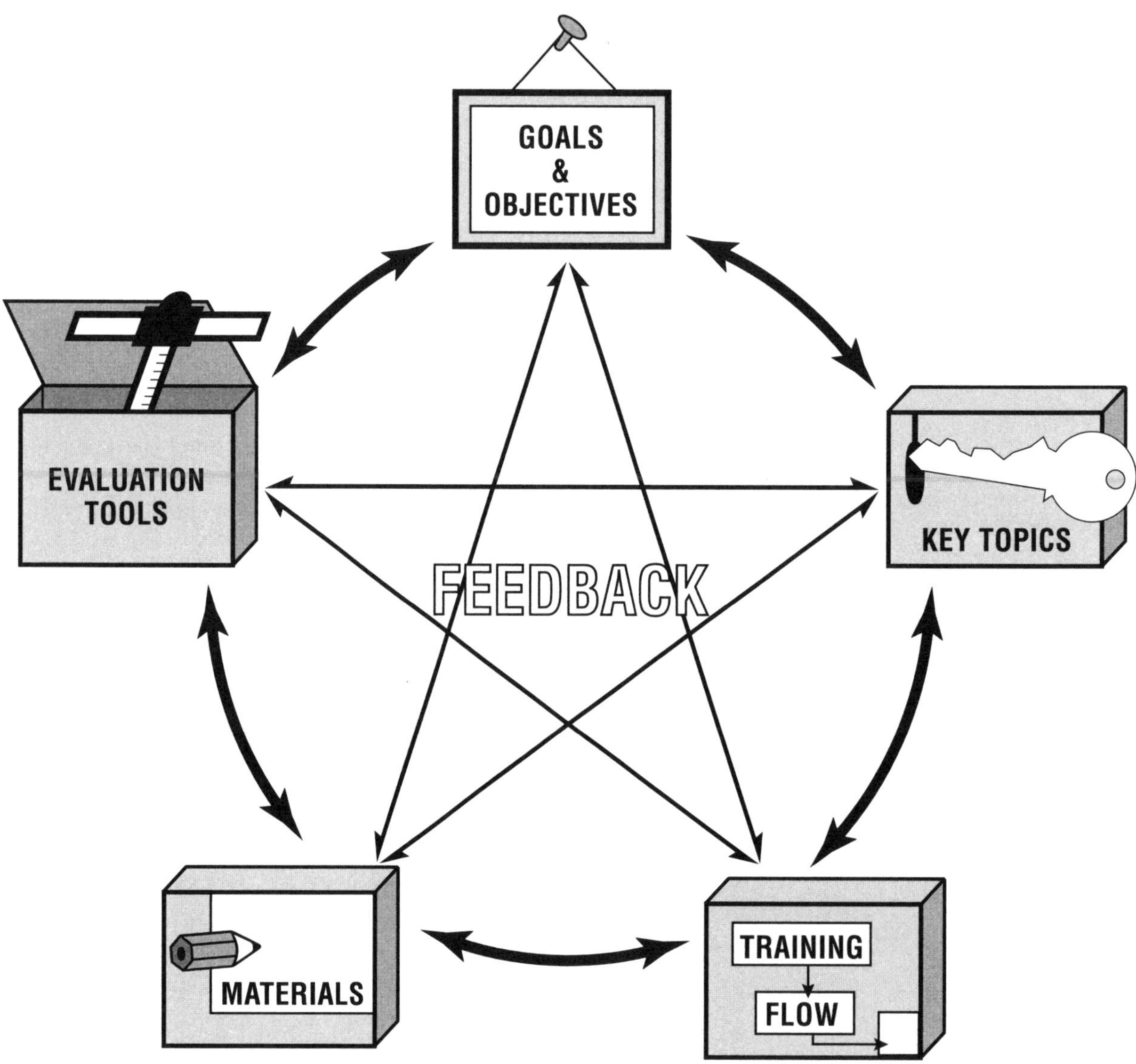

The Sequential-Iterative Model for Training Design

Training Goals and Objectives

This is the first stage of training design. It relies, of course, on the needs assessment (see Chapter Five). Before you can write goals and objectives, you use a needs assessment to gain as much clarity as possible on six key factors:

- Training needs and desired performance—what must participants be able to do?
- Participant analysis—who are they, and what do they know?
- Context for learning—how does this training fit into the bigger picture of the participants' environment?
- Subject-matter expertise and resources—what role are you equipped to play in the design process?
- Skill level of trainers—what are their competencies with respect both to content and to process?
- Logistical requirements—what factors will constrain or support the training?

In the Goals and Objectives stage, you will be assessing the desired behaviors and skills to determine which ones are essential and must be articulated in the objectives. You do not want to overload your design with objectives relating to skills that really are not essential.

The point of the Goals and Objectives stage is to describe both the outcomes for the training and the criteria that you and your clients will use to evaluate the effectiveness of the training. When you have completed this stage, you will have defined a goal and a set of clear, behavioral objectives that will guide the next stages of the design process.

Key Topics

In this second stage, you focus on identifying what content the learner must understand in order to perform the desired behaviors successfully. When you have completed this stage, your product will be a list of the content to be taught in the training, grouped into categories that will help you continue the design process.

At the Key Topics stage, you will often be involved in content research, particularly if you are not a subject-matter expert. As a part of this stage, you will now be sorting through all the possible content to decide what is essential and what is merely nice to know—perhaps with the help of a subject-matter expert. It is a challenge to focus on what is essential, particularly if the designer is a subject-matter expert, to whom everything may seem essential.

It is also important at this stage to resist creating an outline. Many of us learned long ago to arrange information in outline form, and we may be tempted to carry this skill into design. Outlining at this stage is premature. An outline would define a sequence for training delivery that might not be the best way to engage adults in learning the content—especially those who have learning styles different from your own.

During this stage, however, you will consider some *possible* organizational structures for the training. As you define the essential content, you will be looking at it in relation to your learners and to the objectives for the training. You will begin to play tentatively with the question, What sequence might work?

In the Goals and Objectives stage, you defined what you want participants to be able to do by the end of the training. In the Key Topics stage, you have selected the required content for the training. Voila! You now know what you have to cover so that participants will be able to perform the desired behaviors that are the focus of the training.

Training Flow

What you address next is how the content will be taught—what the methods of training will be. This is the third stage of the SIM, the Training Flow stage. Here you select and sequence learning activities that will respect the integrity of the content and will draw the learners toward the desired outcomes. In other words, during this stage of the SIM you will be searching for methods and a sequence that will make your training design effective, efficient, and engaging.

Unfortunately, many designers begin their design work with methods and sequence, wasting precious time as a result. Here is what happens: they have some very creative ideas about how they might teach something. Perhaps they went through some innovative training; they loved one of the methods or activities, and they want to use it. Yet, unless this engaging activity relates to actual application in the workplace, it will not be an effective or efficient way to position participants for the desired behaviors. Starting with methods and sequence is a potential waste of time—both for the designer and for the participants. With the SIM, you address methods and sequence only after the goals, objectives, and key topics have been addressed.

The SIM guides you to approach this stage of design at two levels. First, you produce a *macro*design—a training outline that includes the proposed sequence of learning activities with associated key content. After you are satisfied that your macrodesign meets your goals and objectives, that it addresses your key topics, and that it meets the needs of adult learners, then you design at a much more detailed level—the *micro*design. The level of detail in the microdesign will vary according to your needs and the skills of the trainers. In any case it will be detailed enough for you to make accurate time estimates and to visualize the flow of the training from moment to moment.

When you have completed the Training Flow stage, your products will be the macrodesign and the microdesign.

Training Materials

In the fourth stage, you will focus on materials—generally, trainer's materials, participant materials, and learning aids (audiovisual materials). When you have completed the Training Materials stage, you will have these materials as your products.

The SIM process for this stage begins with defining requirements for each category of materials. The requirements will depend on two factors: your client's needs and resources and the key characteristics of your learners. For example, if you are designing materials for a group of participants with, say, a sixth-grade reading level, your participant materials and learning aids might use fewer and simpler words than if your audience reads at a higher level. In another situation, you might be designing resources for trainers who are subject-matter experts. Then you would include only brief content notes, but the notes on process would probably be extensive.

After you and your client have agreed on the requirements, you will review your microdesign to identify where you need participant materials and learning aids. You then prepare these materials to meet the requirements. You will also finalize the trainer's materials, which grow directly from your microdesign. At this point, you have all the materials required for the training.

Evaluation Tools

In this, the last stage of the SIM, your products will be a final evaluation strategy and the tools to be used for evaluating the training. You will, of course, start thinking about evaluation and discussing it with your client at the beginning of your design work. Early on, when you are clarifying desired performance and training objectives, the question of how to measure success will be one of your main considerations.

To many people, the words "evaluation tools" mean the forms that participants often fill out at the end of a training session. That is not the only possible time to evaluate; evaluation data may be gathered before the event (to establish a baseline), during the event, or some time after the event. Taken from another point of view, the evaluation of training can address one or more of four outcomes—the classic four levels described by Donald

Kirkpatrick (1994): "Reaction" (Did they like it?); "Learning" (Did they get it?); "Behavior" (Do they apply it back on the job?); and "Results" (Does it really make a difference?).

Some design strategies would have you design your evaluation tools immediately after you define the training objectives. There is a strong rationale for this approach: the tools will measure exactly what the training is supposed to accomplish—that is, how well the objectives were met. We recommend, however, that you wait until you have completed the other design stages before finalizing your evaluation tools, for two reasons: (1) at each stage of the SIM, the objectives are among the key criteria upon which you assess your product (if you follow the SIM, you cannot possibly lose sight of evaluating against objectives); and (2) the SIM helps you to design or select training methods that are effective and efficient, and often the methods themselves will provide feedback to the trainer and the participants on progress toward the objectives (if there is enough good evaluation during the training, you may not need to do more at the end).

Evaluation is a fairly complex process. In many situations, training designers are responsible primarily for evaluation at the levels of reaction and learning, and evaluation specialists take responsibility for the levels of behavior and results. Therefore, the Evaluation Tools stage of the SIM focuses on helping designers develop evaluation strategies and tools to be used before, during, and immediately after training events. It makes good sense, then, to finalize your evaluation strategy and the tools related to these two levels of evaluation only at the end stages of the design process.

By the end of the Evaluation Tools stage of the SIM, you will have a design that includes goals and objectives, the key content, a training flow, training materials, and a strategy for evaluating the success of the training event. You will be able to say, "My design is complete and ready to be tried out."

A FEW LAST WORDS

The SIM itself is a process for designing training, but designing powerful training takes more than a process. It takes self-knowledge and commitment, and it requires a sound understanding of the foundations. Before going into detail on how to use the SIM, let's look carefully at the foundations: meeting the needs of your participants as adult learners (Chapter Three); examining the critical elements of the designer's role (Chapter Four); and clarifying the relationships between organizational needs and the design process (Chapter Five).

3 The Adult Learner

"To children, experience is something that happens to them; to adults, their experience is *who they are.* . . . The implication of this for adult education is that in any situation in which adults' experience is ignored or devalued, they perceive this as not rejecting just their experience, but rejecting them as persons."[1]

Malcolm S. Knowles

Knowles expresses the essence of adult learners: their experience is who they are. Keep this truth in your mind, your heart, and your soul as you design. What is essential to designing training for adults is to engage the experience of the learners as a resource for understanding, as the criteria by which they analyze and evaluate what is presented, and as the core of who the learners are. The experience and the learning are intimately interconnected. In fact, David A. Kolb, in *Experiential Learning,* defines learning as "the process whereby knowledge is created through the transformation of experience" (1984, p. 38). If learning creates knowledge, it also continually re-creates the learner.

This chapter provides background and a framework on the relationships between adult learning and the design of training. As a designer of training, you are well aware that one of your key client groups is your participants. Of course, each group of learners brings specialized needs, abilities, and preferences. (See Chapter Five for more information on the importance of assessing the characteristics of each particular group.) However, the general characteristics of adult learners must undergird the work of training designers who hope to create learning events that are effective, efficient, and engaging.

This chapter addresses six principles that flow from those general characteristics—and one of them, the fact that adults learn in a variety of ways, in considerable detail—as well as the implications for designers of training.

[1]From *The Adult Learner: A Neglected Species,* p. 60, by Malcolm S. Knowles.

GENERAL CHARACTERISTICS OF ADULT LEARNERS

Malcolm Knowles is widely considered to be the father of adult education. In *The Adult Learner,* Knowles puts forth the following "foundation stones of . . . adult learning theory":

1. Adults are motivated to learn as they experience needs and interests that learning will satisfy; therefore, these are the appropriate starting points for organizing adult learning activities.
2. Adults' orientation to learning is life-centered; therefore, the appropriate units for organizing adult learning are life situations, not subjects.
3. Experience is the richest resource for adults' learning; therefore, the core methodology of adult education is the analysis of experience.
4. Adults have a deep need to be self-directing; therefore, the role of the teacher is to engage in a process of mutual inquiry with them rather than to transmit his or her knowledge to them and then evaluate their conformity to it.
5. Individual differences among people increase with age; therefore, adult education must make optimal provision for differences in style, time, place, and pace of learning [p. 31].[2]

Principles for Design and Training

Building on Knowles's five "foundation stones" and other research about adult learners, we have devised six key principles. We believe that these principles have significant meaning for the design and delivery of training.

PRINCIPLES FOR TRAINING AND DESIGN

- Personal experience is the key learning tool.
- Motivation for learning is driven by needs: problem solving or personal satisfaction.
- Adults are independent learners.
- Protecting the learners' self-esteem is critical.
- Adults have clear expectations about training.
- Adults learn in a variety of ways and have preferences in learning styles.

[2]From *The Adult Learner: A Neglected Species,* p. 31, by Malcolm S. Knowles, Copyright © 1990 by Gulf Publishing Company. Used with permission. All rights reserved.

Personal Experience. Adults come to training with a vast reservoir of personal experience that they want to use in the learning situation, and they learn best when they are able to use it. In general, they learn quickly those things that fit well with their experience base; they need more time to process information that does not fit.

Adults want to be involved in the learning process through mutual objective setting and participation in activities that tap into their expertise, intuitive knowledge, and interests.

Driven by Needs. Adults are most motivated to learn about things that relate directly to their perceived immediate needs. They are problem solvers in their learning motivation. Although many adults enjoy learning for its own sake, the vast majority see learning as a means toward an end—a way of meeting a need. It may be something like developing a skill required for their work, finding ways to save money on taxes, learning to negotiate better with their children, or simply bringing balance and enjoyment into a hectic life.

The more immediate the need, the more motivated adults are to learn whatever will help them meet it.

Cyril Houle, in *The Inquiring Mind* (cited in Merriam & Caffarella, 1991, p. 83), described three "orientations" toward learning that put "needs" into a larger context: goal, activity, and learning.

- *Goal*-oriented learners are motivated to learn because they have set a goal, and learning is one critical way to achieve it. It may be a long-term goal, such as a degree or career advancement, or a specific short-term goal, such as mastering a particular software program.
- *Activity*-oriented learners engage in learning events for the sake of the activity itself. They are motivated by being involved with others in the learning process.
- *Learning*-oriented people are those who love learning for its own sake.

Even in Houle's typology, each of the learner types is motivated to address a personal need.

Independent Learners. This principle is related to what Knowles calls being "self-directing." Adults interpret information according to their personal values and experiences. They may value the trainer's opinions, and they may wish for approval, but they are the ultimate judges about the relevance of the content for their lives. They may appear to agree with something in order to complete a training activity successfully, but the ultimate test of the training is whether they apply it in their lives, and the question of application depends largely on whether they judge the learning to be personally valuable.

Self-Esteem. Unless the environment is safe, little learning is likely to occur. Learning takes energy and freedom. If the environment does not feel safe to the learner, large amounts of personal energy will go into protecting the self, attempting to alter the environment, or both; little will be left for inquiry, information processing, and analysis. Leslie Hart, whose work focuses on the relationships between brain research and human learning, builds a case for four conditions for learning that are compatible with brain functioning. His fourth condition, "absence of threat in an environment where risk-taking is encouraged and safe" (quoted in Dhority, 1991, p. 23), is a prerequisite to the other conditions.

Adults need to feel that they can question what is being taught and discuss their personal experience without threat. This need is particularly critical in work settings, in which participants may be concerned that if they say something "incorrect" or ask "the wrong question," their actions will be remembered outside the training and will somehow limit their career possibilities.

Expectations About Training. When adults enter into a training event, they bring with them a variety of expectations (based mostly on their experience of education and training) about what will be trained and how it will be trained. These expectations will largely determine participants' behavior, especially at the beginning of the training event. Expectations about what will be trained range from the general ("It won't have anything to do with my job") to the specific ("This communication workshop will tell me exactly what to say to my boss about X"); they may well reflect concerns not only about the content itself but also about how applicable it will be to participants' lives.

In terms of how the training will be presented, participants have expectations about activities, about the trainer, and about their own roles. Some adults expect training to be like school, which often means that they anticipate mostly listening to the trainer and then repeating what he wants to hear. Others expect training to include highly interactive and engaging activities.

In any case, the expectations are filters through which each participant experiences what is going on in the training. The designer has the task of planning what can be done early in the training to clarify expectations and to meet or modify them as appropriate.

Preferences in Learning Styles. Each learner has preferences that affect the ways he learns. Some learners prefer certain types of learning situations that feel more comfortable. Some prefer to learn certain types of content because they are naturally drawn to it. Some learners prefer to listen and observe, while others cannot wait to roll up their sleeves and try the new skill. The challenge for designers is clear: to design training that will appeal to and engage a variety of learning styles so that participants can learn in ways that work best for them.

Implications for Design

Let's take each of the six principles and see how they affect your work as a designer. In this section, we will look at the implications for design in general. In the chapters on the SIM (Chapters Six through Eleven), we will explore specific processes and techniques that will help you address how to honor the needs of your adult learners.

Personal Experience. Because the experience the adult brings to the training is such a significant resource, it should be directly addressed in the design. One way is to have the trainer or the materials refer to it—but that approach is fairly passive and may be perceived as patronizing. A much more productive way is to actively use the experience of the learners as part of the learning process. When the experience of the learners is parallel to what is being taught, it can be a great clarifier and reinforcer. When it is different, it can still serve to clarify what is being presented because the experience of cognitive dissonance may create a need to know and understand. In either case, analyzing personal experience is, as Knowles puts it, "the core methodology of adult education" (1990, p. 31).

As a designer, you will frequently be faced with the challenge of presenting a desired way to do something that does not fit with participants' experience. If your design encourages people to compare their previous experience with what is being presented, then the comparison can be processed in the training room—where other participants, as well as the trainer, can influence the learner. If the design does not call for the dissonance or resistance to be processed as part of the learning event, then it will come out in some other way or time—when there is much less opportunity to influence that processing.

Many designers, when faced with the challenge of trying to "sell" participants on a new skill or a new way of doing things, fall into the trap of simply designing a presentation of one benefit after another. There is nothing wrong with addressing benefits in training designs, but there can be problems in hoping for participants to be so "wowed" with the new way that their old experience will just melt away. It will not. Besides, if the old experience is not addressed in the training, chances are it will emerge after the training as a reason for not trying the new skill or as a rationale for why the new skill did not or would not work. The goal is to help learners integrate new information with what they already know and believe, thereby increasing comprehension and retention.

In short, training designs must include activities that encourage the learner to analyze the content in terms of the wisdom of previous experience—experience that is inseparable from the person of the learner.

Driven by Needs. The focus on performance outcomes and application needs has become a cornerstone belief in training and training design. Practitioners say that design processes must begin with the specific need that generates the training. In organizational settings, the need is usually a desired performance that the organization determines. In any setting, it may be a need perceived by individual learners for performance improvement, career development, or life enhancement.

As Knowles puts it, "The appropriate units for organizing adult learning are life situations, not subjects" (1990, p. 31). Almost everyone in training and development claims to subscribe to this principle. Yet blatant violations of it are rife in training objectives—objectives like "you'll know the ten ways to negotiate for success" or "you'll recognize the importance of listening." When we see these kinds of objectives, we always want to know, "*Why* do we want to learn this stuff?" and "*How* do these objectives help the learner perform more successfully on the job?"

In asking these questions, we are not necessarily questioning the importance of the information; we just want the designer to think about why this content or these skills are valuable—in terms of the learners' needs. Even for intuitive, big-picture learners who like to figure out their own applications, the designer must think about making the training efficient and effective. To do this, the designer should begin with the application and then think about what must be included.

In this book, as you work with the SIM, you will find that we dedicate a lot of time to developing a clear picture of application before writing goals and objectives, before determining content, before selecting learning activities. The designer's task is to put the training into the learner's frame of reference, and that means beginning with the end—the performance that will result from the training. Performance is not something you add onto the training. It is where you begin the design process.

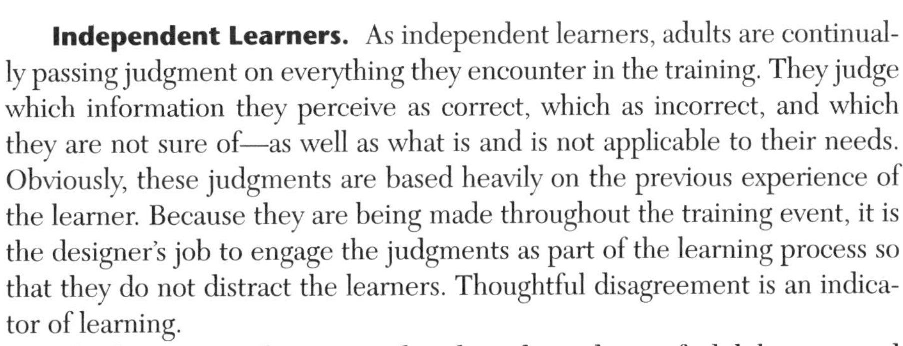

Independent Learners. As independent learners, adults are continually passing judgment on everything they encounter in the training. They judge which information they perceive as correct, which as incorrect, and which they are not sure of—as well as what is and is not applicable to their needs. Obviously, these judgments are based heavily on the previous experience of the learner. Because they are being made throughout the training event, it is the designer's job to engage the judgments as part of the learning process so that they do not distract the learners. Thoughtful disagreement is an indicator of learning.

The designer needs to remember the independence of adult learners and address it in the design. There are two primary ways. First, when there is an opportunity to let the learner make choices about focus, objectives, or learning activities, the designer should do so. For example, in many of our workshop designs we present the objectives that have been negotiated with the client organization, and then we invite participants to identify those that they feel are most important for them and to add additional objectives. The design calls for the trainer to be honest about what objectives can and cannot be addressed and to direct participants toward resources. The design also calls for the trainer to return to the workshop objectives and the participants' objectives throughout the training—as a way of giving the trainer, the group, and each individual an opportunity to assess progress.

TWO WAYS TO ADDRESS THE INDEPENDENCE OF ADULT LEARNERS

- Let the learners make choices about focus, objectives, or learning activities whenever possible.
- Encourage the learners to analyze and evaluate what they are learning.

The second way to engage the independence of adult learners is to plan activities that encourage them to analyze and evaluate what they are learning. The emphasis is not on total acceptance or rejection, but on analysis. For instance, a design might call for an activity in which participants will look at what they are learning and identify what parts they are excited about and what parts they are not comfortable with. Some designers resist such activities because they do not want to encourage "negative thinking." We call it "analytical thinking," and we see it as an effective and efficient way to accomplish objectives. We also believe that avoiding the negatives in the training does not change the reality: they still exist, and they have an impact on application afterward. Training should be about learning—and learning, especially when it involves changing behaviors and beliefs, can be messy. The best training designs acknowledge that messy reality.

In addition, a large percentage of what is labeled "difficult behavior" from participants is rooted in resistance to what is being taught or the way it is being taught. If the learners are not permitted to process their resistance, then the energy may go into undermining the success of the event. If the learners feel that they can talk about their resistance safely, then the energy can go instead into frank and analytical discussion of what is being learned.

Self-Esteem. It is a great art for the designer to create a learning event that includes inquiry, dialogue, and perhaps disagreement in a safe environment. Imagine that you are designing communications training for an intact work group. On the one hand, you want participants to bring up real situations and be honest about disagreements; on the other, you want to protect the self-esteem of the participants by avoiding activities that could result in finger-pointing and blaming. The challenge is to create a learning situation that is not threatening to the learners, one that allows the learning to happen because there is a safe place for honest dialogue.

Certainly, much of the responsibility for creating the environment rests on the trainer, who will actually be present during the event; the way he treats participants during the learning event is a very strong message about how he values them and their experiences.

The designer has a huge responsibility as well. Long before the event, the designer—whether or not she will even observe the training—can do a great deal to protect the self-esteem of the learners. She can develop goals and objectives that, while recognizing the organization's desire to encourage certain desired behaviors, also address the needs of the learners. She can select and present content at the appropriate level for the learners, neither too simple nor too complex for their abilities or their application needs. She can choose and design activities that encourage an exchange of ideas, and still clarify when there is a "right answer."

To maintain learners' self-esteem in a situation in which there is a "right" way being presented, here is what we might do: design a discussion, either before or after the "right" way is presented, about other ways that participants know of. By asking participants to talk about "ways it is done" rather than "ways you do it," we engage participants' experience while also making it safe for them to talk. In addition, by acknowledging that the thing is done in other ways, we enhance the safety of the training environment. The design might then move on to a discussion geared toward identifying reasons why there is an approved way, the advantages of the approved way, or what's in it for participants when they follow the approved way.

Expectations About Training. As noted earlier, participants have expectations about what will be trained as well as how it will be trained, and the designer can do a great deal to help manage those expectations. In some cases, the designer has uncovered specific expectations through the needs assessment and may be able to respond to them directly in the design. In other cases, the designer can provide an activity for the trainer to use to identify and manage participants' expectations during the training. No matter what, managing the expectations will involve comparing the participants' expectations with the plans for the training event and trying to adjust both as much as possible, in an attempt to meet the participants' needs while also meeting the organization's needs.

Here are some techniques you can incorporate in your design process to help manage expectations.

General Expectations. These suggestions may help you address overall expectations about the content and the methods of the training:

- Work with a team of participants in your design process so that you have access to expectations and can respond to them.
- Communicate with participants in advance to help bring expectations into alignment. The way the objectives are written will provide strong

cues about the content of the workshop and its applicability to the lives of participants. You can also give participants a sense of how the training will be managed and what it will be like, perhaps by describing learning activities and the learning environment.

- Early in the event, include an activity to clarify for participants exactly what will be covered in the training and how.
- If possible, write the goals and objectives from the perspective of the learners and their application needs, rather than from the viewpoint of the content.
- Use participants' experience and language as a source for content and activities when possible. If you can learn about the experience and language through your needs assessment and can plan it into your design, so much the better. At the very least, include in the design some opportunities for participants to share their own knowledge, concerns, and tips related to the content.
- Shape learning activities to fit expectations, as long as the activities will support the objectives. For example, if you hear a concern about case studies being unrealistic, you might design the shell of a case study, including just the elements essential to your objectives, and let the participants fill in the details during the training. Such an approach will ensure that the case study will be as realistic as possible.
- Include additional optional content and learning activities in your design when possible, and have the trainer poll participants to make choices that best fit their needs.

Expectations About What Is Trained. These suggestions address the designer's role in managing expectations related to content:

- Respond to participants' needs in your design. If you know their expectations and can integrate them in a powerful training design, do so. For example, if you learn in your needs assessment that participants would like a certain question addressed, and if addressing it would not detract from accomplishing the objectives, be sure to include it in the training.
- Give participants input on objectives. If possible, make their input part of the design process. Otherwise, include a dialogue around the objectives. For example, you might have participants each state one personal objective as part of the introductions, or if the training is limited to certain nonnegotiable objectives, your design can at least solicit from participants some specific things they hope will be covered within the confines of the fixed objectives.

- Edit out nonessential content so that everything in the learning event is focused on application.

Expectations About How the Material Is Trained. Here are a few techniques to use in the design process to address possible expectations about training methods and environment:

- Include time early in the training to define ground rules about participation and desired behaviors during the training event.
- If you believe, on the basis of the needs analysis, that the learning event may be uncomfortable for the learners, have your design build up to the activities that will be more of a stretch for people—both in how you sequence the activities and in how you advise the trainer to give directions.
- Make certain that your activities and practices reflect the real world of the participants as much as possible.
- Use language carefully and flexibly. For example, calling an activity a "role play" may cause anxiety. Sometimes, simply calling the same activity a "practice session" or an "application exercise" does not cause the same anxiety. If you can make such an adjustment with integrity, by all means do so.
- Encourage analysis and interpretation. Design ways to let participants examine how the new learning compares with their experiences on the job and how they might use it in the future.

Preferences in Learning Styles. The sixth principle is so significant and so detailed in its application that it merits its own section, which follows.

LEARNING STYLES

The sixth principle relating to the characteristics of adult learners is that "adults learn in a variety of ways and have preferences in learning styles." David Kolb says, "As a result of our hereditary equipment, our particular past life experience, and the demands of our present environment, most people develop learning styles that emphasize some learning abilities over others. Through socialization experiences in family, school, and work, we come to resolve the conflicts between being active and reflective and between being immediate and analytical in characteristic ways" (Kolb, 1984, pp. 76–77). In other words, each of us has preferred ways to engage in learning. These preferences or styles of learning may be quite conscious or fairly unconscious. Either way, even in day-to-day conversation a careful observer can quickly recognize whether someone has a preference for details or for concepts. That preference will surely be a large component of that person's preferred way to learn.

There are many theories and models that describe learning styles or preferences. Each lends some important insights into how adults acquire and process information—and into why some adult learners are more drawn to certain subjects, treatments, or activities.

Models for Preferences in Learning Styles

In the next few pages, you will find overviews of several widely used models for understanding style preferences in adult learners. As a designer, you are responsible for identifying one or two models of learning styles (here or elsewhere) that will guide your own design processes; you are an adult learner yourself, so seek out models that make sense to you. The key is to be guided by some principles that will ensure variety in your training designs so that you will meet the needs of a variety of learning preferences. It does not make a great deal of difference which model or set of labels you use for the preferences; what matters is that your designs meet the needs of a variety of learners.

USING MODELS: SOME CAVEATS

Models and theories provide a context for making decisions. The danger lies in trying to take the models as absolute. When working with the various models of preferences in learning styles, bear in mind the following:

- Theories and models describe group behavior rather than individual behavior. When you read the description of a certain preference in learning style and its accompanying behaviors, you will often find that you know someone who seems to be that style but who doesn't display all of those behaviors. Remember, the descriptors are true for the overall population of those who share that preference—not necessarily for each individual within that group.
- A person's learning preferences tend to be fairly consistent over time, but immediate preferences are very much influenced by circumstances. For example, you may have a strong preference for concrete learning that focuses on practical application. If someday you take a music-appreciation course simply to expose yourself to a variety of music, you might find yourself preferring learning activities that simply open possibilities and do not focus on practical application. That would not mean that your learning preference had changed; it would simply mean that in a particular situation you preferred a different approach.

- Learning preferences give an important piece of information about the learners—but only a piece. Learners are much more complex than just their learning preferences. Participants also come to a learning event with their values, personality, and experience. In your design work, recognize that the theories and models about learning styles are just tools. They help you to understand your learners, but they give only partial insight into the complex beings that learners really are.
- Most learners have more than one preference in learning styles. Some have very strong primary preferences and rarely feel comfortable using other styles. But most learners, either through innate personality preferences or through learned behavior, are able to function effectively and comfortably within a range of learning styles.

Kolb's Learning Styles. David Kolb describes four basic learning styles: convergent, divergent, assimilation, and accommodative.

Convergent. The convergent style seeks to bring together information into the one correct answer. This style does best in situations in which there is a single answer to a question or problem.

- Greatest strengths: problem solving, decision making, and practical application
- Prefers dealing with technical rather than interpersonal issues
- Controlled in expression of emotions

Divergent. The divergent style seeks to generate alternate ideas and implications. This style does best in situations in which there are several possible answers to questions and the generation of possibilities is part of the learning task.

- Greatest strengths: imagination, awareness of meaning and values, ability to view situations from many perspectives and organize relationships into a meaningful whole
- Emphasis on learning by observation rather than action
- Interested in people, tends to be feeling-oriented

Assimilation. The assimilation style seeks to create and understand theory that is logically sound and precise. This style does best in situations in which it is possible to question and clarify theory.

- Greatest strengths: inductive reasoning and ability to create theoretical models
- Emphasis on assimilating disparate observations into an integrated explanation
- Focus on abstract concepts, less on people and practical application

Accommodative. The accommodative style seeks to respond to the circumstances in which it finds itself—it adapts and acts. It rolls up its sleeves and figures things out.

- Greatest strengths: practical application, new experiences, getting things done
- Emphasis on a trial-and-error method of problem solving
- Focus on the task rather than the plan or theory; generally at ease with people, but task orientation is primary (adapted from Kolb, 1984, pp. 77–78)[3]

Silver and Hanson's Learning Styles Inventory (LSI). Harvey Silver and J. Robert Hanson's model of learning styles is based on the work of Carl Jung and uses some of the labels associated with the Myers-Briggs Type Indicator®. This model presents four styles, all of them based on two of the Myers-Briggs preference dimensions.

The first dimension has to do with the preference between concrete and abstract information, or sensing and intuition. The preference for information that is concrete and can be experienced through the senses is labeled S for "sensing"; for abstract or conceptual information, N for "intuition." The second dimension has to do with whether the learner's orientation is more rational and analytical or more person-centered.

[3]From *Experiential Learning,* by David A. Kolb, © 1984. Adapted by permission of Prentice-Hall, Inc., Upper Saddle River, N.J.

Learners with a preference for the analytical function are labeled T for "thinking"; those with more of a focus on the personal or interpersonal, F for "feeling."

Silver and Hanson's Learning Styles Inventory delineates four learning styles: *S-T,* sensing-thinking; *S-F,* sensing-feeling; *N-T,* intuitive thinking; and *N-F,* intuitive feeling.

Sensing-Thinking. Learners with a preference for the sensing-thinking (S-T) style generally

- Are concrete and pragmatic in their approach to learning and enjoy topics and activities that have practical application
- Like clear, sequential directions and want to know precisely what is expected of them
- Are most comfortable with learning tasks that have right and wrong answers
- Are motivated by being able to see the usefulness of what is being learned
- Aim for results, factual mastery of skills, and practical application
- Frequently ask, "How?"
- Prefer structured, organized, and trainer-directed learning environments
- Learn best by firsthand experience
- Prefer to learn by action, repetition, and feedback

Sensing-Feeling. Learners with a preference for the sensing-feeling (S-F) style generally

- Like to work with others and seek their approval
- Enjoy activities during which feelings can be expressed
- Like situations in which they can be helpful to others
- Prefer to learn about things that affect people's lives, rather than impersonal facts and theories
- Strive for harmonious relationships
- Enjoy learning environments that are friendly, energetic, and focused on the well-being of people

Intuitive Thinking. Learners with a preference for the intuitive thinking (N-T) style generally

- Enjoy theory and abstract concepts
- Want intellectual challenge and highly value competency
- Like to think things through and make a plan before embarking on a project or assignment
- Frequently ask, "Why?"
- Look for logical relationships in any data and relish the challenge of bringing order from chaos; think in terms of cause and effect
- Prefer environments in which they can be independent, follow their own inspirations, and talk about ideas; prefer to learn by discovery and experimentation with ideas
- Appreciate and value precision in thinking and language; will argue for the sake of learning and achieving clarity
- Are interested in facts only to the extent that they can be used to prove or disprove a theory or belief

Intuitive Feeling. Learners with a preference for the intuitive feeling (N-F) style generally

- Enjoy freedom and creativity in the learning environment; prefer to follow personal insights
- Are oriented toward personal values and want or need to express themselves in ways that are personally meaningful, new, or unique
- Are motivated by personal interests; need to be intrigued to be engaged
- Like environments in which they can be curious and imaginative
- Prefer few restrictions, lots of activities; enjoy finding personal creative solutions to problems
- Are interested in belief systems and values and how they compare with their own
- Like new projects and exploring possibilities; are oriented toward the future (adapted from Silver & Hanson, [1980] 1994, pp. 3–5)

ADDITIONAL MODELS

Seven Intelligences

Howard Gardner (1993), in *Multiple Intelligences: The Theory in Practice,* describes seven intelligences:

- Linguistic
- Logical-mathematical
- Spatial
- Musical
- Kinesthetic
- Interpersonal
- Intrapersonal

Brain Dominance

Ned Herrmann (1995), in *The Creative Brain,* links learning preference with brain dominance in terms of four quadrants of the brain:

- Analytical
- Sequential
- Interpersonal
- Conceptual

The VAK Model

Collin Rose (1989), in *Accelerated Learning,* presents the VAK model for learning preferences, which includes three types:

- *Visual learners:* prefer to learn through seeing.
- *Auditory learners:* prefer to learn through hearing.
- *Kinesthetic learners:* prefer to learn through action.

Implications for Design

As you were reading through the different models and comparing them with what you already know, you were probably struck by the diverse ways of considering learning preferences and by the commonalities among the models. There is a lot of information here, and we are not suggesting that you internalize it all. Select a model or models for learning-style preferences, and let the models guide your design work. Pick ones that appeal to you and make sense to you. Pick ones that also help you to know and balance your own preferences well, to help ensure that your preferences do not dominate your design processes and products.

Remember, your designs do need to appeal to a variety of learning styles. True, any one moment in a training event will likely appeal more to one learning style than to another. That is perfectly fine. What is important is that the entire event contain elements that appeal to a variety of learning styles, for that is the only way to engage a variety of learners.

Let's look at the application of this concept for the designer in terms of several key elements of the design process. We have used Silver and Hanson's LSI categories to illustrate the applications.

Training Content. As you select essential content for the training presentation, keep the various preferences in mind. Some topics lend themselves naturally to concrete application; others are more suited to abstractions. Still, to engage a variety of learners, make certain that you have appropriate content. For example, you will want to balance "why" content (N preference) with "how" content (S preference), and balance content about people (F preference) with content about facts (T preference). Even though you may have to emphasize certain types of content more than others because of objectives or subject matter, be sure to include content that engages all learning preferences.

Training Methods. When you are choosing or designing learning activities, you will again consider learning preferences. Although some methods may seem naturally suited to particular preferences, most methods can be adapted to broaden their appeal to a variety of learning preferences.

To use an example from a workshop on creating visual aids: suppose you determine that you want to begin with a lecturette on the principles of good design for visual aids and the importance of these principles. To engage different learning preferences, the design might assign a simple task at the beginning of the lecturette, such as asking participants to jot down their notes in four categories during the lecturette:

- Techniques I want to use next time I create a visual aid (S-T)
- Techniques that will help my learners (S-F)
- What fits with what we know about adult learners? (N-T)
- What has personal meaning for me? (N-F)

After the lecturette, the design could call for a large-group discussion that would address each of these four categories. They are simply prompts that correspond with learning preferences. Individuals with a strong preference for one style might wish to jot down notes in the other areas as well. Individuals might even put entries in the "wrong" category (such as a practical application in the fourth category), but who cares? The design is not being built to teach learning styles. It is being built to enable participants to create visual aids for presentation. You, the designer, have determined that a lecturette is a good method for a particular piece of the training, and you have just designed that lecturette in a way that engages a variety of learning preferences.

Training Materials. You can do simple things with your design of materials to respect and engage a variety of learning preferences. Simply balancing text with graphics will help your visual learners. Encouraging participants to develop their own "pictures" for concepts will engage creativity, visual learning, and kinesthetic learning (the act of drawing).

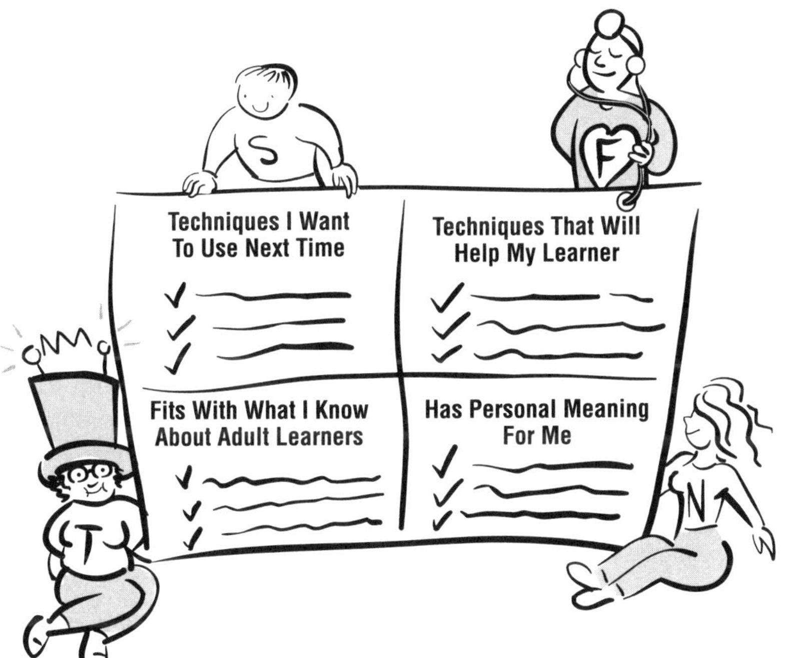

For the example above, there could be a simple worksheet for participants to use during the lecturette and during the discussion that follows it. The worksheet not only provides a place to keep notes; it also provides an ongoing visual reminder of the cues or categories for listening, to help participants keep focused during the lecturette and discussion.

As in managing content, it is important to use language and examples that will appeal to a variety of learning preferences. Even balancing the terms "think" and "feel" as well as "why" and "how" is a simple linguistic technique to engage different learning styles. Balancing examples that highlight facts with those that highlight people is another way to engage different learning preferences.

Evaluation Tools. Evaluation is a rich, complex opportunity to engage learning preferences. Let's look at some evaluation questions that could be asked to appeal to the four different preferences:

- What have you learned that you can use—insights, skills, or both—on your job? (S-T)
- What have you learned that you can use to help others? (S-F)
- What have you learned that has helped you understand and/or support the strategic objectives of this organization? (N-T)
- What have you learned that has personal meaning for you—that you find personally enriching? (N-F)

Of course, not every question will apply to every situation. Still, these examples serve to illustrate ways in which evaluation tools can be constructed to bring different learning preferences to bear.

From the beginning of the design process to the end—not just in the training room—being responsive to learners' preferences can help shape training that is effective, efficient, and engaging.

A FEW LAST WORDS

The job of a training designer is a sacred trust. The designer creates situations in which learning can occur—safe and engaging environments in which personal experience is brought together with new experience. If the designer does the job well, the training event becomes a rich adventure in learning. It is a place of individual transformation, of re-creating knowledge, behaviors, beliefs—ways of being. In the best-designed training events, individual experience comes face-to-face with the experience being presented in the training, and dialogue allows participants to clarify meaning. In many cases, that meaning will include a desired organizational understanding as well as individual assignment of meaning and value to what is learned. Good design not only acknowledges but truly incorporates the diverse experience of the learners in the room. It also engages and meets the needs of the diverse learning preferences that are present in the group.

Throughout this book, as you learn to apply the SIM in your work as a designer of training, you will find ways again and again to fulfill that sacred trust by designing training events that honor your adult learners.

4 The Designer

We have looked at what makes training powerful, at the SIM process for design, and at the adult learner. It is time to look at you—the person who creates powerful learning experiences for adults. We will look at the balancing acts that the designer is always performing, the challenges the designer faces, and some strategies for meeting those challenges.

BASIC COMPETENCIES

Let's start with a quick look at some basic design competencies:

- Establishing goals and objectives on the basis of needs assessment data
- Researching content materials
- Selecting content that is essential to meeting objectives
- Selecting and designing learning activities that will support objectives
- Sequencing learning activities and content
- Estimating time for activities
- Selecting and developing learning aids (audiovisual materials for instructional use)
- Developing materials for trainers and participants
- Designing evaluation tools to measure the success of training

You might think of the designer as a caterer who plans, prepares, and provides the directions for the serving of a wonderful meal. Here is what the caterer would do:

- Translate the needs of the host into a theme and menu: goals and objectives.

- Determine what ingredients will be essential to creating the meal: key topics.
- Make decisions about how the meal will be served (buffet or sit-down) and in what order the courses will be served: training flow.
- Determine what serving pieces and dinnerware will be needed, as well as the settings and decorations that will help create the theme the host desires: materials.
- Propose what indicators she and the host can agree on to determine the success of the event: evaluation tools.

In Chapters Six through Eleven of this book, as you work with the SIM, you will find considerable help with each of these essential design competencies. The SIM will provide steps and guidelines to ensure that these competencies are brought to the design task at the times that they are most needed and in ways that are efficient.

THE DESIGNER'S BALANCING ACT

This chapter focuses on three other sets of competencies, less obvious and less frequently discussed, but equally fundamental to all your work as a designer. We call them the designer's balancing act:

- Balancing your own talents during the design process
- Balancing the impact of your learning preferences on design products
- Balancing your roles as expert and partner, as solo designer and member of a design team

Balancing Talents: The Design Process

Each designer brings particular talents to the design process. Think of a *talent* as a combination of natural tendencies and developed skills. You probably have found that there are certain areas of ability, behaviors, and ways of being that feel natural and comfortable to you. If you are like most people, you probably lean toward behaving in those ways and using those abilities; doing so makes you even more comfortable, and you may tend to behave that way even more. In the process, you probably become even better at it.

Each talent is a gift, and each talent presents some challenges. The major challenge in terms of designing is to develop complementary abilities, behaviors, and ways of being, especially including those that do not feel natural or comfortable.

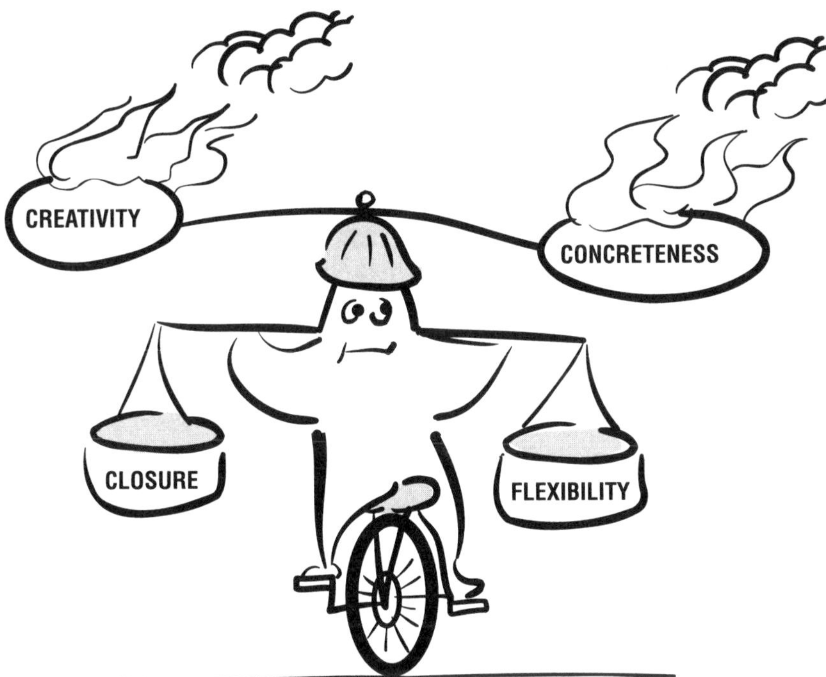

As we have coached and trained many people in the design process, we have identified two complementary pairs of talents that heavily influence how a person designs. The first pair has to do with the tension between creativity and concreteness; the second has to do with the tension between bringing order or closure to things and remaining flexible and open to emerging possibilities.

Most individuals tend to be more comfortable—more talented—with one side of the pair than with the other. In classic Myers-Briggs terminology, the first pair includes "intuition" (N) and "sensing" (S); the second, "judging" (J) and "perceiving" (P). Although the Myers-Briggs typology is describing preferences rather than talents, the language is directly applicable to this discussion.

Creativity and Concreteness. Designing training takes a lot of creativity. For example, you will be searching for ways to present objectives that are true to the needs of the organization while also being intriguing to your learners. You will be designing conceptual or visual models to organize content. You will be coming up with efficient and engaging learning activities. You will be designing visual aids and learning materials for your participants. All of these tasks require you to engage in a creative process.

At the same time, you will be attending to concrete details. You will be checking that every objective is met in the design. You will be writing detailed directions for the trainer (such as how many people should be in small groups and what to do if there are not equal numbers in the groups). You will be estimating time for activities, including how much time it will take for participants to move into groups. You will be preparing materials in such a way that they match the oral presentation and the visuals to be used in the training. These tasks require a disciplined focus on the concrete.

All in all, throughout the design process you are constantly called on to be both creative and concrete. Most designers—like most people in general—have greater talent with one or the other. The designer's job requires balancing the two.

Maintaining the balance is no small challenge. Designers whose greater talent is creativity often begin the design process by thinking about creating ingenious learning activities or novel visual models to organize content. They are enthralled with the possibilities of creating, say, a game for a stress-management workshop. Creativity is a critical design skill, but overusing it can lead to designing activities before determining the objectives for the learning event. The energy and enthusiasm poured into creating those activities can result in holding onto them tenaciously in the design, even when they do not support the objectives. A strong natural tendency toward creativity can also, if not managed and balanced, siphon attention from the more concrete design functions, such as establishing times for activities and developing detailed trainer's materials.

Designers whose talents lean more toward concreteness and detail, in contrast, often begin the process by creating a content outline. It seems practical and concrete. The problem is that content is not what should be driving the training design; application and objectives should. The ability to think pragmatically and concretely is vital in design, but it needs to be balanced by creativity. Attention to the concrete, if not balanced with attention to the creative aspects of design, can lead to training designs that are dull, predictable, and nonengaging.

Order and Flexibility, Closure and Openness. Design is a messy process. It requires a continual balance between achieving some order and remaining flexible; the designer must bring some closure to the work at various stages, while remaining open to refining, or even drastically changing, that work later in the design process. Some people seem to have a special talent for keeping things open-ended, "going with the flow"; others find their talents are most comfortably expressed in organizing, deciding, and finalizing. The designer of training needs both approaches, and the challenge is to keep the two in balance throughout the process.

For example, when you are putting together your training flow (Chapters Eight and Nine), you will be selecting and sequencing training methods. You must make those decisions in order to proceed with the design, but you also need to remain open to revisiting those decisions when you are designing participant materials. You may find as you design a worksheet for a particular activity that the activity does not really focus the learners' energy efficiently on key topics. If that happens, you need to revisit your earlier work.

As you use the Sequential-Iterative Model for Training Design (the SIM), each step of the process invites you to go back and check what you have done. Designers with a strong talent for order and closure may find this approach very unsettling—believing, perhaps, "If I do the work right the first time, I won't have to repeat it. Having to go back is a sign that I didn't do it right." This belief can cause the designer to waste time trying to perfect something that should not yet be perfected. Worse yet, it can lead to keeping a piece of a design even when it is not the best approach—because going back to redesign it would seem to signify that it was not done correctly in the first place.

A TALENT MISDIRECTED

Lee, a designer with a talent for closure, has established three objectives for a workshop in coaching skills for supervisors and managers. He has spent a lot of time getting these objectives just right—in fact, he has already created a beautiful wall chart to display them during the training. Much later in the design process, Lee is working on handouts for the participants. He discovers a graphic model that might help supervisors and managers to remember three key coaching principles. But the principles are not worded to fit well with the objectives—the objectives that are already on that beautiful wall chart. Now what? Lee has three choices—none of them particularly appealing:

- He could go back and re-create the wall chart to include the modified objectives, but that would mean extra work and changing what he has already brought to closure.
- He could drop the model because it does not fit with his earlier work, but to do so would deprive the learners of something that could support their learning.
- He could design some kind of bridge between the language of his objectives and the model; but a bridge would take training time and learner energy that would be more efficiently used by focusing directly on the content and activities related to the training objectives.

None of these is an ideal solution. If Lee had created his objectives in a form finished enough to guide the next stages of design but still open to modification (that is, if he had not brought them completely to closure), then he could simply change the vocabulary of the objectives to fit the language of the model. He would expend much less energy that way than he would either by rewriting the "finished" objectives or by creating a bridge, and the learners' energy would be focused exactly where it should be.

Lee created this situation by relying primarily on his basic talent for closure and not balancing it with the complementary skill.

What about the opposite or complementary skill: flexibility or open-endedness? Designers whose talent is in open-endedness and leaving things flexible for as long as possible (and who are less comfortable and skilled at bringing things to closure) will also have challenges in the design process. Unless there is some sense of closure—tentative closure, anyway—on training objectives, there are no criteria for determining which potential content is essential. Likewise, selecting or designing efficient learning activities is nearly impossible until there are decisions about what content is essential to support the learning objectives. Achieving this sense of tentative closure in each stage of the design process does not mean that you will never go back and change earlier decisions about objectives or content; it just means that you have arrived at enough clarity to help you make decisions at the next stage. Without it, you end up with designs that are unfocused, messy, and often confusing to learners.

Strategies for Balancing

The challenge is to be aware of and take advantage of your talents while using techniques to keep them in balance as you design. Balance requires two efforts: first, keeping in check the potential to overuse your talents, those skills with which you have greater comfort and ability; second, building in your complementary skills.

The caterer has the same need for balance. While putting together creative themes and menus, she is also calculating exactly how long she will have between courses to prepare the next course. The challenge is to do both—to be creative and attend to concrete details throughout the planning process—even though one approach surely comes more easily for the caterer, just as it does for the designer.

The proper balance between creativity and concreteness, as well as between closure and open-endedness, is not easy to find and maintain. Here are some strategies that will help you achieve this balance in your design work:

- Follow the steps outlined in each stage of the SIM (Chapters Six through Eleven). The SIM will help you achieve this balance in two ways. First, each stage includes creativity steps (brainstorming) and concrete steps (editing and focusing); the deliberate pairing will help bring balance to your design work naturally. Second, each stage of the SIM creates a product that leads you to the next stage; the products are carefully defined to be complete enough to carry you to the next stage (closure) but flexible enough to encourage reiteration and refinement on the basis of additional design work (open-ended).

- If during the design process you find that one of your talents is cropping up when it is not needed, reap the benefits without letting it take over. For example, if in one of the detailed steps of the process you start having some great ideas about creative learning activities, listen to your wisdom. Quickly jot those ideas down and put them into your file folder for learning activities. Include enough detail so that you will remember them, but do not waste time fleshing them out until you are certain you will use them. By following this approach, you will develop the discipline to notice what your mind is doing, gain the benefits, and return to work that may be less appealing but is equally important to the overall success of your design.
- Take some time to assess yourself in terms of these four areas of ability. Make note of which ones are more comfortable and natural for you and which are a bit of a stretch. Develop some personal notes or checkpoints for yourself to achieve balance. If you are not certain where your talents lie, ask for feedback from trusted colleagues.

ONE DESIGNER'S CONFESSION

I enjoy dealing with specific details, and I find it satisfying to settle things and tie up loose ends. I'm not so crazy about big-picture conceptualizing, and I hate having to reconsider decisions once they've been made. I guess you could say that my talents are in concreteness and in closure. To keep those personal preferences from being in my way in the process of designing training, I've made some rules for myself:

- When I become stuck brainstorming, get some help.
- When I think I'm out of ideas, try for two more.
- Use at least one creativity technique for each major brainstorming step.
- Move on when each design stage is "done enough," even though I want to keep going until it's perfect.
- Ask a colleague who is more talented at creativity or more comfortable keeping decisions open to work with me as a consultant or a reviewer of my design work.
- Follow the SIM steps to keep myself in balance.

My rules remind me of what I need to do to create powerful training designs. If your talents are different from mine, your personal rules will be different, too.

You do want to capitalize on your strengths, of course; you just do not want them to get in the way of balance. The SIM, designed to incorporate and balance talents in the design process, will be very helpful in this regard. Some steps in the SIM may seem a bit frustrating to you, while others will seem quite natural. Those that seem frustrating will probably be the steps that ask you to work from your less developed skills, and you may be tempted to avoid them. We urge you: be especially sure to follow those steps, because they bring in the skills that you might otherwise overlook. In doing so, you will improve how you design (the process) and what you design (the product), because you will be adding to your natural gifts and talents; you will also learn to save time. We promise!

Balancing Preferences: The Design Product

Just as your talents affect *how* you design, your learning-style preferences can strongly affect *what* you design. Your learning preferences have worked to help you attend to certain types of information and learning activities, which now are part of the bag of tricks from which you draw. Similarly, when you are considering possible new content or activities during the design process, you probably are most attracted to the ones that engage your own learning style, and therefore you are more likely to include such content and activities in your design. Unless your learning-style preferences are conscious and consciously managed, they can limit how well your design will engage a variety of learning styles. For example, if you favor factual and sequential approaches and tend to avoid conceptual and creative approaches without being conscious of that preference, your designs will most likely not engage learners who prefer those more intuitive ways of approaching content.

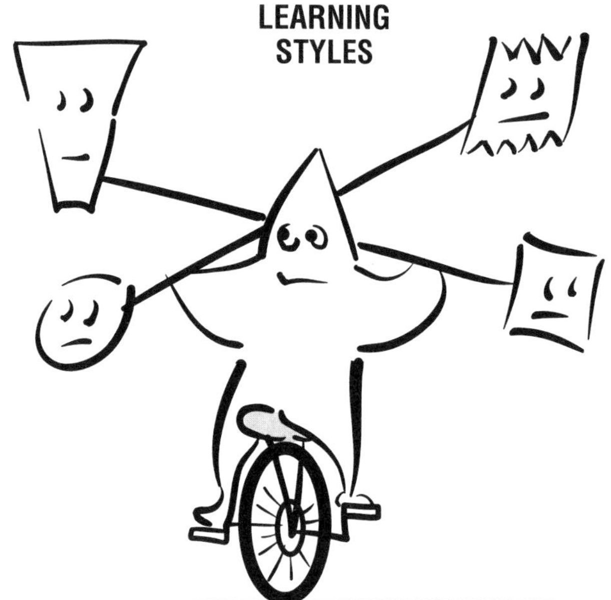

In our experience, most designers seem to design training that would work well for them; their designs reflect their learning preferences. Why? We believe that most designs, even from designers who are fairly sophisticated about varied learning preferences, still reflect how the designer processes information and makes design decisions. The bias is probably unconscious. For example, if you strongly prefer intuitive, abstract, and conceptual information, you will probably put more emphasis on "why" than on "how" in your content as well as in learning activities. Maybe you simply tend to pay closer attention to such information during your research; maybe there are other explanations. In any case, the effect is that the design itself will be more heavily weighted toward particular preferences.

Learning Styles. Designing for adult learners means taking diverse learning-style preferences into account. No matter what model you use to categorize learning-style preferences, you can count on all or almost all of the preferences being present among your participants—even if certain organizations or professions may have higher representation of certain styles.

Creating learning events that will engage the spectrum of styles is no small challenge. In some ways, it is a greater challenge than balancing the personal talents that affect your own design process. The reason is that, although most designers may be quite aware of their overall talents, their learning-style preferences tend to be less conscious. Biases can creep in unrecognized. Often, a designer tends to gravitate toward certain types of content and activities simply because they would work well for his own style.

For example, consider a designer whose learning-style preference is what David Kolb would call divergent (Chapter Three). He might tend to design training that included many possible answers, many opportunities for interpretation, and an emphasis on open-ended discussions. He would be less likely to include activities in which there would be a single right answer. Or take a designer with a strong visual preference in learning style—to use Colin Rose's VAK model (Chapter Three). His training designs might be heavy on art, color, and beautiful models, but they quite possibly would pay little attention to specific verbal explanations of content or activities.

It is human nature to be most attentive to what is personally appealing. The challenge for designers is to move beyond these biases in order to design learning that will appeal to a variety of learners.

Think again of the caterer. She has her own tastes in food and ambiance; those tastes, unless carefully managed, will surely affect her choices when planning for others. If she is conscious of her natural preferences, she can monitor them to make certain that they are balanced by the needs of her host and by her own intention to create a meal that will appeal to a wide variety of tastes.

Strategies for Balancing. The most powerful thing the caterer can do to balance her own preferences is to become aware of the subtle ways they affect her decisions. When she is aware, she can make choices that are more directly focused on meeting her objectives and pleasing her diners. The same is true for the designer. The first step in balancing learning preferences is to become aware of those preferences and how they affect design decisions.

In addition to the fundamental skill of recognizing your learning-style preferences and how they affect your design decisions, here are some additional suggestions and techniques for balancing your preferences and their effects on what you design:

- Familiarize yourself with a variety of learning-style models, and select one or two as a framework for your approach to design. Look for what appeals to you and what has the potential to bring balance to your preferences by helping you work consciously with your nonpreferred styles.
- Develop the skill of analyzing designs for learning styles. Go through several designs created by other people, and mark where they appeal to various learning styles. Ask some colleagues to do the same, and compare your analysis with theirs. Soon you will find that you can quickly review a design and determine which learning preferences will be engaged and which will be less engaged.
- Further develop this skill by reviewing resource books of learning activities. Analyze those activities for their appeal to various learning styles; figure out how they could be modified to engage additional learning styles.
- Increase your sensitivity to how your learning-style preferences influence your design work. One powerful way to do this is to review some of your previous designs and look for signs of your preferences in your work.
- Ask a colleague, someone who is familiar with the model of learning styles that works for you, to review your designs and analyze them for balance in learning styles.
- Develop a personal checklist that will guide your design work. This list should include reminders that speak to your personal gifts and needs for balance.

BALANCING PREFERENCES IN DESIGN PRODUCT

You can use a personal checklist to help keep your own learning-style preferences balanced in your design products. Here are a couple of samples:

An N-F's Checklist

______ Make sure to balance whys with sufficient how-to's.
______ Use the word "think" as often as you use "feel."
______ Write out directions for activities in detail; have someone else read them to see if they are clear.
______ Keep sentences short.
______ Look for opportunities to provide sequential steps for skill building.

An S-T's Checklist

______ Make sure to balance how-to's with sufficient whys.
______ Find opportunities to give participants some freedom and creativity with activities—do not overdirect them.
______ Create a visual of the big picture for the training.
______ Include discussions on opinions and personal judgments, which do not have right or wrong answers.
______ Include some things that are fun just to keep the energy going.

If your learning-style preference is S-F or N-T, of course, your own personal checklist will be different from either of these.

- After you have roughed out your overall design, review it for style balance before you go into any great detail. Mark each learning activity to indicate which style or styles of learning it appeals to. Then review the entire plan to see if there is a good balance.

In summary, in order to create designs that engage a variety of learning styles, first recognize the effect that your own learning preferences have on the designs you create. These effects may be quite subtle. You must then develop the ability to analyze designs for their appeal to different learning styles and develop personal techniques to balance your own style. The point is to create a training event that not only engages a variety of learning styles but makes comprehension and retention as easy as possible for each of those styles.

Balancing Roles: Working with Others

Yes, there is more to the designer's balancing act. Whenever you work as a consultant with clients (either internal or external), you will often be trying to find the appropriate balance between being an expert and being a partner. As an expert, you bring your ability to convert training needs into effective, efficient, and engaging training; as a partner, you work with your client to make decisions that will help reach organizational objectives. The designer must also have the skills to maintain another kind of balance: the balance between being able to design alone and being a member of a design team.

Expert and Partner. Whether you are an internal or an external consultant, you help your client make decisions about training. In some situations, you act as the expert and make the decisions. In other situations, you function more as a partner, giving the client information she can use to make her decisions. Obviously, this is a delicate balance.

This type of challenge may take a number of forms: the client may have unrealistic expectations about your expertise—for example, asking you to function as a subject-matter expert when you are not. Or the client may assume that she does not have to be involved in design decisions—that once the request is clarified, the next thing she will see is the completed design. In contrast, a client may want total control of the design and view you simply as someone who carries out her wishes—especially frustrating if she is not sensitive to the needs of adult learners.

Strategies for Balancing. Most of the challenges related to balancing the expert role with the partner role result from neglecting to clarify roles and responsibilities at the outset. Here are some specific suggestions:

- First, read Peter Block's *Flawless Consulting* (1981). Block thoroughly discusses the roles of the consultant and the process of contracting to clarify these roles.
- Determine what roles are appropriate for you in a particular design project. In one instance, your expertise may be solely in the area of design; for another project, you may also be a subject-matter expert.
- Discuss expectations early and often with your client. Part of your job as a consultant and specialist in training design is to educate your client about the design process. This does not mean that you will be teaching her about the technical aspects of your work, but about a process for working together to create a training event that meets her needs, the organization's needs, and the learners' needs.
- Be honest about your expertise. Even though you may want to meet all of your client's expectations, it is unwise to agree to do things that you cannot do.
- Employ your collaboration skills. The client may ask for something that just is not possible or at least is not good training—for example, reducing the time allotted to training so much that there is no opportunity for learning activities other than an extended briefing. In such a situation, an effective collaborative approach would be to offer your client some choices, along with their business implications, rather than to play the expert by giving a lecture on how adults learn.

CONSULTANT: EXPERT OR PARTNER?

Yvonne, a designer working in a telemarketing center, is designing a module on overcoming customer resistance to a new product. Yvonne and the client have agreed to objectives and essential content. Now, as Yvonne is discussing the plan for the training, she tells the client it will take two hours. He tells her to cut it to one hour and drop all the activities: "Just tell them what they need to know, because we can't afford to lose time they could be selling on the phone."

Yvonne could play the expert role here, explaining all the reasons why just telling them will not result in much learning or changed behavior. But it would be better for Yvonne to act as a partner and make the same point by offering the client some options related to business needs. Yvonne might say, "I see three choices here. The first is that we can cut it to one hour and simply present the information, but we will not be able to measure whether they got it until they are back on the job and we are monitoring calls. That might be too late to meet your needs. Second, we could use ninety minutes—which would allow us, during the training, to measure their ability to respond in a written format to the most common types of resistance. It is closer to what you want. Third, if we can find a way to take the full two hours, we can measure their ability to respond to common types of resistance on the telephone during the training. That way, we can ensure that they can really deliver the information to customers the way they actually are required to do on their jobs. What can we do to get close to what you want for increased sales while respecting the time constraints?"

- Work with a mentor. Balancing the expert role and the partner role is one of the most complex and sensitive aspects of working as a design consultant. A mentor can share with you the benefit of his experience and also help you analyze and strategize about your relationships with your clients.

Solo Design and Design Teams. The ability to function well in either situation is a critical competency for almost all designers, as very few function exclusively on their own or exclusively on a team. There are advantages and disadvantages either way, and the most successful designers are those who can do both—while creating designs that are effective, efficient, and engaging.

Challenges of Solo Design. For the designer who spends a lot of time working alone—as many do—brainstorming may be quite a challenge. Even if you are a naturally creative person, brainstorming can be very frustrating. Some days, you may feel as if you have only about three ideas, but as soon as you talk to someone else, the ideas just start flowing. Perhaps you may find that turning your attention to another project, even for a little while, helps to free up your ideas.

In addition to the challenges for brainstorming, working alone takes two kinds of discipline. The first is that now-familiar discipline of balance; working alone requires that you build into your process all the preferences that you do not personally have. Obviously, achieving this balance is much easier when you are working on a team and can count on your teammates for certain skills, talents, and preferences that are different from yours.

The second is the kind of discipline that keeps you focused on the specific task and on the design process. When working alone, it is very easy to go off on a tangent without knowing that you have done so. For example, you might have an idea for a great worksheet early in the design process. If someone else were there at that moment, she might remind you to put the idea into the "participant materials" file for later. But on your own, you might pretty quickly become involved with the idea and spend too much time with it.

Strategies for Solo Design. Even if you are an independent contractor or a one-person training department, you do not have to rely solely on yourself all the time. Here are some ideas:

- Talk with colleagues elsewhere, share resources, even ask others to review your work or brainstorm a few minutes with you.
- In the absence of other people to work with, make use of the wonderful variety of learning activities and prepared training packages that are widely available.

RESOURCES FOR PREPARED ACTIVITIES

Creative training techniques (monthly newsletter). Minneapolis, MN: Lakewood.

Scannell, E., & Newstrom, J. (1995). *The complete games trainers play: Experiential learning exercises.* New York: McGraw-Hill.

Silberman, M. (1995). *101 ways to make training active.* San Francisco: Jossey-Bass/Pfeiffer.

- Use techniques that help you stimulate your creativity when you are alone. (For more thoughts on stimulating creativity, see Chapter Eight.)
- To achieve learning-style balance when working alone, develop and use a personal checklist (such as "Balancing Preferences in Design Product," which appeared earlier in this chapter).
- Follow the SIM, which will help you in three very powerful ways. First, each stage of the SIM will help you to focus on a critical portion of the design process so that you can work efficiently and avoid being overcome by the complexity of the task. Second, the steps within each stage will

engage all of the skills you must apply to create powerful training. Third, you will review the products you create at each design stage to see that they support your objectives and meet the needs of your learners, including appealing to a variety of learning styles.

- Put large visual cues in your work space to remind you of the major stages of the design process—for example, a set of flip-chart pages bearing the names of the design stages. They will serve as reminders of where you are in the process and also will provide space for recording valuable ideas so that they will not be lost.

Challenges of Design Teams. Working with others presents its own set of rewards and challenges. When a team designs training, the reward is the wonderful richness of diversity; if team members can listen to one another and appreciate their differences, they have the capacity to design training that speaks to a variety of learning styles. The challenges, too, are significant; they include confusion about roles and responsibilities, differing design processes, and interpersonal problems.

Confusion about roles and responsibilities frustrates people and reduces the likelihood that they will function as a team. If someone is unsure whether she is responsible as both subject-matter expert and designer or simply as subject-matter expert, it is pretty difficult for her to determine how she is to function in the group.

Similarly, if there is uncertainty about who decides what, it will detract from the team's effectiveness; team members need to know who does what and who decides what—ranging, for example, from who will find and review potential videos for the training to who has final accountability for the design.

The second major challenge, differing design processes, can be a very sticky one. The members of the team are likely to have individual preferences in the process each uses for design. It may be a conscious process, such as the SIM, or it may be a less conscious approach. In either case, these personal processes are based on assumptions about what makes training good and how to create it. Without a certain level of agreement about the criteria for powerful training and about the process the group will use to develop training, there are likely to be constant misunderstandings and disagreements about how to do the job.

Finally, in any team there will be interpersonal issues that may affect the way the group works. With the richness of diversity come also many sets of assumptions and behaviors related to working in groups. No matter what the task of the group, it takes members with good interpersonal skills to arrive at norms for group behavior that promote the good of the group.

Strategies for Design Teams. To maximize the rewards and address the challenges of designing with a team, try the following suggestions:

- Agree on your criteria for success—how you will assess your finished training design. This discussion will clarify any underlying assumptions about what constitutes powerful training and design.

- Clarify roles and responsibilities early in the process. Part of your project plan should be to determine who will be doing what on the team, who is accountable for what, and how decisions will be made.
- Agree to a design process that has definite deliverables. This process will not only guide the work of the group and individuals within the group; it will also form the basis for the project plan that the group will use to guide its work. The SIM has clear deliverables, which can be mutually agreed on not only within the group but with clients. It also focuses the work of the group on major design stages, permitting the group to assign specific tasks that will fit the expertise of individual team members.
- Use large visual cues—just as you would if you were working alone. You might create a large poster of the SIM—perhaps with a moveable arrow to indicate the stage you are working on.
- Assign one person the role and responsibility of managing the design process. If the group comes up with ideas that are more relevant to another stage of the SIM, this person records them in enough detail to help the team remember them when they are needed and then refocuses attention on the stage at hand.
- Particularly when working with a subject-matter expert (SME), be sure to negotiate and define roles. Often there is tension between the SME

and the design expert, but it can be minimized by making some preliminary agreements. Determine who is to consult and who is to decide when there are differences of opinion about such elements as theoretical models, essential versus nice-to-know content, technical accuracy of content, learning activities, time allocated for various components of the training, evaluation methods, job aids, and so on.

- Agree on some norms for group behavior. The agreements can be added to and amended whenever necessary. Human nature tends to make us avoid such discussions until there are interpersonal problems in the group, but waiting only makes the discussions much more difficult.
- Review the product and the process on a regular basis. The SIM, along with your project plan, will provide clear, specific criteria against which to measure the design product. Brief reviews of how members are working together will serve to reinforce productive group behaviors and to help the group agree on changes when necessary.

This third part of the balancing act, balancing your roles, is a lifelong learning process for all professionals. Maintaining your awareness of this essential process will help you become better and better at balancing as you progress in your work as a designer.

In the SIM design process (Chapters Six through Eleven), the focus is on helping you develop the basic design competencies listed at the beginning of this chapter, while balancing your talents during the design process and balancing the effects of your learning preferences on your design products. The balancing of your roles—as expert or partner and as a solo designer or team member—will always remain a part of the backdrop against which the other aspects of the design process are played out.

A FEW LAST WORDS

Training design is not an easy task, but it is among the most fascinating and challenging of professions. It requires sophisticated skills and processes. It also demands utter honesty with ourselves. We need to be honest about the differences between our own preferred styles of learning and what will work for a variety of learners. We need to be honest about learning activities that we avoid because we are not comfortable with them. Sometimes we need to force ourselves to let go of a learning activity that enthralls us in order to design an activity that might be less appealing personally, but that is a more effective and more efficient way to engage a variety of learners and move them toward the desired performance. We must sometimes embrace content that we do not find personally stimulating, and we must omit content that is nonessential, even if we are in love with it.

Difficult, yes! But when we are finished—if we have applied our design competencies and if we have succeeded at our balancing act—we have, like the caterer, planned a buffet brimming with nutritious offerings that appeal to a variety of tastes. It may not be the meal we would have prepared for ourselves, but our satisfaction comes from knowing that many people with a variety of tastes will leave the learning event nourished and enriched.

5 Needs Assessment

> Much of human resource development, organizational improvement, and training are concerned with *solving* problems. As important as these efforts are, it is just as important first to identify and justify the actual problem. While objective setting is often the starting place for applying performance technology, it is often much more important to make certain that the objectives are the right ones and that their accomplishment will lead to both individual competence and organizational success.[1]

In other words, if you want to improve performance, first figure out what the performance gaps are. In addition, if you want to envision future successful performance, situate that performance in the context of anticipated organizational needs. That is what needs assessment is all about.

What would a book on training design be without a chapter on needs assessment? For training to be effective, efficient, and engaging, the design has to be rooted in real needs—and the tool with which the organization clarifies them is the needs assessment. Broadly speaking, a needs assessment compares "what is" with "what is desired" to uncover the gap between the actual and the hoped-for situations. The gap represents the needs. When a decision is made that certain of these needs are genuine training needs, the designer creates a learning event.

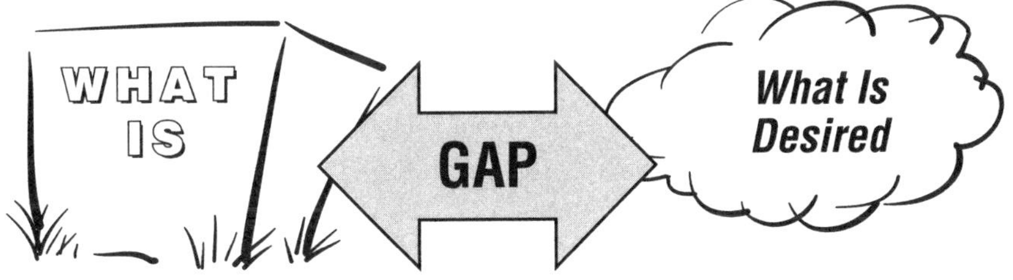

Because *Designing Powerful Training* focuses on design, it is beyond the scope of this book to discuss in detail how to plan and execute a needs assessment. However, two particular aspects of needs assessment have special relevance for design, and we will address them in this chapter.

[1]From "A Needs Assessment Primer," *ASTD Trainer's Toolkit.* Copyright © 1990, the American Society for Training and Development. Reprinted with permission. All rights reserved.

RECOMMENDED RESOURCES FOR NEEDS ASSESSMENT

If you are new to needs assessment, investigate the following resources:

Block, P. (1981). *Flawless consulting* (chap. 11, "Getting the data"). San Francisco: Jossey-Bass/Pfeiffer.

Goldstein, I. L. (1993). *Training organizations* (3rd ed.; chap. 3, "The needs assessment phase"). Pacific Grove, CA: Brooks/Cole.

Kaufman, R., Roja, A. M., & Mayer, H. (1993). *Needs assessment: A user's guide*. Englewood Cliffs, NJ: Educational Technology.

Ulschak, F. L. (1983). *Human resource development: The theory and practice of needs assessment.* Reston, VA: Reston.

Zemke, R., & Kramlinger, T. (1982). *Figuring things out: A trainer's guide to needs and task analysis.* Reading, MA: Addison-Wesley.

The first is how needs assessment and training design fit into the larger context of the training process. As a designer, you will always be balancing the details of a particular learning event with the bigger picture: "How does this event fit with and support organizational objectives?" The first part of the chapter briefly describes the relationships among the major components of the training process.

The second part of the chapter focuses on converting needs assessment data to design requirements. At times, you may be the person who is responsible both for managing the needs assessment and for developing the training. At other times, you may create your design on the basis of needs assessment data gathered by someone else. In either case, there is critical information you need in order to convert the needs assessment data to design requirements; we will describe exactly what data you will analyze from a needs assessment in order to move into the first stage of the design process, formulating training goals and objectives.

THE TRAINING PROCESS

Learning happens only partially during the training event; it also happens during the application on the job. In organizations, real learning manifests itself in the changes that take place in people's knowledge, skills, and attitudes. Training design is just one part of the larger training process, and in most organizations the training process goes hand in hand with the organization development process.

The training process is dynamic, although it is often described in a linear fashion, as certain components do precede others. (Needs assessment, for example, precedes training design). But in vital organizations, all of the steps are happening all the time, and they are continually influencing one another.

The core of the training process, of course, is organizational objectives. In fact, the reason for training is to support organizational objectives, both short-term and long-term, by helping people perform in the ways that the organization needs. That is what chiefly distinguishes training from education: the focus on meeting organizational objectives through the application of specific skills.

Surrounding and supporting the organizational objectives are the five key components of the training process: needs assessment, design, delivery, transfer, and evaluation.

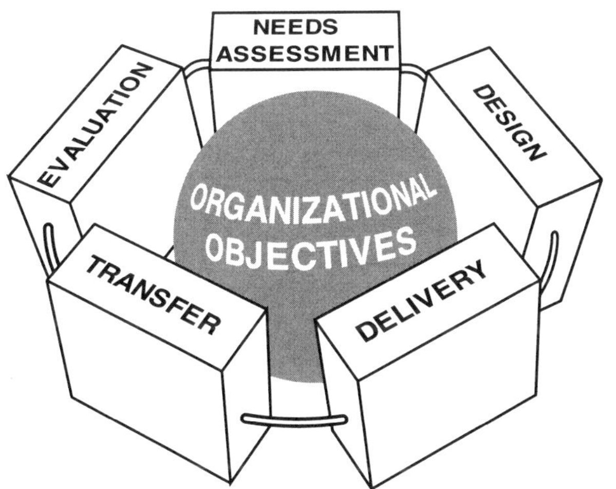

Needs Assessment

Generally considered the first component of the training process, effective needs assessment begins with the organizational objectives. A needs assessment may uncover needs in many areas: systems, procedures, structures, resources, or employee competencies. Some will be organizational needs, some training needs; often, the two overlap. The training needs are those that can be met through learning.

In addition, the needs assessment also helps define the key characteristics of the learners and of the organizational context in which they learn.

Design

The design component, of course, is the development of learning events that will enable participants to perform the desired behaviors. Starting with the data gathered by the needs assessment and converted into design requirements, the designer translates training needs into goals and measurable objectives, selects the essential content, and develops and sequences learning activities through which the participants will master the skills included in the objectives. In addition, the designer determines appropriate delivery platforms—computer-based training, independent study, facilitated discussion, instructor-led workshops—and develops the necessary materials to support and evaluate the participants' learning.

Delivery

During the delivery phase of the training process, the learners participate in activities that have been designed to allow them to reach specific training objectives, which in turn support the desired behaviors. Delivery may be a single event, a series of events, or a curriculum of learning events in any combination of delivery platforms.

Transfer

Another component of the training process is ensuring that participants retain and apply, or transfer, what they have learned. In any situation, forgetting a lot of what is learned is normal—unless the learning is reinforced. Not only that: regardless of how closely the training situation simulates real life, a great deal of the learning actually occurs later, during on-the-job application. In fact, research by Bruce Joyce suggests that, while 25 percent of learners will transfer learning back to the job after a training event that includes practice and feedback, that number jumps to 90 percent when on-the-job coaching is added to the learning process (cited in Gottesman & Jennings, 1994, p. 14). So organizations must plan for the transfer of learning—through systems and structures such as coaching, peer mentoring, supervised or unsupervised application activities, check-ins, and reinforcement activities.

Evaluation

Every performance-based objective becomes a criterion for evaluation: if participants are to be able to perform a certain behavior by the end of the training event, then the training itself ideally will measure their success. As part of the larger training process, evaluation should also address how the new skills are applied back on the job and what the impact of the training is on organizational objectives; if people fail to apply the skills or if there is no positive impact on business outcomes, the training process has failed.

That's right. It is not the training that has failed; it is the training *process*. Even the most brilliant training design and delivery—unless organizational objectives are clearly supported by the critical links of needs assessment, evaluation, and transfer mechanisms—is unlikely to improve performance. Overall success depends on an integrated training process.

FROM NEEDS ASSESSMENT TO DESIGN REQUIREMENTS: SIX DATABASES

As a designer, you may or may not have an active role in the needs assessment. Even if you do not, you must have access to the needs assessment data. You will convert the raw data to a set of design requirements that will guide your design process and help you continually evaluate your design products. If you are actively involved in the needs assessment, you can ensure that the needs assessment tools will gather data in the areas you need for your design requirements. If you are not actively involved, then as you review the needs assessment data to convert them to design requirements, you may find that you need data beyond what are provided in the needs assessment.

Think of the design requirements in terms of six databases that you would like to fill before you begin designing the training.

SIX DATABASES

- Training needs and desired performance
- Participant analysis
- Context for learning
- Designer's subject-matter expertise and resources
- Expertise of trainers
- Logistical requirements

Desired Performance

It is your job as the designer to create a training design that will enable learners to perform the desired behaviors. But where do you begin? Although education may begin in subject matter, training begins in application. In order to root all of your design decisions in the world of application and also to begin very early in the design process to think in the language and experience of your learners, you must create a clear picture of present performance versus desired performance.

We suggest, in fact, that you literally draw a picture of people successfully performing the desired behavior in their work or life situation—yes, even if you "can't draw." This drawing will force you to attend to details about the application environment, and it will help you focus on behaviors rather than on content. In some cases, the drawing will clarify that a single training event can realistically produce the desired performance. In other cases, the drawing will depict a desired behavior that is fairly complex. Then you might need to limit the scope of the training by selecting those aspects that will have the greatest impact and are the most realistic to achieve, given whatever constraints you may be working under. Or you might decide that a series of learning events will be required in order for participants to achieve the desired behavior. For example, in drawing someone

giving a successful presentation, you may note desired behaviors related to preparation techniques, presentation skills, and management of group dynamics. That may show that there is too much for one learning event. At that point, you and your client may decide to limit the scope of the learning event to just *one* of those areas of the desired behaviors.

Once you have made the initial determination of the scope, then ask yourself these questions:

_____ What skills do learners possess that are required in performing the desired behaviors?

_____ What new skills are required in order for learners to perform the desired behaviors?

_____ What existing skills will need to be modified or enhanced in order for learners to perform the desired behaviors?

_____ Assuming that learners acquire all the skills necessary for performing the desired behaviors, what else in the system will hinder their ability to do so?

Responses to the first question tell you what base of experience is already present among the learners. You will be able to build upon this base in your training design. Responses to the second question begin to delineate the new skills your training must introduce.

The third gives you some sense of participants' previous experience. That experience may help the new learning feel familiar; but it may also be an obstacle, as unlearning the familiar can be difficult. The responses to the fourth question identify organizational issues that need to be addressed in order for employees to reach the desired behaviors.

Participant Analysis

The more you know about the particular group of learners for whom you are designing training, the better able you will be to engage those learners. In some cases, you may know the exact group of people who will participate in the training, and you will be able to design it specifically for them. In other cases, you will not know exactly who will be participating, but you will at least be able to identify critical information about the overall group. For example, if you are designing an open-enrollment workshop, you can still make some general assumptions about the kinds of participants who are likely to be interested in the subject area.

We find the following audience information useful for clarifying design requirements about our participants:

SIGNIFICANT INFORMATION ABOUT PARTICIPANTS

- Number of participants
- Expertise related to topic
- Positions/titles/reporting relationships
- Diversity
- Politics
- Anticipated response
- Other issues

- *Number of participants:* You will need to know the number to guide design decisions such as selection of activities, as well as to estimate times for activities.
- *Expertise related to training topic:* Knowing the level of expertise can help you determine which content and skills are essential to include in the training and which may be left out because participants have already mastered them.
- *Positions/titles/reporting relationships:* Knowing the positions of those who will participate in the training gives you critical information about their application needs. Also, to protect the self-esteem of learners (Chapter Three), you may have special considerations—about putting participants into small groups, for example—if there are management and nonmanagement trainees in the session or if there are people in the training who report to others in the same training.
- *Diversity* (age range, gender composition, culture, socioeconomic group, differing abilities, and so forth): All training—no matter what the audience—should respect diverse groups. Still, knowing about your participants ahead of time can greatly influence your design. For example, on the one hand, if you know that you will have a broad age range, you can plan to draw out different experiences related to age, if germane to your topic; on the other hand, if the majority of your participants are in their twenties and thirties, you will want to select examples that would be familiar to that age group. Similarly, using examples of holidays celebrated in your country or culture may not work well for participants who are unfamiliar with those holidays. If you can find out before the training about differing abilities—around spoken or written language, vision, hearing, or mobility—you can design activities that engage all participants and make accommodations for special learning needs.

A STORY OF AGE

Once in a workshop about learning and memory, as an illustration of profound memories, a trainer followed the instructions in the design and asked, "Where were you on the day President Kennedy was killed?" The room was quiet. No one responded—because most of the participants had not yet been born when Kennedy was assassinated. It would have been a great example—for the right group.

- *Politics:* We find two questions related to politics to be especially useful: first, are there any politics among the people who will be in the training? For example, if you know that there is a lot of departmental competition, you will want to use the competition to facilitate learning rather than hinder it. Second, are there any political issues in the organization that may have an effect on the training? For example, in some organizations there are strong feelings around certain issues, such as teamwork or performance appraisal. If you know of such hot issues, you can avoid using examples or case studies in the training design that would bring them up—unless, of course, they are the focus of the training.
- *Anticipated participant response to the training:* Having some sense of how participants will respond to the training is very helpful to the designer. If you know that there will be resistance to the training, you will need to design ways of managing the resistance; you do not want to pretend that it is not there. Your design strategy will differ in each situation, but it is useful to know ahead of time when willingness or motivation to learn may be very low at the beginning of training.
- *Other issues:* An upcoming reorganization (or even rumors of one) can make it very hard for participants to focus on the training. Changes in the workplace or in reporting relationships can also be distractions. The more you can anticipate such external issues, the more able you will be to design learning that will work in the environment.

Context for Learning

Knowing about the context in which the learning will occur will help the designer achieve the best fit with that environment. For example, if you decide during the design process that you would like to introduce the training with a video by the CEO, the CEO's reputation is a critical factor in how the video will be received by trainees. Similarly, if you design an action plan that participants are to review with their supervisors, it is likely to receive one type of reception in an organization that takes seriously the role of the supervisor in ensuring transfer of learning, another in an organization in which there is no such expectation of the supervisor.

Sharon B. Merriam and Rosemary S. Caffarella in *Learning in Adulthood* provide a very practical framework for analyzing the context for learning, using three factors:

- *People:* Who in the organization supports training? Who makes decisions related to training? Who gets to participate in training?
- *Structures:* What are the processes and procedures for enrolling in training? What is the physical environment of the training room? What kinds of equipment are available for training? What structures and systems are in place to promote the transfer of learning (for example, mentors, coaches, informal application discussions)?
- *Culture:* What are the beliefs and values of the organization concerning training? Is training valued as an integral part of the organization? Are there norms that may affect the training—for example, a scientific environment that prizes analytical data, an activity-oriented group with little patience for in-depth analysis, a high or low probability that prework will actually be completed by participants? (adapted from Merriam & Caffarella, 1991, p. 28).

Having the answers to these questions can help the designer in two important ways: first, the information can be used to make the training design realistic for the environment. Second, the answers give a clear indication about what will be available to support the motivation to learn and the transfer of learning. In other words, knowing about the context for learning tells you to what extent you are designing an isolated learning event that will have little support and to what extent it will be part of a much larger training process designed to ensure that learning is valued and applied on the job.

Designer's Subject-Matter Expertise and Resources

As you review the needs assessment data and start to consider the design process that lies before you, you may realize that you know a lot about the subject matter of the training, a little about it, or next to nothing. In any case, assessing your own level of expertise is essential to clarifying your role in the design process—as is knowing what resources are available to you.

For example, if the needs assessment uncovers a gap in time-management skills, you might conclude (even if you have never designed training in that subject area before) that you could research the content and design a powerful training program. In contrast, if the needs assessment uncovers a significant gap in writing skills and you are not an expert in that subject area, you might be wise not to embark on designing the training yourself; it is not a subject area that lends itself to quick study.

If you do not have the expertise, what are your options? Here are some suggestions:

- You could collaborate with a subject-matter expert, combining his content expertise with your design skills and knowledge of the situation.
- If you are an external consultant, you might elect not to take on the assignment at all; perhaps you might refer the client organization to another source. If you are an internal consultant, you might recommend hiring an external consultant who specializes in designing and/or delivering custom training in the particular subject area.
- You could consider bringing in a packaged training program—whether computer-based or classroom-based. In this situation, you could use the criteria described in Chapter One to assess the program.
- You could choose to recommend sending people to outside training.

Whatever you decide, your own expertise has a significant impact on your role in the design process. Naturally, you continually assess your expertise throughout the design process, as you learn more and more about the subject matter. However, even at the beginning it is helpful to have some sense of whether you are dealing with subject matter for which your level of expertise is sufficient to make key design decisions or whether you will need additional resources throughout the design process.

Expertise of Trainers

Another important factor is the skill level of the people who will deliver the training—skill in the content area, of course, but also skill in presentation and facilitation. If you are conducting the training, this database will be easy enough to fill. If others are conducting the training, you may need to do research to learn more about them before you plunge into designing.

What is their level of subject-matter expertise? If it is high, the trainers will not need much supporting information in the training materials to help them master the content. If it is low, you will want to provide learning resources for them.

What is their facilitation experience? If it is strong, they will not need a lot of guidance on managing learning activities. But if they are inexperienced, you will select training methods that can be easily managed, and you will provide detailed guidance on exactly how to manage them.

The skill level of your anticipated trainers, then, will shape not only the materials that you develop for their use, but even the training methods that you select.

Logistical Requirements

In a world that would be ideal for designers, the designer would create a design on the basis of mutually agreed-on objectives; then the designer would simply tell the client organization how much training time is needed, what equipment and resources are required, and what number of participants is appropriate for the learning event. In the real world, this is the delightful exception that happens only on occasion. More likely, the client organization has requirements that must be met.

In our work, we recognize that the requirements may need to be negotiated during the design process, but we prefer to begin the process by identifying those logistical requirements that will affect our design. Here are the most important issues:

- Time available for training
- Number of participants per session
- Participation: voluntary or mandatory
- Training space and equipment
- Financial and other resources

Before beginning the actual design work, you will fill this last database by finding answers to as many of these logistical questions as possible.

A FEW LAST WORDS

When you have all six databases completed to your satisfaction, you have extracted the relevant needs assessment data and converted them into requirements for your training design. You have identified the following:

- The gap between present and desired performance (the training need) for which this training is being designed
- The predictable characteristics and demographics of the learners who will participate in the learning

- The relevant characteristics of the context for learning that will affect your design
- Your level of related subject-matter expertise and the resources that are available to assist you or collaborate with you in the design process
- The expertise of the potential trainers, in terms of both content and process
- The logistical requirements for the training design

At this point, you and your client will revisit the scope of the training event. Looking at the information in the six databases, you may agree that the scope you have defined is just right, or you may decide to broaden or narrow it. Then, with the design requirements in hand and the scope of the learning event defined, you will be ready to start the design process. Using the SIM, that process will begin with formulating goals and objectives.

Running Example: Needs Assessment

Let us introduce Simone, who has been successfully using the SIM (the Sequential-Iterative Model for Training Design) for several years and is about to embark on her next design assignment. For this particular assignment, Simone has been directly involved in planning and conducting the needs assessment.

We will take a look at how Simone planned the needs assessment and how she converts the needs assessment data to design requirements. Later, we will follow her as she uses the SIM all the way through her design process.

Background

Simone works as a training design specialist at the Jexon Corporation.

The Organization. Jexon is a seven-year-old software-development organization specializing in Internet software. The organization has more than eight hundred employees in three locations and has annual revenues in excess of $87.9 million.

The Request. Simone has been asked to develop performance appraisal training for all supervisors and managers at Jexon who have employees reporting to them. According to the senior management team, there has been a steady increase in employee complaints about written appraisals in the past sixteen months. Management has asked Simone to design half-day sessions for 185 supervisors and managers. The sessions are to be held within the next three months, so that the training will be completed before the end of the annual appraisal cycle, at which time the appraisals will be written. After that, the training is to be offered to all new supervisors and managers within the first three months after their promotions.

Senior management has emphasized that this training is very important. Everyone, including senior managers, will participate, and the senior managers have promised to do whatever is necessary to reinforce the training effort. They pride themselves on Jexon's reputation of being responsive to its employees, and they see an opportunity to reinforce that commitment. They also realize that the majority of Jexon's supervisors and managers have very little management training, most having been promoted into supervisory or management roles from technical positions.

Needs Assessment Strategy. Simone has decided to use five tools to clarify the needs related to written performance appraisals:

- *Review of written appraisals:* She received a representative random sample of written appraisals with all names removed. She analyzed these appraisals for trends, both positive characteristics and weaknesses.
- *Focus groups with supervisors and managers:* She met with four representative groups of supervisors and managers to hear their thoughts on the following: characteristics of effective appraisals; purposes of appraisals; what they are doing well in this area; challenges in writing appraisals; and their expectations, hopes, and concerns related to the training.
- *Interviews with senior managers:* Simone met with each of the senior managers to gather the same information as from the focus groups. She asked the senior managers to focus first on their subordinate supervisors and managers in response to the questions, then to answer the questions from a personal perspective.
- *Employee questionnaire:* She sent a brief questionnaire to all employees, explaining that she was developing training for writing performance appraisals. She asked them to indicate strengths and weaknesses in written appraisals at Jexon. She also asked what they considered to be the three major characteristics of a well-written appraisal.
- *Interview of director of employee relations:* The director handles all employee complaints related to performance appraisals. Simone asked him the same questions that she asked the focus groups.

The Data. The following findings were consistent in all five needs assessment data sources:

Characteristics of Effective Appraisals

- Honest
- To the point
- Brief, but complete
- Fair
- Not "cookie cutter" approach
- Written to help the employee improve if necessary
- Balancing the good and the bad
- Giving examples and evidence of both good performance and problem performance

- Focusing on performance, not on the person
- Linking individual performance to the big picture

What They Are Doing Well

- Good systems to monitor performance (many of them automated)
- Not avoiding problems (addressing them as they come up and in the appraisal)
- Finishing appraisals on time (formerly a problem)
- Using the salary matrix to calculate increases (on basis of performance)

Challenges in Writing Effective Appraisals

- Time
- Managing all the data—too much to say
- Trying to summarize
- Writing objectively about "gut feelings"

In addition, Simone's review of the written appraisals has identified the following problems:

- Many performance issues are described in attitudinal rather than behavioral terms (supports what was said about translating "gut feelings"); reviewers tend to "label" the performance or the employee in these situations.
- Very rarely do reviewers describe the impact of performance (positive or negative) on the work and/or the work group.
- Among appraisals in which problem performance is discussed, few contain any strategies for improvement.
- The level of detail in appraisals is uneven. Some give only very general overviews of performance with nearly no supporting data. Others, especially when there is a performance problem, include too much detail (supports what was said about the difficulty of summarizing).
- Performance often is not described in terms of trends. Incidents are described in ways that make it very difficult to tell if they are meant to illustrate a performance trend or a single performance incident (supports what was said about the difficulty of summarizing).

Here are Simone's observations and conclusions from the focus groups and interviews:

- There is a willingness to learn any tools and techniques to make the process less of a burden on supervisors and managers.
- There are continual time pressures, and there is concern about being away from the job for half a day.
- Only a few supervisors or managers express an understanding of appraisals as part of a performance management process. More often, the appraisals are seen as just an organizational requirement. Simone thinks that there may be ways in this training program to begin changing the perceptions of the role of appraisals in performance management.
- Many supervisors and managers say that because they are supervising people in very creative jobs, it is "impossible" to quantify performance objectively. They speak frequently about having to go on "gut feelings" and the few key things that stand out over the year. Simone will have to come up with some compelling examples to help convince this group.
- Performance expectations in the organization are very high.

Converting Data to Design Requirements

On this assignment, Simone was able to plan the needs assessment herself, so she is confident that she has everything she will need to convert the raw data to design requirements.

Desired Performance. In analyzing the data from the needs assessment, Simone has asked herself the four critical questions about desired performance. Here is what she has concluded:

- *What skills do learners already possess that are required in performing the desired behaviors?* The supervisors and managers are capable writers, use the performance appraisal forms acceptably, do appraisals on time, conduct regular feedback sessions with their employees, and are able to address problem performance directly.
- *What new skills are required in order for learners to perform the desired behaviors?* A number of skills will be new for most of the participants, including the following: describing the performance in behavioral terms; describing positive and negative impacts of the performance on the work and the work group; determining appropriate levels of detail; describing performance trends; incorporating significant performance incidents; and summarizing.
- *What existing skills will need to be modified or enhanced in order for learners to perform the desired behaviors?* The major one has to do with

development plans. Virtually all of the supervisors and managers do discuss development with their employees; they simply have not included these discussions in the appraisals. In addition, they are already doing coaching, but they need to put it into their written summaries.

- *Assuming that learners acquire all the skills necessary for performing the desired behaviors, what else in the system will hinder their ability to do so?* The major hindrance to the desired behavior in this organization will be time constraints. They are very busy working managers. Also, given the current appraisal cycle, all appraisals are due in the same week; this is a considerable strain for supervisors and managers who have large teams.

Participant Analysis. In analyzing the group of likely participants, here is what Simone has found:

- *Number of participants:* There are 185 supervisors and managers. There will be 16 to 20 in each session.
- *Expertise related to training topic:* Expertise is quite mixed. Each of the supervisors and managers has received at least one performance appraisal. Most of the twelve senior managers have considerable experience, but it does not necessarily correlate with high skills. The majority of managers have some experience, having been through one or two appraisal cycles. More than 50 percent of the supervisors have never written an appraisal and have had only the introductory training they received at the time they were promoted to supervisory positions.
- *Positions/titles/reporting relationships:* There is agreement that, even though senior managers have more experience, it is politically important to have them attend the same training sessions as everyone else. Supervisors and managers will be mixed in the training sessions, but there will be registration restrictions so that no one will be in the training with an immediate supervisor.
- *Diversity:* The population is diverse in several ways:
  - The senior management team ranges in age from twenty-nine to fifty-five. Supervisors and managers tend to be quite young at Jexon, with an average age of twenty-seven.
  - Gender mix is fairly even among supervisors and managers. Of the twelve senior managers, nine are men.
  - Jexon has a wide variety of cultures represented in its employee base. Supervisors and managers reflect the diversity of the employee base.

  - Nearly 95 percent of Jexon employees are college-educated. The other 5 percent are mainly in administrative and support positions.
  - All the supervisors and managers are fluent at reading and writing English. For 12 percent, English is not their first language, and some of these people are uncomfortable speaking in English in front of groups. Two of the supervisors are mobile by wheelchair; the training space is accessible.

- *Politics:* There are no "hot" political issues in the organization at this time. The environment is very competitive—but competition holds true across the board, not with regard to any particular departments.
- *Anticipated participant response to the training:* As long as it is brief and practical, participants will be quite receptive. If it seems to be theoretical, there will be resistance. The announcement that senior managers will be attending the training has been well received.
- *Other issues:* A favorable factor for this training is the schedule. The appraisal cycle will end soon after the training, and appraisals will need to be written at that time; so the need to know is very high. A less favorable factor is the rollout of a new product just before the training. If the rollout goes smoothly, it will create positive energy. If it does not, people will be distracted. For this reason, senior management has agreed that those supervisors and managers who are directly involved in the rollout will not be scheduled for early sessions of the training.

Context for Learning. Using Merriam and Caffarella's three-point framework, Simone has come to the following conclusions:

People

- Senior management has often included training as part of an intervention to address organizational needs. Most of the senior managers will support what is presented in the training, although several of them have a reputation for supporting ideas only as long as they "don't interfere with the work getting done." Simone knows she will want to work with these senior managers before and after the training to convince them that the extra time spent writing appraisals will be less than the time they now spend following up on employee complaints about appraisals.
- All senior managers have agreed to participate in the training and to send all their supervisors and managers. In addition, each has promised to hold a meeting after the training to discuss implementation issues. In the past, such promises have been kept.

Structures

- A new automated registration process is accessible to all who will attend the training.
- The training rooms are equipped fairly well, with adequate space and equipment for this type of training. However, interruptions are a threat because of two factors: a phone bank directly across the hall and the fact that half of the supervisors and managers work in the building in which the training will be held. It will be important to get help from senior management on managing interruptions in order to meet the half-day requirement.

Culture

- Training is taken fairly seriously, but two significant aspects of the culture are likely to affect this training. First, the culture is very technical (many engineers) and there is sometimes a disregard for the "human side of management." Second, training is often used as part of an intervention, but there is no long-term strategic approach to training; the message sometimes seems to be that as soon as the problem is fixed, training will focus on a new problem.

Subject-Matter Expertise and Resources. Overall, Simone is confident in her ability related to the subject matter. She has extensive experience in performance appraisals and has designed training in this area before. In addition, she works in the Human Resource Department with key people who manage parts of the appraisal process and handle the employee complaints related to appraisals. Simone also has access to written resources. For this topic, she is recognized as an expert at Jexon; she can proceed with the design and does not need a separate subject-matter expert.

Skill Level of Trainers. There are two skilled corporate trainers, and one or both will offer these workshops. Simone is not concerned about the trainers' ability to facilitate whatever activities she may choose to include, but because some of the content will be new to the trainers, Simone notes that she will want to include background material and resources for them.

Logistical Requirements. Senior management has certain logistical requirements, and Simone has decided to consider them "givens" at this point. However, she has also told her key client on the senior management team that she will be in touch if it seems advisable during the design process to reconsider any of the requirements.

Here are the requirements as they stand now:

- Half-day sessions.
- Development time—senior management would like to offer the training beginning three weeks from today.
- Sixteen to twenty participants per session. Therefore, all participants will go through the session within about one month (assuming two or three sessions per week), without too many supervisors or managers being off the floor at any one time.
- Participation is mandatory; however, participants will be given options about which session they wish to attend. An effort will be made to mix participants from the three sites.
- Conducted on site in the headquarters training rooms.
- Budget—normal development costs.
- One trainer per session.

Summary

Simone and the senior management team have agreed to limit the scope of this particular training to the *writing* of performance appraisals. Information about the actual delivery or discussion of the appraisal, as well as about procedural issues, will be handled at another time. Virtually all of the legal requirements are already being handled in a separate briefing; only a few legal points will need to be reinforced in this training.

At this point, Simone has enough information from the needs assessment to begin the design process. This needs assessment has given her a good idea of the gap between present performance and desired performance. Her sense is that she has a clear view of the desired behavior, and it is consistent with what she has heard in all of the needs assessment findings.

Simone feels fairly confident that the identified issues will be manageable within the scope of this half-day session. In addition, she has communicated the issue of time pressure to the senior managers, and they have agreed to consider staggering the due dates on appraisals to reduce the pressure on supervisors and managers. The decision will be announced before the training begins.

Simone has now finished converting the data to design requirements, and she is ready to move into design. She knows that she will become even clearer when she does the Goals and Objectives stage of the SIM, because it will force her into greater detail.

Part Two

Using the SIM

Using the SIM, or Sequential-Iterative Model for Training Design, is what the second part of the book is all about. Here, you will learn how to design training by using the SIM—stage by stage, one step at a time. In addition, with the assistance of Simone, a training designer at the Jexon Corporation, you will see the SIM at work in the Running Example.

The SIM is divided into five stages:

- *Goals and Objectives:* setting the foundation for the training design by starting with the design requirements (derived from the needs assessment) and answering two critical questions: Why are we doing this training? and What will participants be able to do at the end of it?
- *Key Topics:* determining the essential content for the training, based on the goals and objectives, and answering another question: What do participants need to know in order to be able perform the desired behaviors identified in the needs assessment?
- *Training Flow:* determining the sequence of learning activities. The question here is: How are we going to engage learners in mastering the content and skills required to meet the training objectives? This stage of the SIM is divided into two phases:
    - *Macrodesign:* taking an initial big-picture look at possible learning activities, sequence, and approximate times, culminating in a rough outline for the training.
    - *Microdesign:* laying out each activity in detail—how it fits with the others and exactly how it will be accomplished—and ending up with a precise outline for the entire learning event.

- *Training Materials:* developing all the materials called for in the training flow by answering this question: For the training to succeed, what materials are needed for the participants, the trainer, and the training environment?
- *Evaluation Tools:* finalizing the evaluation strategy and the tools that will be used to measure the success of the training. The question here is Besides the evaluation points embedded in the training activities, what else is needed to assess what has been achieved?

By following these five stages of the SIM, you will be working with your client to develop training events that are effective, efficient, and engaging. And remember, you don't have to say "the Sequential-Iterative Model." Do as we do: just rhyme it with Kim and call it the SIM.

6 The SIM

Training Goals and Objectives

After the needs assessment data have been converted into design requirements and you and your client have agreed on scope, the first stage in designing a training event is to determine goals and objectives.

Goals are general statements that articulate the relationship between the training you are designing and the desired performance on the job. *Objectives* are descriptions of specific behaviors that participants will be able to demonstrate by the end of the training. These behaviors support the goal or goals of the training.

PRODUCTS OF THE GOALS AND OBJECTIVES STAGE

When you have completed this stage of the SIM, you will have two products:

- *Goal:* A clear statement that answers the question Why are we doing this training?
- *Objectives:* Behavioral descriptions of what the participants will be able to *do* by the end of this training.

For example, for a half-day workshop on listening skills for medical professionals, the goal and objectives might look like this:

- *Goal:* To save you time and improve efficiency by increasing your ability to gather essential diagnostic information from patients.
- *Objectives:* By the end of this workshop, you will be able to
  - Identify three personal habits that get in the way of listening and select one technique to manage each.
  - Demonstrate your ability to ask closed- and open-ended questions to gather information from a patient.
  - Demonstrate your ability to ask questions to check your understanding of what a patient is saying.

Clearly, the overall goal—improving listening so that essential diagnostic information is heard—is a desired behavior for a medical professional. The three objectives define behaviors that can be measured during or after the training and that position the medical professional to listen more effectively. A good way to picture goals and objectives is to think of the goal as an umbrella under which the objectives fall. When they are well crafted, the relationship between the training event's goals and objectives should be obvious, just as the relationship between the goal and the desired performance on the job should be obvious.

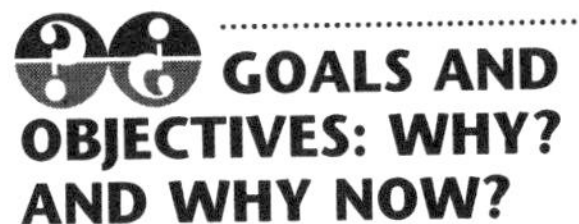

GOALS AND OBJECTIVES: WHY? AND WHY NOW?

A well-written goal statement answers the question "Why are we doing this training?" It provides the answer for participants, designers, supervisors, managers, and the organization. The goal statement must be broad enough to encompass the major desired performance on the job and narrow enough to define the scope of the training. For example, a designer might say that the goal of a supervisory training session is "to increase productivity." That may be true, but the statement is so general that it does not convey much; it might as well be the goal for *all* of the organization's training. A better answer to the question "Why this training?" would be "to increase productivity through better planning."

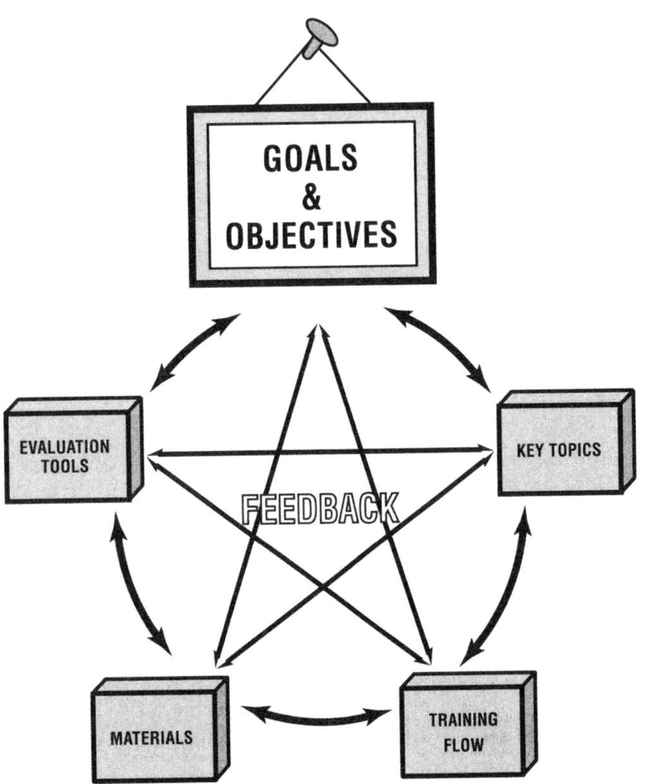

To strike a balance between goals that are broad enough to encompass many related competencies and narrow enough to communicate meaningfully about the training, the designer can ask some key questions:

_____ Does the goal statement answer the question "Why are we doing *this* training?" in a way that is clear to most who hear it?

_____ Is there a clear relationship between this goal statement and the requirements for successful job performance?

_____ Does the goal statement create an umbrella under which objectives will fall?

After the goals come the objectives, and objectives are the grounding for all good training design and delivery. Many designers have love-hate relationships with objectives; they know that objectives are important, but they still feel that writing objectives is an artificial task to be done at the end of the design. In our work, we have learned that objectives are the pot of gold upon which we can design a great rainbow.

Objectives and Design

Well-written objectives facilitate the design and delivery process in several ways. First, objectives define an end point in relation to desired job behaviors. They help the designer determine what content is absolutely essential to include in the training and what content is nice to know but not required for performing the behaviors described in the objectives. Second, objectives help the designer make informed decisions about methods to select for the training, methods that are closest to the performance described in the objectives. For example, if the objective for a computer software training is that participants will be able to save and retrieve a document, then a skill practice is the best method. The design could call for a lecture and even a demonstration (and if equipment were limited, that might be all that would be possible), but without skill practice neither the trainer nor the participants could evaluate during the training whether the objective had been met. Finally, clear objectives also define for the designer what is essential to evaluate.

Objectives and Delivery

Clearly stated objectives become a kind of contract the trainer makes with participants, guiding every decision she makes. Objectives help a trainer determine which questions to process thoroughly and which to answer briefly. They allow participants to evaluate their own progress throughout the training. They help the trainer make decisions about time. There is no need to continue a learning activity after the related objectives have been met, but other activities may have to be extended beyond the allocated time in order to meet essential objectives. To make changes on the spot, the trainer must know the objective—the desired outcome of the activity. Then, and only then, can she consider alternate ways to reach that outcome.

Objectives and Communication with Clients and Participants

Objectives are significant tools for communication with clients and prospective participants. With clients, well-written objectives can become tools for negotiation and for agreement on what the training is to accomplish. The designer has to articulate objectives to describe specific behaviors that the client sees as essential to successful job performance. In our work, we often ask the client to choose from a "buffet" of choices and explain those choices to us. This process helps our clients and us to clarify the needs of the organization.

For example, in working to design a career-management program, one client opted against an objective that described resumes, cover letters, and thank-you notes as "marketing materials." (Some of our other clients, in contrast, have liked this business-language approach to career management.) This particular client, in explaining her choice, pointed out that certain language was not valued in the culture of her organization. That was very important information, which not only drove the choices we made about language in the training package but also better defined for us the circumstances in which participants would be applying what we taught in the career-management workshops.

Most frequently, discussions with clients have to do with the time to be allocated for training. It is expensive to have employees away from their jobs, so managers usually want to minimize the time. In addition, most managers are not experts in adult learning, so they often request that designers and trainers "cut out all the fluff." (Translation: "Just tell them what they need to know, and forget about doing any activities.") We believe that one of our tasks as training professionals is to educate our clients, including line managers who may request training. Because these clients are adult learners, the most efficient and effective way to educate them is to tap into an immediate problem or need that they have. We find objectives a useful way to engage the client in this learning process.

Objectives and Marketing

Objectives can also be used to market training to prospective clients or participants. Consider the difference between these two objectives for a workshop on communication skills for supervisors:

- By the end of this workshop, you will be able to demonstrate three techniques for communicating clearly with employees.

Or

- By the end of this workshop, you will be able to demonstrate three communication techniques to reduce the likelihood that you will have to spend extra time "fixing" communication with an employee.

Both objectives describe the same behavior (demonstrate three communication techniques), but the second speaks directly to a client's or participant's perceived need (saving time). The essence of the objectives is not changed to communicate with different clients, but the designer recognizes that objectives may be recast to emphasize the interests of a particular client.

A CLIENT AND OBJECTIVES

Avi, a training designer, receives a request from a sales manager in his company. She tells Avi that a new product will be rolled out very soon, and she wants him to design training for her salespeople. Avi knows that the new product is similar to another product in the organization, and he anticipates that customers will have many questions and will find the differences confusing. The client has stressed that this training needs to be as brief as possible—thirty minutes or less.

Avi is concerned that with thirty minutes all he can design is a briefing that reviews the new product, how it is similar to and different from other products, and how to position it for sales. He returns to the sales manager and presents her with two options in the form of objectives:

- If he has only thirty minutes, then by the end of the training her salespeople "will be able to formulate (in writing) the responses they would give to confused customers." He will be able to evaluate these responses after the training and go back to the salespeople for feedback; the feedback, of course, will take Avi's time and theirs.
- With an hour for the training, participants "will demonstrate their ability to actually respond to confused customers on the telephone" (through a simulation that Avi will design). Avi will be able to mimic and measure the application of the skill (responding to confused customers) in a way that is close to the on-the-job situation. Also, responses can be corrected, if necessary, before the learners are back on the phone with real customers.

Now Avi's client will be able to make an informed choice. By using objectives to provide options, Avi helps the client to make decisions on the basis of her needs and educates her about how the training can contribute to her business goals.

In short, you begin the design process by focusing on the end—why this training is being offered and what behaviors participants will be able to demonstrate by the end. Your objectives, along with what you know about adult learners, will drive every subsequent decision you make in the design process. The objectives will also be your criteria for evaluating the success of the training.

Before we move to the how-to of developing goals and objectives, let's look at the criteria for objectives and consider how some different types of objectives will support your design process. Much has been written on both of these topics, so we will focus on the aspects that are critically important to the designer.

RESOURCES FOR WRITING OBJECTIVES

If writing behavioral objectives is new to you, investigate the following resources:

American Society for Training and Development. (1985). *Write better behavioral objectives.* Info-Line series. Alexandria, VA: Author.

Mager, R. F. (1997). *Preparing instructional objectives* (3rd ed.). Atlanta, GA: Center for Effective Performance.

GOOD OBJECTIVES: CRITERIA AND DOMAINS

There are numerous models and criteria for what constitutes good objectives. Here is our way of remembering what is important.

Essential Criteria

After you have established your essential goals, good objectives will help you *BAG 'M.* In other words, good objectives describe training outcomes that are

- *Behavioral:* They address something that participants will be able to do by the end of the training. Even if an objective focuses on what participants will know, it still must be expressed in behavioral terms.
- *Attainable:* They are within the participants' reach, given the starting point and the time available, and they are under the trainer's and the participants' control.
- *Goal-oriented:* They relate clearly to the overall goal, which in turn relates clearly to organizational objectives.
- *Measurable:* They are quantifiable—or at the very least observable. They address how the trainer and the participants will assess whether the new performance is successful; measurability is often implicit, sometimes explicit.

BAG 'M

After the goals are established, good objectives will help you *BAG 'M*. Good objectives describe training outcomes that are

- Behavioral
- Attainable
- Goal-oriented
- Measurable

For example, let's start with the all-too-common kind of objective that begins with "to understand X." The objective is not behavioral. The obvious question is "How will the trainer know if participants understand X?" If the designer converts "to understand" to an observable behavior such as "to list," "to describe," or "to identify," then the objective allows both the participant and the trainer to know when it has been met. Another example of an objective that does not describe a behavioral outcome might be "In the training, participants will examine the difference between proofreading and editing." This objective is about the training process (it is an instructional objective), not about what participants will be able to do at the end of the training. A better behavioral objective would read, "Participants will explain the difference between proofreading and editing and describe when each is to be used on the job."

Other objectives are written in terms of precise behavioral outcomes but are not *attainable*—and therefore not effective. Some are simply too big a leap. Others may be outside the participants' control—for example, "By the end of this training, participants will be able to demonstrate their ability to resolve all customer complaints." Still others may be unattainable because they are outside the trainer's control—for example, "After this program, 95 percent of appraisals will be submitted on time."

Objectives should also be *goal-oriented.* Take the example of an objective reading, "At the end of this training, participants will be able to apply standard rules of punctuation." If the goal for the session had been "to increase participants' ability to express themselves in creative writing," then this objective would not be goal-oriented. The objective might be wrong for the goal, or the goal might be wrong. If the needs assessment had shown that punctuation was a big problem, then the goal should have been worded differently. Either way, the objective and the goal should match.

The final criterion is whether the objective is *measurable.* For example, if the objective reads, "At the end of this training, you will be able to jump farther than you could at the beginning," both the trainer and the participants can readily observe (and perhaps even measure) whether the objective has been met. However, if the objective read, "You will be able to demonstrate your ability to listen better," the question of *how* the objective will be measured would surely come up.

Optional Components: Conditions and Standards

Besides the four essential criteria expressed by BAG 'M, in some cases objectives may include conditions, standards, or both. *Conditions* describe the circumstances under which the desired behavior must be performed or the resources available for performance. For example, you might write an objective such as "by the end of this training, you will be able to answer questions about product X, using the on-line help screen at your computer." The condition ("using the on-line help screen at your computer") tells participants that this is not a memory exercise. What is important is to be able to hear customers' questions about the new product and to access information from the on-line help screen. The distinction is important to the participant, and it will drive both the design and the presentation of the training; neither the design nor the presentation itself will emphasize memorization.

The second optional component for objectives is *standards,* which describe how well one must perform the desired behavior. Standards generally describe quantity, quality, or both. Using a standard, the objective above might read, "By the end of this training, you will be able to answer questions about product X, using the on-line help screen at your computer, with an accuracy rating of 92.5 percent." Including standards in an objective makes sense in an organization that has clear performance standards for certain desired job behaviors.

Other Considerations with Objectives

Because objectives are the foundation of the design process, it is not surprising that there are many considerations in constructing good ones. Among those considerations are the *domains* of objectives and the *levels* of objectives.

Three Domains of Objectives. In general, objectives can be used to describe three arenas, or domains, of learning:

- *Application,* or skill, objectives (sometimes called psychomotor objectives) measure participants' ability to apply skills—for example, to change the oil in a car or to verify the data on a form.

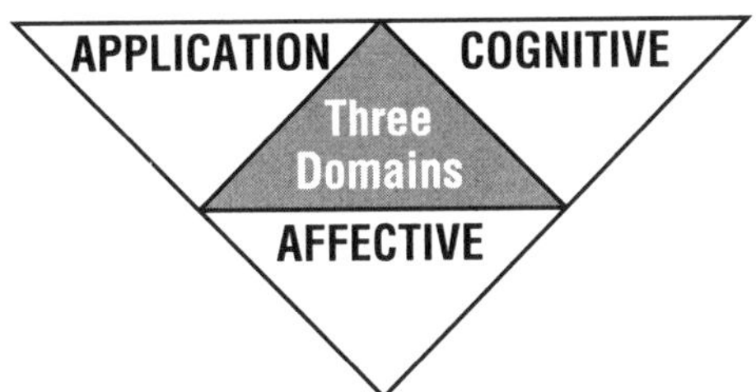

- *Cognitive,* or content, objectives measure what participants know—to explain why it is important to change the oil in a car frequently or to describe what are the essential data to be verified on the form.
- *Affective* objectives measure feelings, beliefs, or values of participants—to list three personal reasons why they want to change their oil regularly or to articulate what is personally most challenging about verifying data on the form.

Application Objectives. The application objective is the primary domain of training. Unlike classic education—in which students are learning for the sake of learning—in training, the participants usually are coming together to learn so that they can do something that they are not doing now or do it more effectively than they are doing it now. So, whenever possible, training designers try to write objectives that link what is being learned with how it will be applied on the job. In writing objectives for a workshop on selection interviewing skills, the designer would be more likely to choose "You will be able to demonstrate your ability to rank candidates for a job" than "You will be able to list the criteria used to rank candidates for a job." The second version—to list the criteria—is an enabling objective; it expresses only part of what goes into being able to rank candidates. The first objective is more powerful because it describes the performance in terms of the end product—to rank candidates—in terms that match what people do on the job (the desired behavior). Whenever possible, powerful design uses application objectives to describe training outcomes.

Cognitive Objectives. A cognitive objective aims to measure what someone knows. In behavioral terms, it may be stated as "list the features of," "explain the steps in," or "describe the process for." Whenever you find that you have developed cognitive objectives for a training program, stop and ask yourself, "What will people *do* with this information?" If the answer is that participants will use the information to perform a certain part of the job, then you should, whenever possible, convert the cognitive objective to an application objective—because the real focus is performing on the job, not just knowing the information. For example, a research librarian, in designing an orientation for new employees, may write, "New employees will be able to explain the differences between the automated catalog and the on-line indexes." That is a cognitive objective. If the librarian asks himself, "Why is it important to explain these differences?" he may conclude that employees must know which resource to use so that they will be able to find certain kinds of information. Therefore, a better choice is an application objective:

"Participants will be able to select which resource to use to find desired information."

If you cannot convert the cognitive objective to an application objective or if the conversion feels like too much of a stretch, then ask, "Can I justify keeping this content?" No one has the luxury of including unnecessary content in training; there simply is not enough time. Also, as a training professional, you know that learning is more efficient if it is tied to an immediate need of the learner. Nevertheless, sometimes an organization elects to provide information to employees for needs that are less tangible than direct job performance. For example, some organizations include an overview of their organizational history as part of their orientation. The reason is not that they expect employees to answer customers' questions by repeating part of this history. Rather, there is a sense that people will feel more included in an organization if they understand something about its roots. In this case, the objective is considered important for overall job success, even though it is not tied directly to any desired performance on the job. That is a justifiable reason for retaining a cognitive objective.

Affective Objectives. When we think of affective objectives, what comes to mind is the image of a minefield planted with a rich harvest of grain. The rich harvest is that these objectives can tap into potent motivators of behavior. People are most motivated to take those actions for which they have both external and internal reinforcers, and the internal reinforcers are their feelings, beliefs, and values. Certainly learning and training are inextricably bound with personal values. All the same, affective objectives are still a minefield—for three reasons: first, the designer and the trainer do not have control over participants' internal reality; second, simply entering this territory can make the training seem intrusive; third, things such as values are very difficult to measure.

But remember the rich harvest? The affective domain is the place in which the adult learner's internal motivators come together with what is being taught. Suppose you are designing a training event to teach supervisors how to use a new performance appraisal rating system. You know that the system can be used mechanically by anyone who understands it. However—and here is the rich harvest—you also know that those who take this system seriously will have a vital tool for communication with employees. For this reason, you want to "sell" the full use of the new tool. Like it or not, you are in the affective domain—because you want to motivate people to use this tool well—and you may choose to address that domain in the training design, directly and respectfully, to increase the probability that participants will see the value in this new tool.

Writing affective objectives is a bit of a challenge. Perhaps you have encountered an objective such as this: "As a result of this training, supervisors will value the new performance rating system." It sounds great, but several flags should go up in your mind: "How will I know if they value it?" "How can I make anybody value anything?" "If I try too hard to sell it, aren't they going to come up with every reason why this new system doesn't work?" With these cautionary questions in mind, you can then decide if the affective domain should be addressed explicitly in the design. If so—recognizing that values cannot be directly measured or controlled—you must try to identify what indicators of the desired value can be measured. For example, wanting supervisors to "value the new rating system" might be articulated as an affective objective in any of the following ways:

- Participants will identify three ways this new system will make their job of rating employees easier.
- Participants will list three things they like about the new system and three concerns they have about it.
- Participants will give an example from personal experience of a time when this system would have made it easier to rate an employee.
- Participants will describe what they like best about the new system.

Each of these objectives respects the personal judgments of participants, while explicitly tapping into their personal motivators related to the topic.

One powerful way to approach affective objectives is to look for the WIIFM ("What's in it for me?"). Whenever participants identify sincerely what is in it for them, then you are in the affective domain, and you are touching on participants' internal motivation to perform in the way being presented in the training.

Enabling Objectives. In any of the three domains, a major objective may depend on one or more enabling objectives. These are sub-objectives that help participants meet the major objective but that do not stand on their own. For example, an application objective for a workshop on changing oil might be "Participants will demonstrate their ability to select the appropriate oil grade." A related enabling objective might be "to describe the criteria used to select oil grade." In your design, you probably will not express the enabling objectives directly to the client or the participants, but you may well include them in the trainer's guide or lesson plan, because an enabling objective often is the reason for a specific classroom activity.

Three Levels of Objectives. Here is one last piece of information about objectives before we move into how to develop them. It is a distinction we find very helpful when working with application objectives and cognitive objectives.

"About" Objectives. These objectives are at the simplest level; participants merely demonstrate that they know about the content. Using the oil-changing example, an objective at the about level would be "Participants will be able to describe what oil does inside an engine." This level of objective is purely cognitive: it simply allows measurement of what someone knows.

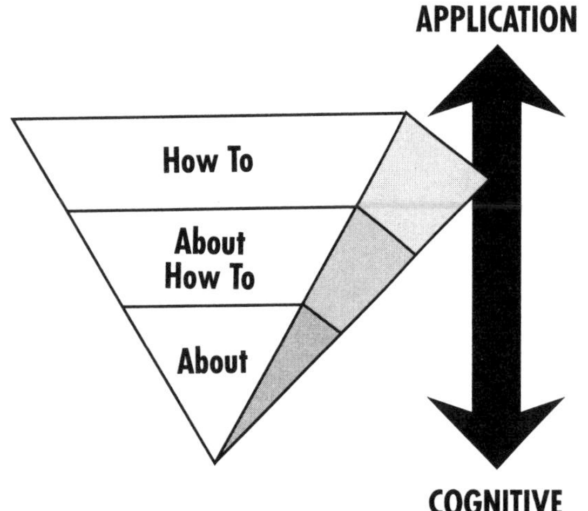

"About-How-To" Objectives. At this second level, you are measuring a participant's comprehension of an application. To use the oil-changing example again, such an objective might read, "Participants will be able to describe the tools and steps required to change the oil in their cars." You do not know if the participant can really do it, but you know more than at the about level. You know that the person can at least describe how to perform the skill. At this level, the participant is demonstrating a cognitive ability about an application. The objective comes closer to measuring the actual demonstration of the competency, but it still is not quite there; many people can talk about something as if they were experts, but they fall far short of satisfactory performance when actually faced with the job.

"How-To" Objectives. This is the highest level; it allows you to measure a participant's ability to perform some task. For the oil-changing example, a how-to objective might read, "Participants will be able to demonstrate their ability to change the oil in their car within forty-five minutes, using the tools supplied." Clearly, this objective commits the training design to actually measuring participants' abilities to perform the task. It will probably take more training time than the other designs, but it will truly measure the application.

So why bother with this distinction? Shouldn't designers always write at the how-to level? Not necessarily. In fact, there is at least one reason why designers cannot always write at the how-to level and one reason why they often should not.

Sometimes you *cannot* do it because there is not the time or the resources within the actual training to commit to measuring the application of a skill. If the training time is very limited, it is unlikely you will be able to evaluate each participant's ability to perform a certain skill. If you are doing computer training with only one demonstration terminal, then participants cannot demonstrate their ability to perform functions. You may have to be satisfied with the about-how-to level of objective—having participants describe how they would perform the function when they returned to their own terminals. Given the constraints, it is as close as you can come to the real thing. In designing training, there are always constraints.

Sometimes you *should not* write at the how-to level: you must consider the expertise of participants. If you are training people who have already demonstrated strong skills and who merely need new information, it would be a waste of time to measure their performance at the application level. For example, if you were designing advanced training on oil viscosity for specific automobiles in specific driving situations, and if your participants were people who had already mastered oil changing, the objectives would clearly belong at the about level or the about-how-to level. To write objectives and measure performance at the how-to level would not only be a waste of time but would show disregard for participants' expertise. The selection of the correct oil viscosity is the only new thing being added to participants' demonstrated repertoire of skills. At the about level, the objective could be "Participants will be able to describe the criteria they will use to make oil viscosity selections." At the about-how-to level, the objective might be "Participants will describe the process they use to make oil viscosity selections."

Being Realistic About Objectives

Having skimmed the surface of the whole range of objectives, you may be feeling somewhat overwhelmed. The best advice we can give is to sweat—and sweat hard—over formulating objectives that help you design effective, efficient, and engaging training. If your objectives are well developed, they will drive your design; they will also focus the presentation of the training, serve as contracts with the learners, facilitate communication and negotiation with your client, simplify marketing, and help participants evaluate their success during the training event.

Do not obsess about the precise articulation of the objectives at this point. Some organizations may require that all objectives contain a range for the standard. Other organizations have only informal criteria for standards.

Some may prefer narrative objectives that describe, in detail, the conditions and standards for acceptable performance. Others prefer very brief bulleted objectives. In any of these cases, the designer simply follows the organization's preferred format.

Frankly, some organizations would prefer to skip the objectives and get right to content and methodology. That's a risky approach. Even if it is the preference in your organization, don't do it! Without agreement on a desired end product for the training, neither you nor your client has any clear criteria for determining what to include in the training or for evaluating its success.

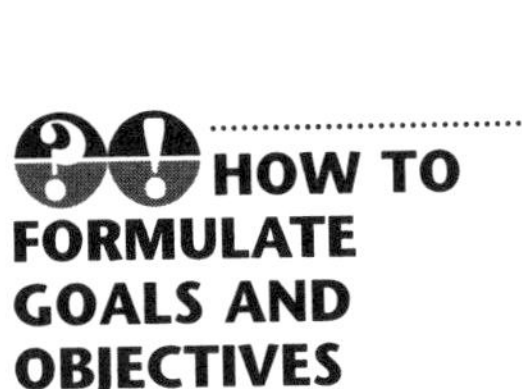

THE DESIGNER AND THE CATERER

As the designer of training, you will end up with two products in the Goals and Objectives stage: one is the goal or goals for the training—an overall statement of what the training is intended to accomplish. The second is a list of specific behavioral objectives—statements of what participants will actually be able to do by the end of the training. The objectives support the goal by moving participants toward the desired behaviors identified in the needs assessment.

Remember the caterer from Chapter Five? As she is planning a party, her work at this stage will also yield two products: a statement of the party theme (a goal) and a menu (objectives).

HOW TO FORMULATE GOALS AND OBJECTIVES

As you begin developing goals and objectives, remember that some of the objectives may still need refining during later stages of design. That is perfectly fine, because designing with the SIM is an iterative process. What you create in the Goals and Objectives stage must be sufficient to meet three needs:

- The goals and objectives are your tools *for further design.* They must define realistic outcomes of the training in behavioral and measurable terms. They must point to the related skills so that you can determine what you must include in the training and which methods are most effective, efficient, and engaging for reaching your objectives.
- The goals and objectives are your tools *for discussions with your client.* You will be meeting with your client to reach agreement before you proceed with the design, and the objectives must be in a format that facilitates discussion. We often tell clients that we do not want to waste their

money on formulating perfectly stated goals and objectives at this point. What we bring to them is a working document that helps both the client and us feel free to make changes as necessary.

- You may also use the goals and objectives *for discussions with subject-matter experts* (SMEs) who may be working with you on the training design.

Eventually, of course, the goals and objectives will be used in delivering, evaluating, and possibly marketing the training. Those steps come later, and you will be doing more work on the objectives before then.

Here is a quick example of how goals and objectives (with related skills) might look at the end of this first stage of the SIM:

Request. Two-hour workshop on taking phone messages

Goals. To present company in positive way to callers and to ensure that accurate data are recorded for following up on phone call

Objectives

- Demonstrate ability to follow organizational guidelines for answering the phone.
  - Skills
    - Select approved greeting.
    - Identify organization.
    - Identify self.
    - Ask how may be of help.
- Record required information.
  - Skills
    - Request name/verify spelling.
    - Request/verify phone number.
    - Identify whom you will be forwarding messages to.
- Describe one way that following organizational guidelines will make their jobs easier.

Let's work through the eight steps.

THE EIGHT STEPS IN GOALS AND OBJECTIVES

1. Review design requirements.
2. Establish a goal statement.
3. Brainstorm the skills for reaching the desired behaviors.
4. Edit: determine essential versus nonessential skills for reaching the desired behaviors.
5. Consolidate: cluster related skills together.
6. Draft objectives.
7. Review and edit the proposed goals and objectives.
8. Review the goals and objectives with your client.

1. Review Design Requirements. The design requirements, which you derived from the needs assessment, are the criteria against which you measure all of your design work, so of course it is necessary to begin with them. Here, in the form of a checklist, are the six databases you used for your design requirements:

_____ Visualize again the gap between existing performance and desired performance.

_____ Double-check your analysis of the participants.

_____ Examine the context for the learning.

_____ Assess your own subject-matter expertise and the need for and availability of resources.

_____ Look at the skill level of the trainers.

_____ Review the logistical requirements.

From this point forward in the design process, you will be focusing on the scope that you determined with your client. The scope may be the desired behavior you identified in the needs assessment, or it may be just a component of the behavior that this training will address.

2. Establish a Goal Statement. Your goal statement articulates the relationship between the training you are designing and the desired performance. It is stated in general terms and establishes a broad foundation for the objectives that will follow. Here is how to create it:

_____ Brainstorm responses to these questions: "Why are we doing this training?" and "What's in it for the participants to develop the skills presented in this training?" Do not edit or group responses; go for quantity rather than quality at this point.

_____ Analyze the responses. Look at whether each one is broad enough to include related training events.

_____ Draft a goal statement.

- _____ Eliminate anything that no longer fits.
- _____ Consolidate and modify remaining responses as necessary.
- _____ As you consider the content and wording of the possible goals, take into account the following: the organization's norms, climate, and standards; the likelihood of grabbing the attention of participants and speaking to their needs; crisp, easy communication; principles of adult learning.
- _____ Select or pull together a goal statement.

Remember, the goal statement becomes the umbrella under which the rest of the design resides. The objectives, content, training methods, and materials should all support the goal for the training.

3. Brainstorm the Skills for Reaching the Desired Behaviors. In order to develop objectives that support your goal statement, you will start by focusing on the specific skills required to perform the desired behaviors. This list of skills will come from your brainstormed answers to the question *What do participants need to be able to do in order to perform the desired behaviors?* Here are some techniques for brainstorming the skills:

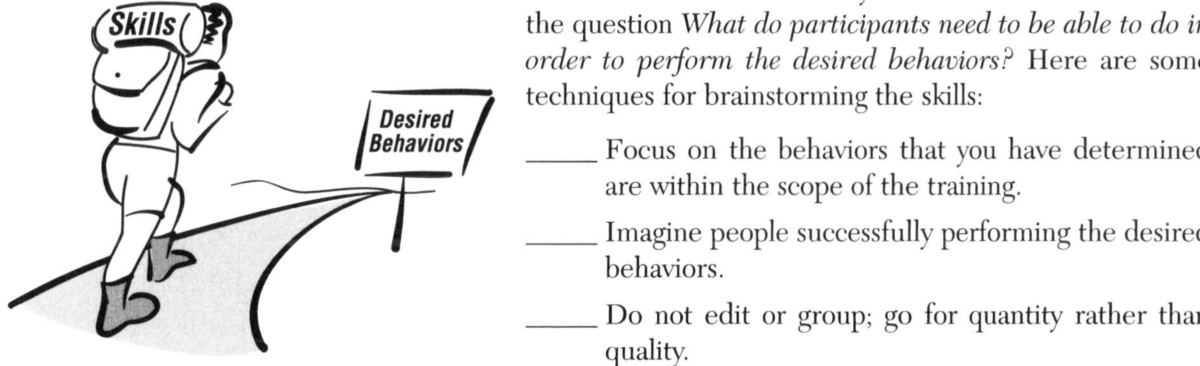

_____ Focus on the behaviors that you have determined are within the scope of the training.

_____ Imagine people successfully performing the desired behaviors.

_____ Do not edit or group; go for quantity rather than quality.

At this point in the SIM, you focus on what you want participants to be able to *do.* This approach serves several purposes: first, you are beginning the design process by focusing on desired outcomes. Second, you are thinking about the outcomes in terms of performance rather than in terms of content or subject matter. Third, by thinking about the outcomes in relation to performance, you are already putting yourself in the mind and the framework of the learner rather than the content expert. Fourth, by using a creative, open-ended process, you may generate novel approaches to conceiving the training that may capture the attention of your learners.

4. Edit: Determine Essential Versus Nonessential Skills for Reaching the Desired Behaviors. After you brainstorm, the list will need editing because, of course, not all of the possible skills that come to mind will truly be essential for reaching the goal or be within the scope of the training that you are designing. Identify which skills are essential to cover in the training you are designing. This is an incredibly difficult step, especially for technical experts who fully appreciate the depth of detail of the subject matter. Here is how to approach the task:

_____ Do not group skills into similar categories at this point. The temptation to do so will be strong, but if you do it now, you will not really be reducing the amount of material the training must cover.

_____ Use the following questions to help determine what is essential to be included in this training and what is not:

  _____ What is the overall curriculum plan? Is this the only time these participants will be exposed to these skills, or are some of the skills covered elsewhere in their training?

  _____ Where is my audience in relation to these skills? What can participants already do?

  _____ Can I look at this task developmentally? Is it the kind of task that participants can do at a certain acceptable level and then improve as they develop? (Here, you are assessing the difference between acceptable performance for someone new to a skill and acceptable performance for a seasoned employee.)

  _____ Is it reasonable at this time to teach just how to identify the problem and what the resources are, rather than insisting on participants' being able to resolve the problem completely?

_____ Go through your brainstormed list and determine whether each item is essential for this training. If you cannot decide, put a question mark next to the item and reserve your decision until later.

This is a key step in the SIM. Almost always, there is far too much material for the amount of time allocated for training. You are trying to find the essence of what participants need to be able to do by the end of this training in order to perform the desired behaviors.

Bringing together all these data to answer the editing questions is a complex task. In addition, you will probably have to resist the brain's natural desire to group similar things rather than eliminate them. If you do start grouping, you may feel better for the moment, because it will seem that you have reduced the list by creating categories of related skills from a list of skills. However, grouping does not really reduce the list; later in the design process, you will still be forced to admit that you simply cannot cram all the desired outcomes into the constraints of your training event. Even if you could, you would not be doing a service to your participants. You would be overloading them with information and skills; instead, your job is to help them to succeed by clearly delineating those skills that are essential to successful performance. In other words, the designer must be rigorous—even ruthless—in distinguishing essential from nonessential skills.

5. Consolidate: Cluster Related Skills Together. Now that you have determined the truly *essential* skills, you are ready to group them into categories. Why? First, you need to make the design process more manageable. Second, by beginning to play with categories of skills, you will once again have the opportunity to focus on them from the point of view of the learners and perhaps to create categories that speak to their felt needs. Third, by grouping skills, you may find that some are enabling skills, which are components of an end-product objective. In order to consolidate your list of required skills:

_____ Play with several groupings until you arrive at combinations that capture all the elements on your list, that make sense, and that may captivate the learners.

_____ Group enabling skills under the outcome category they support.

By the end of this step, you will have categories that contain all of the required skills you have listed as essential. You may find that some skills, in fact, fit into more than one category. That is fine at this point; go ahead and put them in more than one category. You are trying to group the required skills into categories that help you design and help you think about the training in ways that will enhance adult learning. Remember to play with categories as you do this step: try out different possibilities and combinations.

6. Draft Objectives. Next you will develop one or more objectives for each category of skills. The objectives must describe what participants will be able to *do* by the end of the training event to demonstrate that they have mastered the skills within the category.

In the earlier steps, you focused on *skills* necessary to perform the desired behaviors on the job and grouped them into categories. Now, without losing that focus on skills, you will describe the *behaviors* that participants will be able to demonstrate by the end of the training event; these behaviors are what the participants will apply back on the job. Here is how to go about the task:

_____ For each category, develop one or more objectives that encompass the skills in that category.

_____ Make your draft objectives BAG 'M—they should be behavioral, attainable, goal-oriented, and measurable.

_____ Use active, specific verbs that describe what participants will be able to do.

_____ Strive for language that is less related to content and more related to the needs of the adult learner (Chapter Three).

Because you are only drafting the objectives here, you do not have to make them perfect. Think of outcomes and on-the-job application as well as the scope of this training event, and use them as the framework to help you describe training outcomes.

7. Review and Edit the Proposed Goals and Objectives. This stage of the SIM has two products: a goal statement that answers the question "Why are we doing this training?" and one or more objectives that describe specific, measurable behaviors—what the participants will be able to *do* by the end of the training. In this step, you will review these products with your client and any key decision makers in the organization.

Your goals and objectives must be in good enough form for that review, but they do not need to be perfect. Basically, they will serve to help you and your client determine if the focus for the training is on track and, if so, they will guide the rest of your design process. However, they are likely to undergo some changes during the rest of the design process. Because you want to stay open to possible changes that increase the value of your objectives, it is important that you do not insist on absolute perfection at this time. If you do, you will be less open to a change during the later stages of the SIM design process.

Review your goal statement by asking the following questions:

_____ Does it address why we are doing this training?

_____ Does it state what's in it for the participants?

_____ Is it written in language that fits the culture and appeals to the learners?

Review your objectives by asking the following questions:

_____ Are my objectives aligned with the requirements I developed from my needs assessment?

_____ Do they address the characteristics of adult learners? Do they speak to real needs, and are they articulated in ways that maintain and enhance self-esteem?

_____ Are they responsive to the needs, experiences, and abilities of my participants?

_____ Are they stated in a way that is responsive to the organization's norms, climate, and standards?

_____ Do they BAG 'M?

  _____ *Behavioral:* Do they describe behaviors that participants will be able to demonstrate by the end of the training?

  _____ *Attainable:* Can participants be expected to reach these objectives by the end of the training event? Consider time constraints; number of participants; control (are the objectives going to be under the trainer's and the participants' control?); participants' present skills, knowledge, and abilities; resource constraints (equipment, space, and so forth); trainer capabilities; and other organizational constraints.

  _____ *Goal-oriented:* Do they relate clearly to the overall goal drafted for this training event, as well as to major organizational goals that may have surfaced during the needs assessment?

  _____ *Measurable:* Do they state, or at least imply, what level of performance will be considered successful?

Again, you are not trying to create perfect objectives right now. Nevertheless, considering these questions will help you draft objectives that address the needs (as identified in the needs assessment and your design requirements) and the training goals. It will also assist you in the design process and in building relationships and making collaborative decisions with your clients.

8. Review the Goals and Objectives with Your Client. Now is a critical time to make sure that your work meets with the client's approval. All the rest of what you do will depend on the goals and objectives, so ask for feedback and make adjustments as necessary. It is often helpful to prepare the client by saying something like "I don't want to spend too much of your time or money on the exact wording at this point, but I do want to make sure that these goals and objectives will meet the needs that we've been discussing."

After you and the client are satisfied with the goals and objectives, you are ready to move on.

Question: Now that I have my objectives, shouldn't I sequence them? Wouldn't that make the rest of the design a lot easier?

Answer: It may seem that way, but sequencing objectives at this point has two significant drawbacks. First, during the rest of the design process you may well discover that you have to refine, drop, or add objectives. If you have already sequenced them, you will be less willing to make changes. Second, the sequencing of objectives imposes a certain structure on the training design; but that structure may not be the most effective way to sequence the training in order to engage the adult learner, and you do not want to lock yourself in. All in all, it is simply too soon to start sequencing.

Question: I'm not certain what behavioral verb to use in some of my objectives, and it begins to feel like nit-picking. It is pretty frustrating.

Answer: Do not worry about it too much right how. Ultimately, the verb you select is very significant: it identifies the learning that you want to measure. Even at this early stage, you want to be clear about whether participants must be able, for example, to "apply" a policy or merely to "describe" it. But if you're wavering between "describe" and "list the elements of," let it go. Agonizing over that level of precision at this stage is fruitless. Just include several possible verbs or use some symbol to remind yourself that you will have to come back and decide later. Then move on.

Question: I'm having trouble selecting an appropriate number to incorporate in an objective. In designing a skills workshop, I've written the following objective: "Participants will be able to demonstrate their ability to use X number of techniques to ensure that they are getting the speaker's message." I don't have a clue what number to insert—it could be two techniques or it could be twenty.

Answer: What you are doing is developing a measure, or standard: a person will have to demonstrate a certain number of techniques in order to have performed successfully in this training. There are several questions to help you define a realistic and justifiable standard:

_____ When you look at the number of skills you will present in the training, is there a reasonable number that will indicate that participants have, in fact, grasped the material?

_____ Are you presenting different categories of skills/materials that make it desirable that participants demonstrate a certain number from each category?

_____ When you review the desired performance on the job, is there some standard (whether explicit or implicit) that is generally used to judge performance?

You may also want to talk with subject-matter experts to obtain their opinions. Often you are asking, "What will fit into the time allowed for training but still indicate the required level of competence both to the trainer and to the participants themselves?" It often helps to express these numbers as ranges. A range gives a minimum acceptable performance but clearly indicates that desired or optimal performance is higher than the minimum of the range.

If you cannot make a final decision on the right range at this point, pick something for now and refine it later—or simply indicate in your draft objective that a number will be determined later: "to use X–Y techniques."

Question: I'm not sure whether adding conditions to my objectives is worthwhile. How can I tell?

Answer: There are three important criteria to consider to help you determine whether to articulate conditions in your objectives:

_____ Will conditions help the learner learn? If, by including conditions such as "with the help of a job aid," you reduce learner anxiety and/or help the learner determine the real focus of the learning, then by all means articulate the conditions.

_____ Considering your needs assessment data, are conditions integral to the successful desired performance? If a participant can perform a certain function successfully only when wearing protective clothing, then the condition must be included in the objective or you will be measuring behavior that may not lead to successful performance back on the job.

_____ Will articulation of the conditions drive the design in a desired way? If you know that you are going to teach listening skills to people who do all their work on the telephone, then articulating that condition in your objective will drive the design to focus on skills and activities that are not based on face-to-face communication.

Question: You haven't said a lot about time yet, but I can already tell that there is no way I can meet all of these objectives in the time my client has allocated for training. Shouldn't I just drop some of them now and save myself trouble later on?

Answer: We purposely have not said a lot about time. Although time is a critical factor in making design decisions, it should not be the first or the principal factor. In particular, at this point in the design process, time should not drive decisions about what skills are essential to successful performance. If you are training people to use a computer software program and they have never used a computer, then—no matter how limited your time—if they do not know how to turn on the computer and access the software program, they can never perform successfully on the job. You may need to communicate that to your client.

What is critical at this point in the design process is to make decisions about required skills and objectives on the basis of the gap between present and desired performance. If, when you see your objectives, it is apparent that you simply cannot cover the required skills in the allocated time, then the discrepancy becomes a matter for discussion with your client. This discussion might include several possibilities: reallocating the time, providing other means for participants to learn certain required skills, or offering coaching and reinforcement after the training.

Question: You keep referring to my client. I am an independent consultant who wants to design a workshop for a general population. In fact, I don't have a specific organization in mind; I just have a great product that I want to develop into a training program.

Answer: When you are designing a training event that you hope to offer to a variety of clients, you have a special set of circumstances. You will be defining the requirements yourself, some of which would otherwise come from a requesting client. However, you will still do a modified needs assessment. You must determine a target audience for your training and then identify the gaps between that group's likely level of knowledge and skills and the desired level for successful performance. When you do your analysis, you will have to assume a wide variety of participants and design accordingly. You may find that it helps to survey other SMEs and examine some parallel training materials to obtain some insights into likely objectives.

BEFORE YOU MOVE ON

You have done a lot of work in the Goals and Objectives stage to create the foundation for the rest of your design.

Before we go on to the next stage of the SIM, imagine opening a computer file titled Goals and Objectives to see what you have created. Floating on your screen, much like a screen saver, you will find an umbrella that states the goal for the training. Under the umbrella, you will find clusters that resemble large atoms; in the center of each atom, you will find one or more objectives. These objectives describe realistic, measurable behaviors that participants will be able to demonstrate by the end of the training, and each of the objectives has a direct and obvious link to the umbrella goal. Around each cluster, you will find specific skills that a participant must possess in order to perform the behaviors described in the objectives. If you look in one of the lower corners of the screen, you may find a few skills that are still in question. You will return later to decide whether those skills are essential or not.

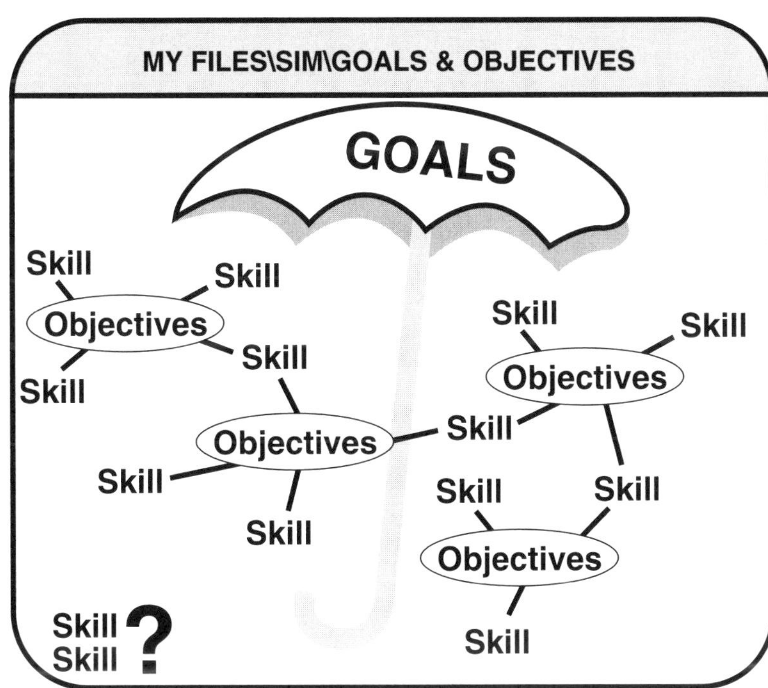

Please note that things will not look perfectly neat on your screen. They will be floating because they are truly in a state of flux. These goals, objectives, and skills may change quite a bit on their way to a final design.

It is time to create a new file called Key Topics. That's the next stage in the SIM design process.

Looking Back

Here is the SIM process up to this point:

Goals and Objectives

1. Review design requirements.
2. Establish a goal statement.
3. Brainstorm the skills for reaching the desired behaviors.
4. Edit: determine essential versus nonessential skills for reaching the desired behaviors.
5. Consolidate: cluster related skills together.
6. Draft objectives.
7. Review and edit the proposed goals and objectives.
8. Review the goals and objectives with your client.

Running Example: Goals and Objectives

With the needs assessment data converted to design requirements, Simone is ready to begin designing the training event. The first stage of her process is to formulate goals and objectives.

1. Review Design Requirements

For the needs assessment on the training at Jexon, see the segment of the Running Example that follows Chapter Five.

2. Establish a Goal Statement

Brainstorm Responses. First Simone lists a variety of possible goals—overall statements of why the training is being offered and what's in it for the participants.

- Stay out of trouble.
- Avoid grievances.
- Write performance appraisals (PAs) that summarize well.
- Become better at making suggestions for improvement.
- Write PAs that will help improve employee performance.
- Build on participants' good coaching skills and make PA part of this coaching process.
- Make PA a tool for managing performance, rather than a yearly requirement.
- Increase the comfort and success levels of supervisors and managers.

Analyze the Responses. Next she examines each brainstormed response. Might it be appropriate as a goal?

Brainstormed Goal	*Simone's Analysis*
Stay out of trouble.	Legitimate organizational concern, but stated in a negative way for a goal.
Avoid grievances.	Legitimate organizational concern, but stated in a negative way for a goal.
Write PAs that summarize well	At the heart of the needs assessment, but too specific for a goal.

Become better at making suggestions for improvement.	At the heart of the needs assessment, but too specific for a goal.
Write PAs that will help improve employee performance.	Good way of articulating why we care about better appraisals.
Build on participants' good coaching skills and make PA part of this coaching process.	Nice, honest way to position this workshop.
Make PA a tool for managing performance rather than a yearly requirement.	Good way to position better appraisals as part of the larger performance management process.
Make the PA process more meaningful for employees.	Nice way to highlight "what is in it" for employees and management.
Increase the comfort and success levels of supervisors and managers.	Nice way to highlight "what is in it" for supervisors and managers.

For your own analysis, you probably won't write all your own comments. The comments are included here for illustration.

Draft the Goal Statement. After analyzing the possible goals that she brainstormed, Simone modifies and condenses the most promising elements. This process leads her to several possible goal statements, such as the following:

- The goal of this workshop is to increase your ability to write appraisals that truly summarize a year's performance, describe the performance in concrete language, and offer suggestions for improvement of performance.
- The goal of this workshop is to build on your existing coaching and counseling skills to improve our written performance appraisals so that:
  - the appraisal is a management tool, rather than an organizational requirement
  - your comfort level and success are improved

    - employee performance is improved
    - the organization meets its legal responsibilities in this area
- The goal of this workshop is to increase your ability to write appraisals that build upon and summarize day-to-day coaching of your employees.
- The goal of this workshop is to increase your skills so that you can better use the performance appraisal process to manage your employees' performance.

Select or Pull Together the Goal Statement. In this case, considering Jexon's norms and the needs of this learners, Simone chooses the third of her four possible goals: "The goal of this workshop is to increase your ability to write appraisals that build upon and summarize day-to-day coaching of your employees." This goal, of course, is still a draft. Simone may modify it later.

3. Brainstorm the Skills for Reaching the Desired Behaviors

Simone's next task is to begin looking at skills that participants will need to have in order to perform the desired behaviors that are the focus of this training. Again, the process is brainstorming. Here is what she comes up with:

By the end of this training, we'd like participants to be able to

- Monitor performance in a way that gives good data.
- Summarize performance.
- Translate gut responses to behavioral descriptors.
- Describe existing performance in behavioral terms.
- Describe impact of performance on the work and on the work group.
- Meet organizational format standards for the performance appraisal.
- Describe desired performance in behavioral terms.
- Not resist discussing problem performance.
- Explain the legal requirements for the performance appraisal.
- Write suggestions for improvement in the appraisal.
- Make employees feel better about the performance appraisal.
- Involve employees in the performance appraisal process.
- Meet deadlines related to the appraisal process.
- Use the salary matrix to calculate salary.
- Leave out unimportant details in the appraisal.

- Avoid labels (positive or negative).
- Identify performance trends and consolidate data into overall descriptors.
- Emphasize positive performance in the written appraisals.
- Balance an employee's strengths and areas for development in the appraisal.
- Manage the appraisal discussion to keep it focused.

4. Edit: Determine Essential Versus Nonessential Skills for Reaching the Desired Behaviors

Now Simone assesses the brainstormed list to distinguish which of the skills are truly critical for participants in this workshop.

Brainstormed Skill	*Simone's Analysis*
~~Monitor performance in a way that gives good data.~~	Nonessential: the needs assessment indicates that participants already do this quite well.
Summarize performance.	Essential: see needs assessment findings.
Translate gut responses to behavioral descriptors.	Essential: see needs assessment findings.
Describe existing performance in behavioral terms.	Essential: see needs assessment findings.
Describe impact of performance on the work and on the work group	Essential: see needs assessment findings.
~~Meet organizational format standards for the performance appraisal.~~	Nonessential: outside the scope of this training; needs assessment does not indicate a problem in this area.
Describe desired performance in behavioral terms.	Essential: see needs assessment findings.
~~Not resist discussing problem performance.~~	Nonessential: needs assessment shows that people are already quite good in this area; topic is handled elsewhere in mandatory training.

~~Explain the legal requirements for the performance appraised.~~	Nonessential: handled elsewhere in mandatory training.
Write suggestions for improvement in the appraisal.	Essential: see needs assessment findings.
~~Make employees feel better about the performance appraisal.~~	Nonessential: feels more like a goal; is broad and does not describe any skills.
Involve employees in the performance appraisal process.	???: could significantly contribute to the goal of improving employee performance, but is not directly related to the problems identified in the needs assessment; can't decide at this time.
~~Meet deadlines related to the appraisal process.~~	Nonessential: needs assessment shows that people are already quite good in this area; topic is handled elsewhere in mandatory training.
~~Use the salary matrix to calculate salary.~~	Nonessential: needs assessment does not identify a problem in this area; topic is handled elsewhere in mandatory training.
Leave out unimportant details in the appraisal.	Essential: see needs assessment findings; seems to be related to the lack of summaries in the appraisals and the focusing on incidents.
Avoid labels (positive or negative).	Essential: see needs assessment findings.
Identify performance trends and consolidate data to overall descriptors.	Essential: see needs assessment findings.
Emphasize positive performance in the written appraisals.	???: could significantly contribute to the goal of improving employee performance, but is not directly related to the problems identified in the needs assessment; can't decide at this time.
Balance an employee's strengths and areas for development in the appraisal.	???: could significantly contribute to the goal of improving employee performance, but is not directly related to the problems identified in the the needs assessment; can't decide at this time.
~~Manage the appraisal discussion to keep it focused.~~	Nonessential: outside the scope of this training.

For now, those skills that Simone could not decide about will be kept out of the essential category. They are skills that would be very nice to be able to include in the training, because they would sharpen the training's focus on using the appraisal to improve employee performance. However, they go beyond the needs as identified in the needs assessment and the scope of this training; she'll include them in the training only if there is time. Simone won't know about the time until she is well into the Training Flow stage of the SIM process.

As a result of editing the brainstormed list, Simone has eliminated the nonessential skills. Here are the remaining skills:

Essential Skills

- Summarize performance.
- Translate gut responses to behavioral descriptors.
- Describe existing performance in behavioral terms.
- Describe impact of performance on the work and on the work group.
- Describe desired performance in behavioral terms.
- Write suggestions for improvement in the appraisal.
- Leave out unimportant details in the appraisal.
- Avoid labels (positive or negative).
- Identify performance trends and consolidate data into overall descriptors.

Questionable—Nice to Include

- Involve employees in the performance appraisal process.
- Emphasize positive performance in the written appraisals.
- Balance an employee's strengths and areas for development in the appraisal.

5. Consolidate: Cluster Related Skills Together

Simone considers several possible ways of consolidating the skills into categories. Here are three of them:

- Summarizing, describing behaviors, and making suggestions
- Writing appraisals that help manage performance
- Tools for describing and summarizing a year's performance, tools for writing the appraisal to help manage performance

The first set of three categories—summarizing, describing behaviors, and making suggestions—works well to include all the essential skills, but it seems quite dry; it sounds academic and removed from the interests of the Jexon audience. The second, a single category—writing appraisals that help manage performance—also works to take in all the skills, but it is so broad that it feels more like a goal, and Simone knows that it won't help her to design, because it doesn't group the elements usefully.

The third set of two categories—tools for describing and summarizing a year's performance and tools for writing the appraisal to help manage performance—appeals to her for several reasons. For one thing, all the essential skills fit into these categories in what feels like a natural fit—no forcing. In addition, Simone now has just two main categories of skills to address in her design. Finally, and most important, these categories seem closest to the needs and language of her participants and to the desired on-the-job performance. Participants will readily acknowledge the difficulty of trying to summarize a year's performance in one appraisal, and they are open to anything that will help them manage employee performance. Using these two categories, Simone rearranges the skills she has identified.

At this point, Simone's design work looks like this:

Category. Tools for describing and summarizing a year's performance

- *Skills*
  - Describing existing performance in behavioral terms
    - Translating gut responses to behavioral descriptors
    - Avoiding labels (enabling skill)
  - Summarizing performance
    - Leaving out unimportant details (enabling skill)
    - Identifying trends and consolidating data into overall descriptors

Category. Tools for writing the appraisal to help manage performance

- *Skills*
  - Describing impact of performance on work and on work group
  - Describing desired performance in behavioral terms
  - Writing suggestions for performance improvement in the appraisal
- *Questionable—Nice-to-Include Skills*
  - Involving the employee in the performance appraisal process
  - Emphasizing positive performance
  - Balancing positive and problematic performance areas

Simone is tempted to add the "nice to include" skills in the category of "tools for writing the appraisal to help manage performance" or to create a third category for them. It's important to resist that temptation and to acknowledge that these three skills are not, at this point, considered essential; one of the keys to successful design is keeping the design as uncluttered as possible. If she finds later, in the Training Flow stage, that she has time to include these skills, she will add them then. She knows that if she includes them now, she runs the risk of crowding her design or later having to cut an essential area because of time constraints. The illustration shows her progress so far.

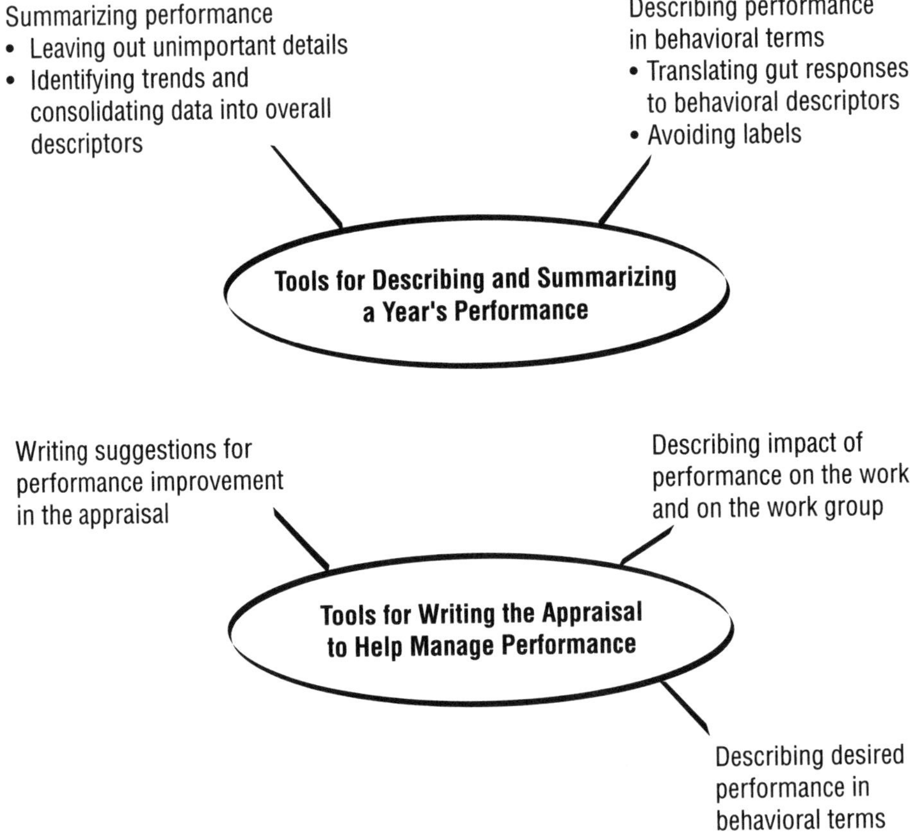

6. Draft Objectives

With the categorization of skills, Simone is now ready to start thinking about objectives—what will participants be able to do by the end of the training? She begins with the first category of related skills.

Category. Tools for describing and summarizing a year's performance.

- *Skills*
  - Describing existing performance in behavioral terms
    - Translating gut responses to behavioral descriptors (enabling skill)
    - Avoiding labels
  - Summarizing
    - Leaving out unimportant details
    - Identifying trends and consolidating data into overall descriptors
- *Objectives.* By the end of the training, participants will be able to
  - Translate judgments about performance into specific, concrete, behavioral descriptions of performance.
  - Describe the process they will use to ensure that they are summarizing performance patterns and trends.

Here is some of the thinking behind these statements of training objectives. Simone has decided that it is realistic, in a half-day training event, for participants to demonstrate their ability to "translate their judgments about performance into specific, concrete, behavioral descriptions." However, she did not feel that they could demonstrate their ability to "summarize a year's performance" during the training event; it seemed much more realistic that they would be able to describe how they would do it. Therefore, Simone decided to write that objective on the about-how-to level, not the how-to level. Participants will apply the skill back on the job, when appraisals are being written.

In working with this first category of describing and summarizing, Simone had an important insight. (This is where the iterative part of the SIM comes into play.) She realized that an essential summarizing skill had not come to mind during the brainstorming step of this stage of the SIM: the ability to "determine critical performance events to include in the appraisal, even though they are not representative of performance trends." Simone reflects now that supervisors and managers, while learning to edit out unimportant details, might have the mistaken notion that only performance trends should be included on the appraisal. This is not entirely true: a significant performance event (positive or negative) might need to be included in the appraisal for a variety of reasons. Thus Simone decides to add it as another essential skill; it is easily covered by the second objective she has already written for this category.

After this reexamination, here is how the objectives read for the first skill category:

- *Objectives.* By the end of the training, participants will be able to
  - Translate judgments about performance into specific, concrete, behavioral descriptors of performance.
  - Describe the process they will use to ensure that they are summarizing performance patterns and trends, as well as including critical performance events that are not part of performance trends.

Simone moves to the second category of critical skills.

Category. Tools for writing the appraisal to help manage performance.

- *Skills*
  - Describing impact of performance on the work and on the work group
  - Describing desired performance in behavioral terms
  - Writing suggestions for performance improvement in the appraisal
- *Objectives.* By the end of this training, participants will demonstrate their ability to
  - Describe in the appraisal the impact of an employee's performance on the work and on the work group.
  - Clarify in the appraisal concrete expectations for desired performance.
  - Include in the appraisal written suggestions for performance improvement.

The illustration shows how this category looks now.

Simone is pleased with the objectives at this point. They help organize skills, they are aligned with the goal, and they will assist her in discussions with the client. Also, from the perspective of what people need to be able to *do* by the end of this training, these objectives BAG 'M!

HOW THE WORK LOOKS NOW

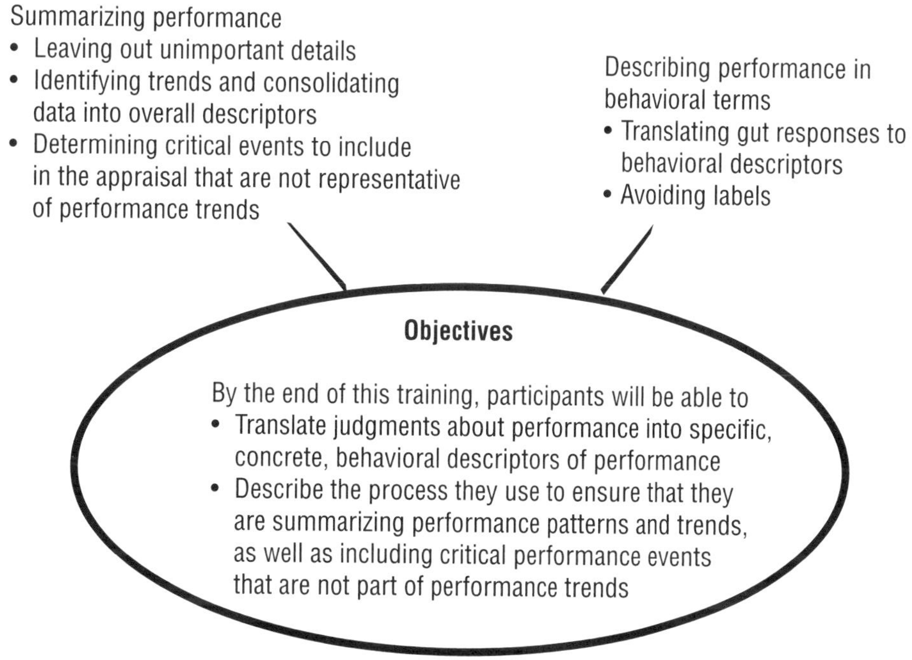

Summarizing performance
- Leaving out unimportant details
- Identifying trends and consolidating data into overall descriptors
- Determining critical events to include in the appraisal that are not representative of performance trends

Describing performance in behavioral terms
- Translating gut responses to behavioral descriptors
- Avoiding labels

Objectives

By the end of this training, participants will be able to
- Translate judgments about performance into specific, concrete, behavioral descriptors of performance
- Describe the process they use to ensure that they are summarizing performance patterns and trends, as well as including critical performance events that are not part of performance trends

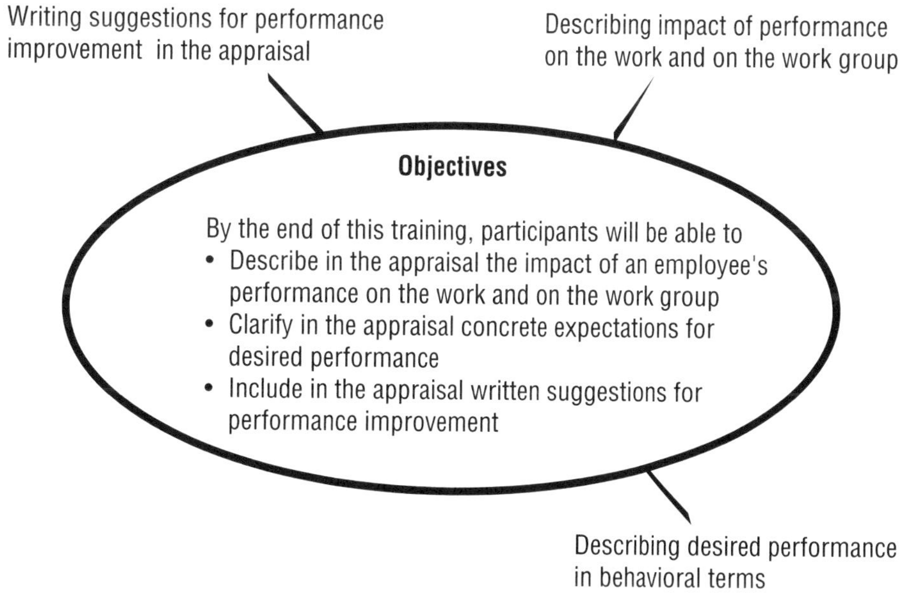

Writing suggestions for performance improvement in the appraisal

Describing impact of performance on the work and on the work group

Objectives

By the end of this training, participants will be able to
- Describe in the appraisal the impact of an employee's performance on the work and on the work group
- Clarify in the appraisal concrete expectations for desired performance
- Include in the appraisal written suggestions for performance improvement

Describing desired performance in behavioral terms

7. Review and Edit the Proposed Goals and Objectives

Simone starts with her draft goal: "to increase your ability to write appraisals that build upon and summarize your day-to-day coaching of your employees," and asks herself the three critical questions about the goal statement:

- *Does it address why we are doing this training?* Absolutely, because Jexon wants to emphasize that the written appraisals are summaries of day-to-day coaching.
- *Does it state what's in it for the participants?* Indirectly, yes. The goal describes building upon skills that the supervisors and managers are already using frequently and well—as shown in the needs assessment. The goal is fine in this regard.
- *Is it written in language that fits the culture and appeals to the learners?* Simone has mixed feelings about this one. She believes that the idea of building on their skills will appeal to the learners. However, the language sounds a little too much as if it came from the Human Resource Department. She decides to keep it for now and ask for input from her lead client.

Next Simone asks herself the five critical questions about the objectives.

- *Are my objectives aligned with the requirements I developed from my needs assessment?* Yes, they position the outcomes of the training in relation to writing the appraisal, and they address the major problems found in the survey of written appraisals in the organization.
- *Do they address the characteristics of adult learners? Do they speak to real needs, and are they articulated in ways that maintain and enhance self-esteem?* Somewhat, but Simone knows she would like to make them even more so. The strength of the draft objectives is that they describe the outcomes in relation to the appraisal, rather than in terms of just enhancing skills for their own sake. However, Simone wants them to be more aligned with the identified needs of her participants, to help grab attention early in the training event. In fact, Simone might even use the objectives as advertising tools to gain interest before participants ever come to training, so she will want to translate the objectives into terms the supervisors and managers express concerns about. Here are some possibilities for translating the objectives.

First draft objective

By the end of the training, participants will be able to

- Translate judgments about existing performance into specific, concrete, behavioral descriptions of performance
- Describe the process they will use to ensure that they are summarizing performance patterns and trends as well as including critical performance events that are not part of performance trends

Translation

By the end of this session, you will be able to

- Translate what is in your gut into language that is clear to both you and the employee and that reduces the possibilities of misunderstandings
- Describe some quick steps you can use to reduce an entire year's performance into brief and meaningful summaries without missing any critical performance data

Second draft objective

By the end of this training, participants will demonstrate their ability to

- Describe in the appraisal the impacts of an employee's performance on the work and on the work group
- Clarify in the appraisal concrete expectations for desired performance
- Include in the appraisal written suggestions for performance improvement

Translation

By the end of this training, you will be able to

- Demonstrate your ability to include in the appraisal the impact of the employee's performance, exactly what you expect, and suggestions for getting there

- *Are they responsive to the needs, experiences, and abilities of my participants?* After the revision in response to the last question, Simone thinks the objectives are better. The inclusion of phrases like "quick steps" really speaks to participants' concerns and to reality. The draft objectives feel much better now in terms of speaking to the identified needs of the participants.

- *Are they stated in a way that is responsive to the organization's norms, climate, standards?* Actually, they are a bit of a stretch. Typically, objectives at Jexon are stated in fairly general language—more in terms of desired performance on the job than behavioral outcomes of training. Nevertheless, Simone will wait to hear what her client says.
- *Do they BAG 'M?* Yep!

8. Review the Goals and Objectives with Your Client

After her own review and edit, Simone is satisfied that her goals and objectives are on the right track. She takes them to her lead client on the senior management team to solicit feedback.

The client's review is generally positive. However, she agrees with Simone that the goal, "to increase your ability to write appraisals that build upon and summarize your day-to-day coaching of your employees," could be reworded to better reflect the Jexon culture. They work together and come up with the following revised goal:

- The goal of this workshop is to turn your great coaching skills into dynamite appraisals.

The lead client thinks the objectives are just fine. Even though Simone and her client know that they may want to refine these objectives, they agree that Simone is ready to move ahead to the Key Topics stage and continue the design.

7 The SIM

Key Topics

Congratulations! You have completed the foundation for your design—a stage of the process that is often challenging and time-consuming. You have established goals and objectives aligned with your needs assessment and with the desired behaviors you identified as the focus of this training, and you have clearly identified the skills that are essential to meeting the objectives you identified. Now it is time to look at what content must be covered in order to build those skills and meet those objectives. In this stage of the SIM, you will be focusing on content; how the content will be taught will come later.

PRODUCT OF THE KEY TOPICS STAGE

When you have completed this stage of the SIM, you will have one additional product:

- *Key Topics:* A list of the essential content that needs to be included in the design because participants need to know it in order to perform the skills that support the desired behaviors.

The list will be organized into categories that address the needs and interests of your participants; the categories will be broad enough to encompass several pieces of content and yet distinct enough to be meaningful divisions.

For instance, in the training on listening skills for medical professionals (as in Chapter Six), the categorized key topics list might look something like this:

Obtaining Information You Can Use

- Kinds of questions—closed- and open-ended
- Why/when to use each
- Probing for more information: how/when
- Reflecting/mirroring what patient says
- Asking for verification/feedback

Keeping Information Flowing

- Listening as part of the bigger picture
- Results of ineffective listening behaviors
- Options/tips for managing ineffective personal habits

Note that these two categories do not bear a one-to-one relationship with the three objectives. They don't need to. The key topic categories cover all of the information or knowledge that participants will need to have in order to meet the behavioral objectives—that is, in order to *do* what they are expected to be able to do. They address two critical needs of the participants: how to get the information needed for diagnosis and how to avoid stopping the flow of information inadvertently or prematurely.

KEY TOPICS: WHY? AND WHY NOW?

"But," you may be saying, "we already have the goals and objectives. Aren't they enough?" No, they're not. Behaviors are different from content, and in this stage of the SIM, you will focus on content. The process of developing key topics is necessary for three reasons: to distinguish need-to-know from nice-to-know information; to double-check your goals and objectives; and to keep the information fluid long enough to consider ways of organizing that may be especially effective, efficient, and engaging.

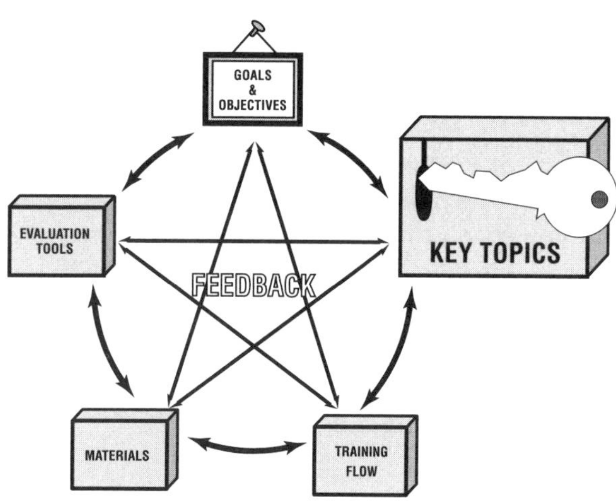

Need to Know and Nice to Know

A big part of your task at this stage is to separate what participants need to know in order to perform the desired behaviors from what would just be nice to know. It sounds like a fairly simple distinction, but bear in mind that training designs are like snowballs rolling downhill—they tend to grow and grow.

Before you know it, you run out of training time. What's more, you risk overloading participants with information. When information is new to participants, they have little personal experience to help them sort out the essential from the incidental. If the design does not do the sorting first, there is a high potential for learner fatigue and limited comprehension. That is why the designer has to zero in on the central question of the Key Topics stage: "What do participants need to *know* in order to be able to perform the desired behaviors that are the focus of this training?"

In order to answer this question, you will focus on the relationship between the potential content and the desired performance outcome—not on the relationship between the potential content and the overall subject area. Keeping this focus will make your work easier, and it will also increase the likelihood that participants will meet the objectives for the training.

Checking Goals and Objectives

This stage of the SIM is also a double-check on your goals and objectives. The process will feel familiar. You will brainstorm, edit, and consolidate again. However, the focus is dramatically different. In the Goals and Objectives stage of the SIM, the focus was on the *skills* that participants need in order to perform the desired behaviors. In the Key Topics stage, the focus is on the *knowledge* participants need in order to perform those skills. You will be developing a list of all the content to be covered in the training.

IDENTIFYING REQUIRED KNOWLEDGE TO SUPPORT DESIRED BEHAVIORS

Imagine that you are designing training for a new word-processing program. One of your desired behaviors might be "to be able to delete text from a document in at least two ways." In order to do this, participants need to know that one way of deleting text ("command" + "cut" keys) saves it to a recycling bin from which it can be retrieved if they change their minds. The second way, though an easier process ("delete"), is a permanent deletion. That is essential knowledge for performing the desired behavior in a way that will serve them when they are applying the behavior in their work.

The familiar process, with a new focus, takes advantage of the iterative nature of the SIM. Frequently, the designers whom we teach realize—by working through this stage and asking questions from different points of view—that they missed some important skills or objectives in the first stage. Sometimes they realize that the participants already have relevant content expertise, and the objectives can be adjusted accordingly.

For example, if participants already have enough content knowledge, an objective originally stated as "to list the major parts of X" might become "to demonstrate two or three ways X can be used in your present job." The designer would be changing a cognitive objective to an application objective. That's great, because application is richer in this case; it is attainable, because participants are already familiar with essential content.

Also, in this stage of the SIM, designers may identify the need for a content objective that is not tied to any specific skill but is essential to success in the organization. For example, participants may need to be able to describe why the organization has a particular policy on performance appraisals. Certainly supervisors could perform the desired behaviors without being able to explain the reasons for the policy; but if familiarity with human resource policies is a high priority for the organization, then this knowledge is an essential bit of content.

Playing with Categories

The Key Topics stage of the SIM encourages you to play with relationships among data. You will categorize your essential content, but you will not create a formal outline of the content. Why not? After all, most of us were taught, early in our education, to think in outline form; we were told that outlines were a way to save time and keep our writing focused. But there is a cost—a cost to creativity, as described by Colin Rose in *Accelerated Learning* (1989). Outlining typically engages the left side of the brain (the logical, sequential side) without also engaging the right (the more creative, abstract side). Most outlines are sequential, chronological, or categorical; the organization of the outline depends somewhat on the material, but mostly it depends on the designer's information-processing preference. In other words, an outline you create organizes the material in a sequence that fits your own preferences in learning and information processing. When this initial outline drives the rest of the design (as it is sure to do), it builds on a structure you have already imposed, although perhaps unconsciously. That structure may not be the most effective, efficient, or engaging one for your learners.

Instead, the Key Topics stage of the SIM suggests a process much more like mind-mapping. It asks you to "play" for a while with potential categories that will help you group the essential content. If you play against the backdrop of a thorough needs assessment, you are more likely to generate categories that have to do with the needs of the learners and with application on the job than with the obvious categories that may be associated with your content. At this stage, all the SIM asks you to do is to arrange the essential content (key points) in categories (key topics) that work for you and your learners and to consider some possible organizational structures for your design. In this way, you are invited to expand beyond your preferred information-processing style to identify some options that might work for your objectives, learners, and content.

Playing with categories has another benefit: it frequently leads to visual or metaphorical models that can be used as core reference points to integrate the content. Once, our team was designing an advanced session on planning and managing discussions. As we played with the content, we noticed that we kept talking about "getting and keeping the discussion on track." Out of that grew the metaphor of a railroad, which helped us to organize all of our content and later became the model for this portion of the training. We talked about "getting people on board" in a discussion, "keeping the discussion on track," and "keeping people on board" throughout the journey. It was a powerful metaphor; it assisted the design and continues to serve as a core reference point for the delivery of the session. Participants are able to use the three aspects of the model to categorize and remember what they learn in the training.

Relating Key Topics to the Design Process

Although new designers often begin with content, it is not a good idea. Training is different from education; the focus of training is performance, not simply content for its own sake. By developing goals and objectives first, you have established the criteria that will help you determine what is essential versus nonessential content. You are considering what participants need to know, and you are doing it immediately after you have identified what skills they need in order to perform successfully.

The Key Topics stage comes before any consideration of training methods in order to save time and maintain a tight focus during the design process. Most designers are tempted to begin selecting appealing methods (because they are novel, feel like a good fit for the organization, or match the designer's preferred style of learning), but those methods may not be effective, efficient, or engaging ways to reach objectives. Just wait. After you have the combination of objectives and key topics, then you will have a framework and some criteria for selecting appropriate training methods.

Of course, you may think of some ideas for activities while you are playing with the content. Great! Record those ideas somewhere so that you can come back to them. You certainly do not want to disregard potentially useful learning activities simply because you are not at that stage of the design. However, avoid the trap of actually designing learning activities at this point.

Why is it a trap? First, you may be wasting time and losing focus. Second—and more dangerous—you may fall in love with the activity. If that happens, then surely the activity will find its way into your design, regardless of whether it is an effective, efficient, or engaging way of meeting objectives.

Also, you may have some great ideas for materials (a handout or a visual aid) or for evaluation tools or techniques at this stage. Jot them down for later. Don't start creating materials until you have made your best decisions concerning content and methods. Remember, it is still quite possible that the objectives for this training may be modified, so it is too early to design your evaluation tools in detail.

Potential Challenges for Key Topics

Determining what is essential to know versus what is nice to know is a very difficult task, particularly for two categories of designers:

- Some designers are subject-matter experts or have been deeply involved in what is being taught. These designers often find that nearly everything seems important. They keenly appreciate all the subtle nuances of the subject, and it can be a stretch for them to imagine the position of someone who is learning the subject for the first time.
- Many designers are highly intuitive and conceptual thinkers, who naturally see multiple relationships among concepts. This wonderful gift brings with it some costs as well as rewards. The ability to see relationships allows such designers to give the big picture, but it may also make it difficult for them to cut out any content, because it all seems related and therefore essential.

Both of these categories of designers must bear in mind a certain painful reality: there is virtually never enough time for training. Decisions to eliminate content—challenging though they may be—are critical to successful design.

Another challenge is that the Key Topics stage of the SIM often feels redundant—particularly to people who are new to the SIM. Yet, even though the process is similar to the one described for goals and objectives, the focus is very different. If you find yourself feeling this way, it will help if you pay particular attention to skills and behaviors in the Goals and Objectives stage and to content in the Key Topics stage.

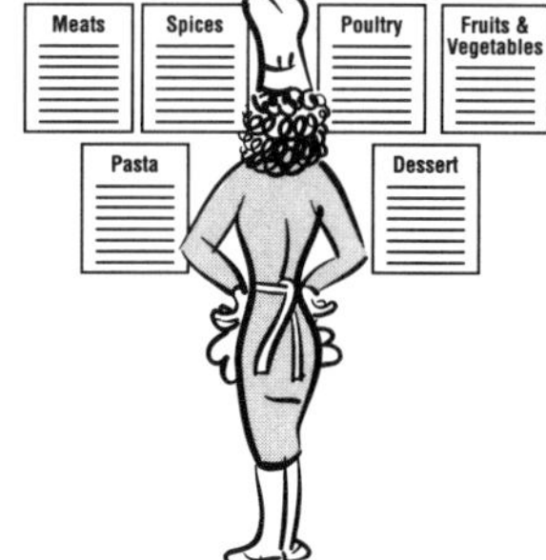

THE DESIGNER AND THE CATERER

Remember the caterer from earlier chapters? At the completion of this stage of her party planning, the caterer will have a complete list of ingredients grouped into categories. These ingredients are what she must include to produce the dishes on her menu—that is, the essential ingredients for reaching her objectives.

HOW TO DEVELOP KEY TOPICS

As you work to determine the key topics for your training, you will be building on what you did during the Goals and Objectives stage. In fact, during the Key Topics stage, the iterative nature of the SIM may cause you to rethink some of your objectives. Remember, that is not a bad thing; it is a sign that the process is working.

During this stage, you will be considering what your learners need to know in order to perform the desired behaviors that you defined earlier, and you will be considering possible ways of arranging the information. As in the Goals and Objectives stage, the work you do in the Key Topics stage does not have to be "perfect"; everything you produce is still a working document.

Some guidelines to keep in mind:

- You will be developing a list of essential content—key points. Then you will be grouping your key points loosely into categories—key topics—that seem promising in terms of engaging your learners. These categories will remain loose; you will not at this stage be committing to specific categories or ways of organizing.
- The key topics will serve as a check on your objectives. As you develop the key topics, you will be going back to the desired behaviors, not to the objectives. If you try to take a shortcut and base your key topics directly on your objectives, you will never find out whether something is missing from your objectives.
- You will be considering organizational structures, but you will not commit to a structure until the next stage of the SIM, after you have looked at possible learning activities.
- As you did during the Goals and Objectives stage, you will be checking the results of the Key Topics stage with your client.

THE EIGHT STEPS IN KEY TOPICS

Step by step, here is an overview of the process:

1. Research the subject.
2. Brainstorm possible key points.
3. Determine essential versus nonessential points.
4. Group key points into key topics.
5. Identify additional points for key topics.
6. Consider possible organizational structures.
7. Review and edit key topics.
8. Check work with your client.

Here is how to implement the eight steps:

1. Research the Subject. If you are a subject-matter expert, you may be able to move on immediately to the next step. However, if you are not a subject-matter expert, you will have to do some research in order to identify content for the training. Depending on the topic and on your own preferred work methods, your research will include some or all of the following:

______ Review your design requirements, derived from the needs assessment.

______ Study published resources.

______ Interview various kinds of experts in the field.

Published resources may include internal resources prepared and used within the organization. They may also be books, professional journals, other training programs, or on-line documents. Check the library or the bookstore, ask your client for recommendations, and look at the bibliographies of the works you are consulting for further suggestions.

When you consider experts to interview, it may help to think in two categories: experts in theory and experts in application. For example, if you are designing training on the use of an automated system, you may want to speak with those who developed the system or who are experts on its inner workings. Beyond that, you may wish to interview people who know how to make the system work for day-to-day job applications—perhaps even including some people who are new to the skill and are performing it quite well for novices. Interviewing broadly will give you the fullest picture of what is essential to know for successful performance of the desired skills.

2. Brainstorm Possible Key Points. To create your list of possible key points, brainstorm as many answers as possible to the following question: *In order for participants to perform the desired behaviors, what information, facts, or concepts might they need to know?* Bear in mind the following points:

______ Remember to use a brainstorming approach—go for quantity rather than quality. You will analyze and edit later.

______ Don't worry about exact wording, format, sequence, training methods, or supporting details. You will do that later.

For example, if you were designing training in how to write checks—for a group of participants who had no experience with checking accounts—your brainstormed list might include such items as when to use checks and when to use cash, essential and optional parts of the check, different ways of writing the date, how to keep checks secure, and so forth.

3. Determine Essential Versus Nonessential Points. During this step, you are deciding what content is essential to include in the training. You will use everything you know about the project so far and apply your own judgment to determine which points from your brainstormed list are essential and which are not. The following questions will help you identify what is not essential:

______ Do participants already know X?

______ Is X available to participants in other parts of the training curriculum?

______ Can participants perform the desired behaviors without knowing X?

The focus of this step is to identify the content that supports the desired behaviors, not the objectives you formulated in the previous stage of the SIM. If you focus on objectives, then the results of this stage of the SIM cannot be any better than what you produced at the previous stage and cannot be used to reassess and possibly improve your objectives.

Be sure to consider your learners in relation to the desired behavior. For example, if the behavior is new, just knowing some basics that will enable a learner to experience success quickly may be enough; more advanced training might need to include more sophisticated content.

This is hard work! You may need to let go of content that feels important. It might help to remember that "nonessential" is different from "not important"; "nonessential" simply means that the content does not absolutely have to be included in this particular training. If you cannot determine whether a point is essential or not, simply put a question mark next to it for now. Identify what resources you will need in order to make this decision, and reserve it for further consideration. Do not group the points—decide! You will group during the next step.

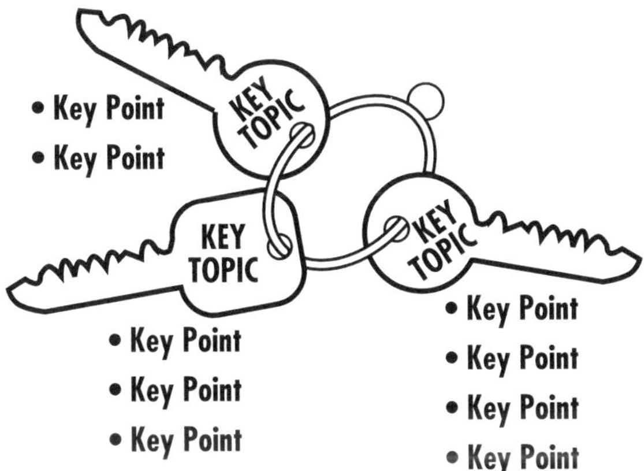

4. Group Key Points into Key Topics. After you have identified the essential key points, it is time to group similar and related points into categories. These categories will become your key topics, which will be more manageable for you during the design process. Remember that you are not trying to create

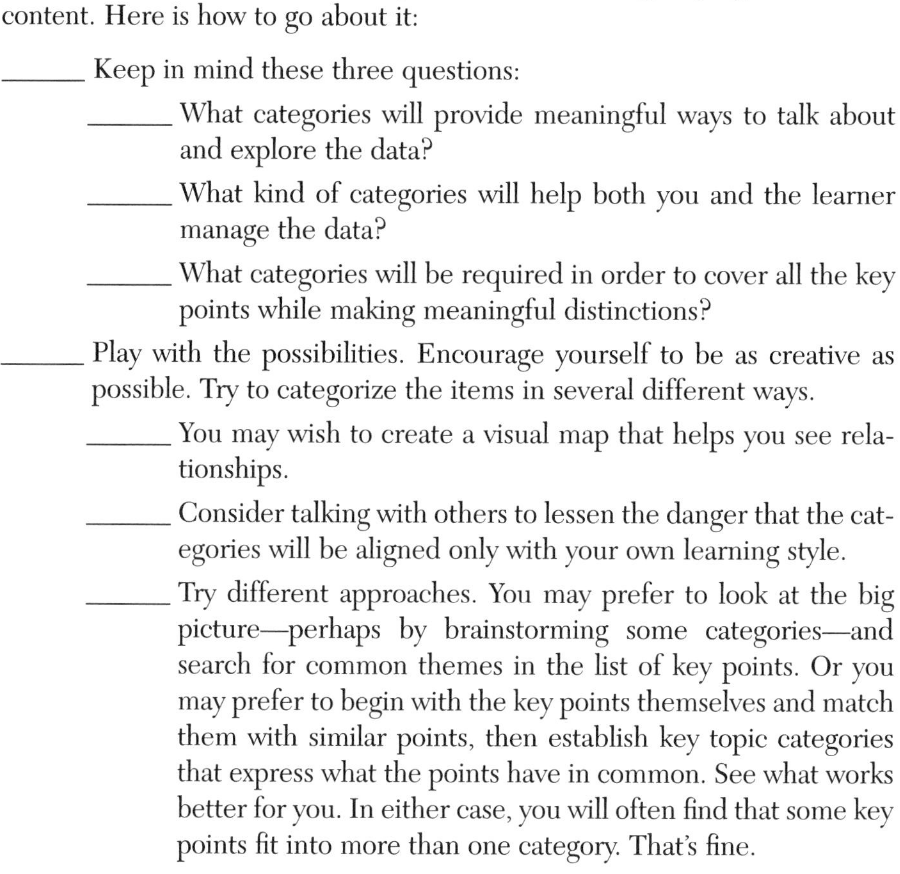

an outline here—it is still too early for that. You want groupings of essential content. Here is how to go about it:

- ______ Keep in mind these three questions:
  - ______ What categories will provide meaningful ways to talk about and explore the data?
  - ______ What kind of categories will help both you and the learner manage the data?
  - ______ What categories will be required in order to cover all the key points while making meaningful distinctions?
- ______ Play with the possibilities. Encourage yourself to be as creative as possible. Try to categorize the items in several different ways.
  - ______ You may wish to create a visual map that helps you see relationships.
  - ______ Consider talking with others to lessen the danger that the categories will be aligned only with your own learning style.
  - ______ Try different approaches. You may prefer to look at the big picture—perhaps by brainstorming some categories—and search for common themes in the list of key points. Or you may prefer to begin with the key points themselves and match them with similar points, then establish key topic categories that express what the points have in common. See what works better for you. In either case, you will often find that some key points fit into more than one category. That's fine.

What you are hoping for is some powerful magic—categories that start to add to the value of the list. This is where the designer is called on to be an artist! The added value may come from discovering unexpected categories that create a model you can use throughout the training, categories that speak directly to the felt needs and experience of your participants.

For example, in the check-writing training, you might at first have fairly obvious key topic categories—such as parts of the check, check security, and record keeping. After playing for a while, you might come up with categories that are oriented more toward benefits—such as putting money into your account, keeping it safe, knowing how much money you have, and cashing checks.

5. Identify Additional Points for Key Topics. You already have a list of essential key points for each key topic category. Now it is time to identify any additional supporting points that you need to include within each key topic to meet your training objectives. This is the approach:

______ Look over your categorized list.

______ Note what additional information or ideas will be required.

______ Keep in mind the distinction between what is essential to know and what is nice to know—always in relation to the desired behaviors.

Here is how all this might work in practice: for example, in the check-writing training, you might have a key topic called "parts of the check." As you look through the key points that support it, you may notice that you have already included several parts of the check, such as signature line, memo line, and amount box. You realize that you have left out other parts of the check, such as amount line and date line. You will add them at this stage of the SIM so that you have a complete list of essential content.

In another design situation, you might have brainstormed an item such as "corporate policy on promotions." At this point, you would want to identify what essential information from that policy would have to be part of the training.

6. Consider Possible Organizational Structures. So far, the SIM has kept you from outlining—and you will be asked to stay away from it a little longer. When you are working with content, the urge to outline will be great; but whatever you do, don't outline now. Yet now is the time to consider possible structures. Notice the two key qualifiers: "consider" and "possible." You will make no final decisions at this point. However, you will consider and identify structures that might offer engaging ways to organize the training. This step is included at this point in the SIM to circumvent any unconscious decisions that may be forming in your mind about organizational structures. So here is what you will be doing in this step:

______ Consider possible structures. Push yourself, if necessary, to examine more than one. (For explanations of nine common organizational structures, see the Appendix.)

______ Analyze the possible organizational structures, considering the following:

  ______ Fit with the desired behaviors

  ______ Fit with objectives

______ Fit with content

______ Fit with real-world application

______ Relationship to expressed needs of learners

______ Potential to create a need to know

Usually, a training session has one main organizational structure, plus secondary organizational structures within the key learning activities. In this step, you are considering structures for the overall design—possible main organizational structures. You will make your final decision on structure in the next stage of the SIM.

How do you know which is the right structure? You really do not need to know precisely; you are simply identifying *possible* structures. Your objectives and content may help you quickly rule out a few structures—because they do not fit (not effective), they are too complex (not efficient), or they are too predictable (not engaging). Your needs assessment data may also help; for example, if focus groups have clearly identified a pressing problem, your design must address that problem early on, or you risk having low interest from participants in the training.

7. Review and Edit Key Topics. The product for this stage of the SIM is a categorized list of essential content—your key topics. The key topics for the training should support the desired behaviors and the goals and objectives for the training, and they should be responsive to the needs of your learners. To review your key topics, ask the following questions:

______ Is there any content missing, without which my design cannot meet one of the stated objectives?

______ Is there any content that is not essential to meeting the desired behavioral outcomes of the training?

______ Does the content respond to the needs I identified in my needs assessment?

______ Does the content address the general characteristics and needs of adult learners? Does it balance the concrete and the abstract, the "why" and the "how," analysis of information and concern for people? Does it respect and acknowledge the learners' experience?

______ Does the content respond to the particular needs and abilities of the learners for whom the training is being designed? Are the vocabulary and level of complexity appropriate?

______ Does the content use language in ways that are understood and supported in this organization? Is it responsive to organizational norms, climate, and standards? If it includes any models or theories that run counter to organizational beliefs and assumptions, does it provide a rationale?

This is an iterative process. If you are not satisfied with your answer to any of these questions, do some more work before going on to the next stage of the SIM. Reviewing and editing your key topics may encourage you to revisit your goals or objectives for additions or modifications, or it may simply send you back to expand or condense your key points or key topics. You might even decide to move on to the next stage of the SIM while acknowledging that there are some key topic areas for which you need to do some more research. In any case, this review and edit will help you assess the progress of your design up to now.

8. Check Work with Your Client. Now is an especially critical time to make sure that you and your client are in agreement; once the client is ready to sign off on your Key Topics stage, you can move ahead with confidence.

Question: Why am I doing this stage? It feels very redundant—didn't I just do it when I identified goals and objectives?

Answer: There is an intentional redundancy of process in the SIM between the first and second stages. The focus is different—though with some inevitable and desirable overlap. The redundancy serves as a double-check on the work of the first stage. The products of the Key Topics stage may confirm your earlier work or cause you to revisit it. As you continue to use the SIM, you will become better at focusing on *skills* in the Goals and Objectives stage and on *content* in the Key Topics stage.

Question: How many categories do I need?

Answer: There's no magic number. The number needs to be large enough to contain all the essential data in some meaningful way and small enough to assist you in the design process. The reason for categorizing the data into key topics is that the list of key points is usually too much to keep in mind while designing. Obviously, the number of categories will have a lot to do with the complexity of the content and the length of the training. When you have completed this process, every bit of essential content should be included in a category; if it is not, revisit your categories or create new ones.

What is more critical than the number is the playful brainwork that goes into formulating the categories. Most designers tend to approach this task from a very logical framework, and as a result they come up with pretty predictable categories. To explore less predictable—and possibly more engaging—categories, try one of the following strategies:

- Ask what categories your potential participants would come up with if they were working with you.
- Study the actual performance of the task to see if it suggests new categories.
- Look for a strong visual image that seems to speak to the content, and then try to generate some categories related to that image.

Question: Why go back to desired behaviors? I have already based the objectives for the training on the behaviors. Why not just begin with the objectives and then brainstorm a list of possible content to support them?

Answer: If you were in a terrible time crunch, you might have to do just that. The problem is that it short-circuits the iterative checks and balances of the SIM. If you use your tentative objectives as the basis for your content in the Key Topics stage, your key topics cannot possibly be any better than your objectives. But if you base your key topics on the desired behaviors that are within the scope of the training, you may be able to improve your objectives.

Yes, it is a lot of work. Starting with the brainstormed potential content, you will label much of it nonessential because it is related to the desired behaviors but beyond the scope of the particular training. Still, we believe that the double-check is more than worth the effort. Both with our own work and with that of participants in workshops, we have seen many profound changes in objectives—usually simplifications—as a result of this stage of design. We cannot overemphasize its value.

Question: What should I do if I have some content that feels very important to me but does not really correspond to any of my objectives?

Answer: First, congratulate yourself for making this distinction and being willing to work with such a difficult decision. Here are a few possibilities:

- Your content may be telling you that some objectives are missing. Ask yourself why participants need to know this content and what they are to do with it. If the content is essential to performing a required skill, then you can go back to include it in one of your objectives or develop a new objective.

- You may have identified some essential content that cannot reasonably be tied to any essential performance objective but that needs to be articulated in a content objective.
- Perhaps this content, although it feels important to you, is not essential for this training. If you suspect this is the case, move the problematic content out of your way for now—otherwise you are likely to include it, essential or not. Put it in a folder to reconsider at the next stage. Later, if you find that you have extra time in your design, you may want to retrieve it.

Question: What do I do with the nonessential but nice-to-know stuff? I don't want to just toss it out. It could be very helpful.

Answer: You have many choices. It can become additional material to be made available before the training, a resource for after the training, or part of a follow-up program. You may even find as you design that you do, in fact, have time to include some of it. However, at this point, you must clearly segregate it from what is essential.

The nonessential may still be valuable. It may provide additional information for people who want to know more; it may provide background or "why" information to help motivate people who learn best when they have that kind of information; it may simply add credibility to what is being trained.

Your job is to help the learners focus on what they must know. Some learners will appreciate additional information, and others will be overwhelmed by it; so if it is clearly identified as additional, each learner can individually decide how helpful it is. If you choose to put nonessential information into handouts for reference after the training or to include it in the materials to be used during the training, be sure to use a special graphic or title to identify it clearly—perhaps "supporting research," "additional resources," or "other applications."

What is critical is to avoid overloading the learner and minimize the trainer's temptation to "cram it all in." You must separate—for the learner and the trainer—what is essential to be learned from what is not.

Question: I have really worked hard to select only essential content, and I still have too much content for the time allocated. What should I do?

Answer: This is a common problem, and you and your client have several choices: together, you can determine what can be cut from the training and handled in some other format; you can extend the time; or you can add pre- or postwork to cover some of the essential content.

Do not pretend the problem will go away. Decisions need to be made now to guide the rest of the training design and to engage your client in the problem-solving process. After all, the client has expectations about the performance that will result from this training, and you now know that the desired performance cannot be achieved in the allocated time. Do not set anyone up for failure: yourself, the participants, or the client.

Question: What can I do about pressure from my client or a subject-matter expert (SME) to add content that I do not think is essential?

Answer: The nature of your relationship with your client or SME will have a great deal to do with how you manage this issue. Peter Block, in *Flawless Consulting* (1981), describes the roles a consultant can embrace. If you are functioning primarily as what Block calls a "pair of hands" (implementing the directives of your client), then your task is to figure out a way to include all the content while making certain that the design highlights what is essential.

If you are what Block calls a "collaborator," the situation is different. That is how we try to structure relationships with our clients. We come to the relationship with expertise in training design and delivery, as well as in adult learning; depending on the subject, we may also have content expertise. Our client comes with expertise in performance issues, in organizational norms and culture, and sometimes in the content. The SME usually has high content expertise and may have performance expertise. As in all collaborative relationships, there is much give-and-take. If the SME and the client push to include content that we do not think is essential, we raise the question but defer to their expertise. If the issue is one of learning strategies, we are much more likely to assert our expertise.

In either case, if your client's request will fit into the time allocated without jeopardizing objectives or essential content, then add it—while making certain that the design highlights what is essential. If you cannot add it within the time allocated for the training, bring the decision back to the client—either to add more time or to reduce some other content.

What is powerful about going back to your client at this stage in the design is that you are simply talking about objectives and content. Our experience in working with clients is that they often wish to make cuts in activities. They will see an experiential activity and suggest that it be changed to a lecture—"just tell 'em about it." We prefer to avoid these discussions when possible. If we discover during the Key Topics stage that there is a potential problem, that is when we discuss it—so that choices can be made before things become more complicated.

Question: I still find that I am most comfortable outlining at this stage. What's the harm?

Answer: The harm is that the sequence of the training will be driven by the content, by your preferred style of learning, or by your learned patterns of outlining. Any of these factors may lead you to a sequence or an organizing principle that falls short of engaging your learners. Instead, the SIM recommends that you organize the content into meaningful categories that are not sequenced—but it also asks you to consider organizational structures that may fit your objectives and content. You will sequence in the next stage of the SIM, Training Flow, after you consider appropriate learning activities; the goal is a sequence that will create the need to know, will build upon the experience of the learners, and will support your behavioral objectives. To do all that, the activities, the content, and the sequence must go hand in hand.

BEFORE YOU MOVE ON

Take a break, and pat yourself on the back! You now have goals, objectives, and key topics for your training design.

It is time to open your imaginary computer files again and see what you have created. First, let's open the file titled Key Topics. As at the end of the Goals and Objectives stage, you will find a screen with data floating on it. This time, all the data form the content that will be included in your training design. Individual pieces of essential content—key points—are grouped together into categories that are your key topics. These key topics are the categories that seem to you, at this time, to be meaningful ways of arranging the key points—ways that will help you design and that will also engage your participants. They are floating because, just like your goals and objectives, they are not yet fixed; they need to remain open to possible change.

In the lower corner of your screen, you may find a few content points that you have not yet decided are essential. You will come back to them later in the design process to make your final decision.

This is the ideal time to reopen your computer file titled Goals and Objectives so that you can compare it with the Key Topics file. If all is going well, the two files are very much aligned. As you look from one file to the other, you see clearly how the key points and key topics relate to the goals and objectives of the training. Every objective is supported by essential content, and all content supports objectives. What you see is not perfect at this point—there are a few pieces of data that you have yet to decide on—but the fit is evident, and you can move confidently to the next stage of the SIM. There you will make decisions about learning activities.

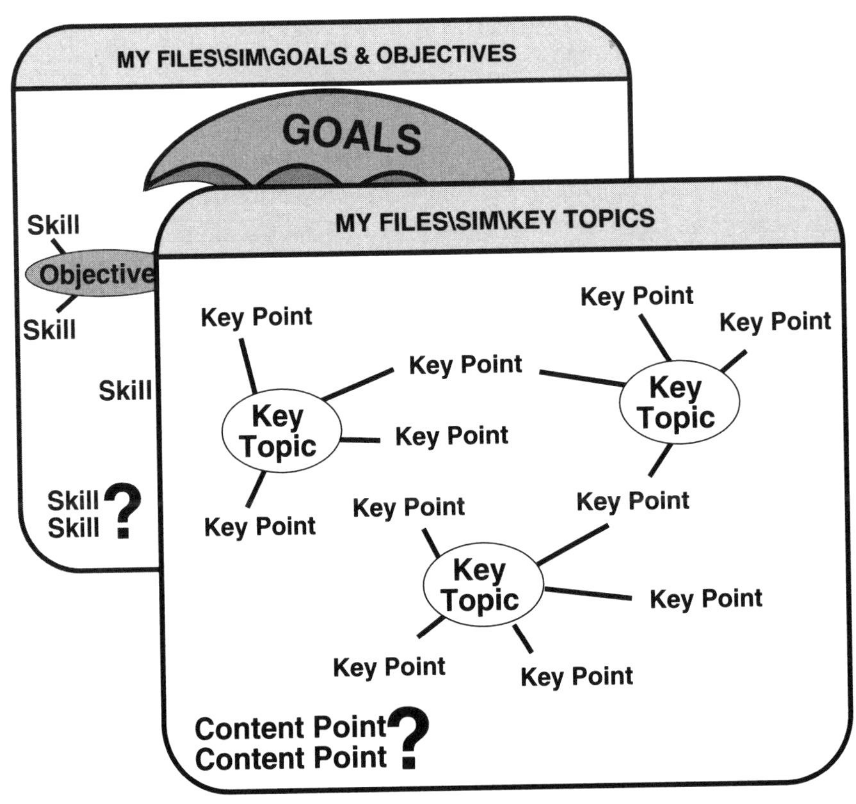

Among the designers we have trained, most report that these first two stages of the SIM are the most challenging and time-consuming, requiring the designer to work with the concept and the possibilities of the design in many different ways. These designers also report that the effort is more than repaid by the benefits. For one thing, the rest of the process seems to flow readily from this work. In addition, designers say that in these two stages they often find interesting ways to structure and position the training—so they feel as if they are well on the way to creating learning events that are effective, efficient, and engaging.

Looking Back

Here is the SIM process to this point:

Goals and Objectives

1. Review design requirements.
2. Establish a goal statement.

3. Brainstorm the skills for reaching the desired behaviors.
4. Edit: determine essential versus nonessential skills for reaching the desired behaviors.
5. Consolidate: cluster related skills together.
6. Draft objectives.
7. Review and edit the proposed goals and objectives.
8. Review the goals and objectives with your client.

Key Topics

1. Research the subject.
2. Brainstorm possible key points.
3. Determine essential versus nonessential points.
4. Group key points into key topics.
5. Identify additional points for key topics.
6. Consider possible organizational structure.
7. Review and edit key topics.
8. Check work with your client.

Running Example: Key Topics

After the goals and objectives have been approved by her client, Simone moves on to the next stage: establishing key topics.

1. Research the Subject

Simone decides to do the following research:

- Review relevant company policies and procedures.
- Consult needs assessment data.
- Review samples of well-written and problematic appraisals (HR person will supply these).
- Read selected books and articles on performance appraisals.
- Review training programs on writing appraisals.
- Interview HR person.
- Interview sampling of supervisors and managers who have a reputation for writing good appraisals (some who have lots of experience, some who are new to the task).

2. Brainstorm Possible Key Points

She brainstorms about what information, facts, or concepts she might include in the training in order for participants to perform the desired behaviors. Here are the results:

- Corporate policy on appraisals
- Differences between evaluative and behavioral/descriptive language
- Why it is important to summarize performance
- What's in it for them to write better appraisals
- Criteria for a well-written appraisal
- Different types of employees (depending on their personality preferences) like different types of feedback
- Need for consistent standards for evaluating employee performance
- Ways to involve the employee in the process
- Ways to balance the appraisal (between positive and corrective feedback)
- Importance of consistency in appraisals

- Relationship between appraisal and performance management
- Legal requirements for writing appraisals
- Some performance incidents are critical and need to be on the appraisal, even if they are not part of a trend
- Importance of documentation of previous performance discussions
- Why it is important to describe the impact of performance on the work and on the work group
- Techniques for ways to describe impacts
- Ways to overcome employee resistance
- Performance as a two-way street: the boss can ask for feedback, too
- Feedback as a discussion rather than a monologue
- Ways to manage the appraisal meeting
- Setting a comfortable climate in the meeting
- The importance of including the impact of performance
- Language/words to avoid in the appraisal
- Techniques for bringing up difficult subjects
- How much detail to put in the appraisal
- Why and how for developmental strategies
- How to handle writing appraisals for employees who are new to your group
- How to document performance when someone is leaving your group
- How to decide what to include and what to leave out of the written appraisal
- Examples of descriptive language
- Importance of describing desired performance
- Ways to write suggestions for improvement
- Ways to obtain the employee's input into the appraisal
- Why it is important to avoid labels—even good ones
- How to use the corporate form
- What to do if the employee refuses to sign the appraisal form
- Separating salary discussion from the appraisal
- Examples of well-written appraisals
- Typical employee complaints about appraisal
- Ways to monitor performance on a regular basis

NOTE TO READER

At this step and at several other steps, the Running Example includes just a few items to illustrate the steps in the process. In a real design project, of course, all the items would be analyzed and included.

3. Determine Essential Versus Nonessential Points

Simone reviews each of the items in the brainstormed content list and determines which ones are essential.

For the training on writing performance appraisals, here is part of Simone's edited list, with nonessential points crossed out and comments in the right-hand column. The comments reflect her knowledge of the organization, as well as what she has learned from the needs assessment and what she knows about general adult learning principles and these particular learners.

Please remember that these decisions are judgment calls; if you were designing this training, you might make some different decisions about what is and what is not essential.

Edited List: Essential Versus Nonessential

Original Point	*Simone's Thoughts*
• ~~Corporate policy on appraisals~~	Nonessential: covered in other training. Also, the policy covers appraisal requirements such as due dates and appraisal cycles, which are beyond the scope of this training.
• Differences between evaluative and behavioral/descriptive language	Essential: supports desired behaviors about translating judgments about performance into behavioral descriptors.
• Why it is important to summarize performance	Essential: supports desired behavior of summarizing performance patterns.
• What's in it for them to write better appraisals	Essential: personal motivation to implement what is covered in training. However, no objective directly relates to this content, so must go back to decide whether to add an objective related to the WIIFM (What's in it for me).
• Criteria for a well-written appraisal	Essential: will support all desired behaviors and can also be used to reinforce what participants are already doing well. May give participants a checklist with these criteria; note the idea in the Materials file.

- ~~Different types of employees (depending on their personality preferences) like different types of feedback~~ — Nonessential: interesting; include it if there is time, but it is more like Level II of this training. For now, will focus on the essentials.
- ~~Need for consistent standards for evaluating employee performance~~ — Nonessential: beyond the scope of this training. It is an organization development issue for Jexon; raise it as an ongoing issue that will continue to hinder supervisors' and managers' ability to perform the desired behaviors related to writing appraisals.
- ~~Ways to involve the employee in the process~~ — Nonessential: hard to let go of, because it's critical to the appraisal process. Supervisors and managers can demonstrate the desired behaviors without increasing employee involvement, so this content is beyond the scope of this training. If the training goes well and yields the desired improvements, can begin a dialogue with senior management about further skill development.
- Ways to balance the appraisal (between positive and corrective feedback) — ???: cannot decide if this is essential; it certainly seems related to summarizing performance. Go back to check the random sample of existing performance appraisals, as well as other needs assessment findings.

In the real world of your own training design, as you perform this step, you will probably simply cross off the nonessential points. Most of your explanations will be just in your head—or in conversations with others on the design team—not written down. We have written them here to make the points clear.

4. Group Key Points into Key Topics

Having made some determinations about essential content in the previous step, Simone has reduced her original list to the following:

- Differences between evaluative and behavioral/descriptive language
- Why it is important to summarize performance

- What's in it for them to write better appraisals
- Criteria for a well-written appraisal
- Importance of consistency in appraisals
- Relationship between appraisal and performance management
- Legal requirements for writing appraisals
- Some performance incidents are critical and need to be on the appraisal, even if they are not part of a trend
- Importance of documentation of previous performance discussions
- Why it is important to describe the impact of performance on the work and on the work group
- Techniques for ways to describe impacts
- The importance of including the impact of performance
- Language/words to avoid in the appraisal
- How much detail to put in the appraisal
- Why and how for developmental strategies
- How to decide what to include and what to leave out of the written appraisal
- Examples of descriptive language
- Importance of describing desired performance
- Ways to write suggestions for improvement
- Why it is important to avoid labels—even good ones
- Examples of well-written appraisals

She has two points that need further consideration in order for her to determine whether they are essential:

- Ways to balance the appraisal (between positive and corrective feedback)
- Ways to obtain the employee's input into the appraisal

The task now is to play with some categories—possible key topics—that will help group the key points in meaningful ways. Here are some of the first ideas that strike Simone:

- Summaries
- Planning for the Future

- WIIFMs
- Do's and Don'ts
- Criteria for Well-Written Appraisals
- Translating What's in the Gut

As she works with these possible categories, she notices that many of the items from the list of essential key points that would go into Summaries would also go into Planning for the Future (for example, difference between evaluative and behavioral/descriptive language, criteria for a well-written appraisal, relationship between appraisal and performance management). With this realization, she moves toward a category that will capture what is critical to a good appraisal, whether one is reviewing the previous year's performance or looking forward to performance improvement.

As Simone plays with these ideas a little more, she realizes that the following four categories feel more engaging:

- *What's in It for Me (WIIFM):* This addresses how new behaviors will benefit the participants.
- *First-Class Appraisals:* This language feels better than "criteria for well-written appraisals" because it is more aligned with the way people talk at Jexon.
- *Looking Back:* This feels broader and less formal than "summaries." Also, it subtly ties into the notion of appraisals as part of performance management.
- *Looking Forward:* Using parallel language will make it possible to link content elements from different categories. For example, summarizing performance rather than going into detail is very important for the review of the previous year, but it also has implications for describing desired behavior when looking forward to performance improvement.

So here is what will fall into Simone's four key topics at this point:

What's in It for Me

- What's in it for participants to write better appraisals

First-Class Appraisals

- Difference between evaluative and behavioral/descriptive language
- Criteria for a well-written appraisal

- Importance of consistency in appraisals
- Relationship between appraisal and performance management
- Legal requirements for writing appraisals
- Importance of documentation of previous performance discussions
- The importance of including the impact of performance on the work and work group
- Techniques/ways to describe impacts
- Language/words to avoid in the appraisal
- How much detail to put in the appraisals
- How to decide what to include and what to leave out of the written appraisal
- Examples of descriptive language
- Why it is important to avoid labels—even good ones
- Examples of well-written appraisals

Looking Back

- Why it is important to summarize performance
- Some performance incidents are critical and need to be on the appraisal even if they are not part of a trend

Looking Forward

- Why and how for developmental strategies
- Importance of describing desired performance
- Ways to write suggestions for improvement

Simone has identified the key points (essential content) and categorized them into key topics, but she is not through yet. In the next step, she will identify additional points that are required to complete each key topic.

5. Identify Additional Points for Key Topics

Now, Simone will determine what supporting points she will need for each of the key topic areas. She marks the points at which she needs to gather additional information or develop original content as she continues to design.

What's in It for Me? The essential content points—the benefits—will come from participants during the training. In the next stage of the SIM, Simone will certainly select an activity that asks participants to generate what is personally in it for them. For now, she just wants to anticipate the kind of data she might get in response to this question. Here is what she comes up with:

- Increased employee performance
- Increased perception of fairness among employees
- Decreased legal liabilities
- Feel better about integrating the appraisal with real performance management
- May decrease dread of writing appraisals
- Will make appraisals sound less "cookie cutter"
- Employees will know that their supervisor or manager is aware of their good performance and how it affects the group and Jexon

First-Class Appraisals. There are three parts to this key topic category: first, Criteria for a Well-Written Appraisal; second, Content and Language; third, The Appraisal as Part of Performance Management. To flesh out the content for this category, Simone has reviewed the literature on written performance appraisals. She is extracting just the points that she and the client have agreed are important for this organization.

Criteria for a Well-Written Appraisal

- Accuracy
- Compares performance with stated work objectives
- Balanced: points out strengths and areas for improvement
- Summarizes performance
- Describes behaviors
- Describes impacts of performance—links with group and organizational success
- Positive tone
- Consistent and fair

KEY TO SYMBOL

In this step, *** indicates a point on which the designer will need to do more work—either additional research or designing new materials.

- *** Legal requirements
- *** Examples of well-written appraisals

Content and Language

- Difference between evaluative and behavioral/descriptive language
- *** Language/words to avoid in the appraisal
- *** Examples of descriptive language
- Why it is important to avoid labels—even good ones
- How much detail to put in the appraisal
- How to decide what to include and what to leave out of the written appraisal

The Appraisal as Part of Performance Management

- Relationship between appraisal and performance management
- Importance of documenting all performance discussions
- The importance of including the impact of performance on the work and the work group
- Why and how to include developmental strategies in the appraisal

Looking Back. Here are the supporting points:

- Why it is important to summarize performance
    - *** Legal requirements
    - Your time
    - Meaningful feedback to employee
    - Length of appraisal
    - You are simply summarizing discussions you have had throughout the year
- Importance of performance trends
- *** Sample summary statements
- *** Sample summary formulae
- Some performance incidents are critical and need to be on the appraisal even if they are not part of a trend

- *** Criteria for determining when an incident is critical enough to be included in the appraisal
- Guidance on how to document such an incident

Looking Forward. Simone identifies these supporting points:

- Why include developmental strategies in the appraisals
- *** Criteria for determining what types of improvement will need to be documented in the appraisal
- How to include developmental strategies
- *** Formats and samples
- *** Do's and don'ts
- Importance of describing desired performance
- Ways to write suggestions for improvement
- *** Formats and samples

A light bulb goes on for Simone. These categories suggest a visual image: a supervisor or manager, checklist in hand, looking back at the previous year and looking forward. Simone knows that she doesn't want to lock onto this image now, but it is appealing. She makes a note in the Materials file.

6. Consider Possible Organizational Structures

As a result of putting the key points into key topics, Simone now has a categorical structure; however, she has put the points into categories simply to make them easier to work with and to suggest some novel ways of treating the content. She does not want to be locked into a categorical sequence for the training because it may not be the most effective, efficient, or engaging.

Three other structures seem to have promise at this time: problem to resolution, theoretical to practical, and known to unknown. She takes a closer look at them. (See Appendix for a review of structures.)

Problem to Resolution. Because the focus groups generated a list of problems, and because some of the people who will attend the training were members of the focus groups, there is a certain appeal to organizing the training so that it offers tools and techniques to manage some of the problems that came up.

Theoretical to Practical. The First-Class Appraisal category will provide many "whys" for doing certain things on the appraisals. The rest of the training could be "how." Or this organizational structure could be adapted a bit: theoretical to practical, then back to theoretical. The training could begin with the criteria for effective appraisals, go right to "how" (as the group is very pragmatic), and then return to some of the "whys" at the end and include the WIIFMs in the "why" section.

Known to Unknown. Simone is uncertain exactly how she could use this as her overall organizational strategy, but she does want to remember it for use within major components of this training. As she was developing objectives and identifying and organizing essential content, she realized that many of the concepts to be included in the training will be familiar to participants. People at least will know that certain things are important in the appraisal, and they may want some quick techniques for doing those things they know are important. So Simone would like to use this organizational strategy wherever possible—for two reasons. First, she wants to honor the principle of valuing the experience that adults bring to the learning situation (Chapter Three). All of these people have had appraisals written about them, most have written many appraisals, and some of them are very good at writing appraisals. Second, Simone wants to organize the training in such a way that participants will not be resistant. Although they have asked for this training and participated in the focus groups, it will be very important to maintain their interest and self-esteem throughout the training. One way to do that will be to surface and use what they already know and then present some tips and techniques that will help them move to a higher level of expertise with regard to writing appraisals.

7. Review and Edit Key Topics

Here is where Simone asks herself several critical questions:

- *Is there any content missing, without which my design cannot meet one of the stated objectives?* No. As indicated with ***, there is more work Simone needs to do, but she believes that she has identified all the essential content areas that need to be included in order to meet the objectives.
- *Is there any content that is not essential to meeting the desired behavioral outcomes of the training?* The content related to the WIIFM is not directly essential—people could exhibit the desired behaviors without

identifying what's in it for them—but Simone is convinced that the likelihood of practicing the new behaviors will increase if people have the opportunity to tap into their internal motivation. For this reason, she decides to add a WIIFM objective for this training.

- *Does the content respond to the needs I identified in my needs assessment?* Yes. Simone was able to eliminate some potential content because people already know it. She is thinking about having the trainer post a list of what is already being done well. This list will not only acknowledge and reinforce participants' expertise, but it will also allow the trainer to provide a rationale for the key areas on which the training will focus. She makes a note in the Training Flow file.
- *Does the content address the general characteristics and needs of adult learners? Does it balance the concrete and the abstract, the why and the how, analysis of information and concern for people? Does it respect and acknowledge the learners' experience?* Yes. Simone has done what she can to acknowledge what they already know. This effort will speak to their experience and maintain self-esteem. She has also tried to include a balance between "why" and "how" content to meet the different learning preferences. In addition, asking people what is in it for them allows them to make personal judgments about the skills and information being presented. Even though the behaviors being taught in this workshop will be Jexon's organizational norms and expectations, it is still important to let the adult learner exercise judgment about what is being learned. Finally, because the design will provide a variety of samples and approaches, learners will be able to select and adapt what they judge to be most appropriate to their needs.
- *Does the content respond to the particular needs and abilities of the learners for whom the training is being designed? Are the vocabulary and level of complexity appropriate?* Again, yes. Simone is satisfied that she has edited potential content appropriately on the basis of the needs and abilities of the group, and she is particularly pleased with the categorical names that she has selected for the key topics. They sound very much like people talk at Jexon. The categories also suggest a potential visual model that will serve to simplify information that could be technical and complex and will aid in retention.
- *Does the content use language in ways that are understood and supported in this organization? Is it responsive to organizational norms, climate, and standards? If it includes any models or theories that run counter to organizational beliefs and assumptions, does it provide a rationale?*

Things are looking pretty good in this regard. The content and objectives are supported by Jexon's corporate policy as well as by the expressed interest of both management and employees. What is newest in this content are the ideas of using behavioral language and defining impacts. The other content will be somewhat familiar, though not commonly practiced. Simone knows that the design must quickly explain what is meant by the new concepts and make a compelling case for using them.

8. Check Your Work with Your Client

At this point, Simone is confident that her decisions about key points and key topics are good ones. She takes the list of key topics, with the key points for each one, to the lead client on the management team. The client approves them, and Simone is ready to move on to the next stage of the SIM—Training Flow.

8 The SIM

Training Flow—Macrodesign

It's time for some of the real magic of training design, and it's time to play again. At this stage, you will be playing with learning activities. Through your work with the SIM so far, you have addressed why the organization is doing the training (goals) and the behaviors that participants will be able to demonstrate by the end of the training (objectives). In addition, you have determined the content that needs to be included in the design (key topics). In the Training Flow—Macrodesign stage, you will focus on appropriate learning activities and the sequence of the activities. You have laid the groundwork. Now you are ready to think about how to engage your learners through learning activities.

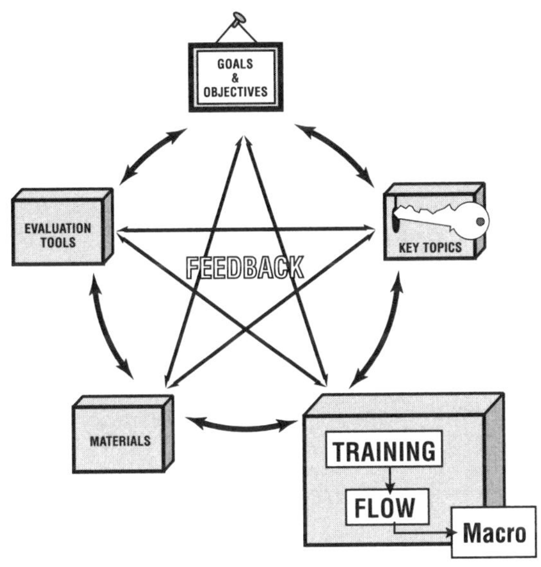

In the Macrodesign phase of the Training Flow stage, you will select and sequence creative learning activities that will engage your adult learners in mastering the essential content and skills. You may choose predesigned activities that support your objectives, or you may design activities yourself.

PRODUCT OF THE TRAINING FLOW—MACRODESIGN PHASE

When you have completed this stage of the SIM, you will have one new product, your big-picture plan for meeting your goals and objectives:

- *Training Flow—Macrodesign:* An outline—at last. It shows the learning activities, grouped into segments; an objective for each segment; the related content and time estimates for each activity; and notes on some key transitions. It does not yet include the details of individual learning activities. The

Macrodesign phase is the first of two in Training Flow; in Microdesign, which comes next, you will add detail and polish (Chapter Nine).

For example, in the continuing development of the design on listening skills for medical professionals, the designer might plan a segment called "What makes it hard to listen and really hear." It would be preceded by an introductory activity and some information on objectives and agenda.

Starting with a transition to follow the piece on objectives and agenda, the macrodesign for this segment might look like this:

Transition. Our first objective is about techniques for managing personal habits that get in the way of listening. We all have them. In fact, you have already mentioned some in your introductions. Let's go back to them and make some additions.

3. What Makes It Hard to Listen and Really Hear. (40 min.)

   Objective. Participants will identify delivery characteristics and three personal habits that are challenges to listening and hearing.

   A. Brief video demos.
      - Small groups identify what about delivery in video made it difficult to listen and hear.
      - Large-group list of challenges.

   B. Large-group discussion: personal habits that get in the way.

   C. Individual work: pick three that are personal habits.

Because the macrodesign is an overview, it does not specify details of process, content, or time. For example, this macrodesign does not describe how to run the discussion, which video clips to use (although by this time the designer probably has a pretty good idea), or how the forty minutes of the segment will be divided. All of that comes later. The macrodesign focuses on the big picture.

TRAINING FLOW—MACRODESIGN: WHY? AND WHY NOW?

Surely it is obvious that the designer must select learning activities and determine a sequence for them. Or is it? Perhaps you have seen, as we have, so-called training designs that were little more than goals, objectives, and content outlines—possibly with copies of participant materials, but with little indication of how the participants might interact with the material, how the content might be presented, or what the time frame might be.

That's not enough. The designer is also tasked with deciding what activities will be effective, efficient, and engaging. In other words, she is looking for activities that will support the goals and objectives, deliver the key topics, and meet the needs of participants. In addition, she must figure out how long the activities will take and in what order they should be arranged. That is what the Training Flow—Macrodesign stage is all about.

Notice that we said, "in what order." Yes, it is finally time to begin to sequence your training flow. One of the assumptions behind the SIM is that the best time to determine the sequence is when you are considering appropriate activities. Now is that time.

What is the designer looking for in activities? They must support the objectives and content, of course; ideally, they will also create a need to know, lay the groundwork for future activities, build upon the expertise of the participants, and allow the trainer and participants to evaluate success throughout the training. In short, the activities you select must be effective, efficient, and engaging.

- *Effective* learning activities will cover the content and help participants meet the explicit objectives for this training.
- *Efficient* activities will do it in ways that are sensitive both to time and to the energies of the learners—that is, they will not make the learning unnecessarily complex.
- *Engaging* activities will invite learners to participate actively in the learning—to interact with one another, with the trainer, and with the content, and to bring their past experience to all of these interactions. Activities that are engaging will also invite the learners to think critically and independently about what they are learning so that they can assign personal meaning and thereby increase comprehension and retention.

This stage of the SIM comes before you design trainer's materials, participant materials, or visual aids. The reasons are simple—to save you time and to keep you from becoming invested in a product that may later prove not to be the best choice. If you find yourself wanting at this stage to design these products, put a note about your idea into your Materials file.

This stage also comes before your definitive work on evaluation tools. That is intentional, too. Often, you will select an activity that allows participants to demonstrate a particular competency during the training. If you do that, there probably will be no need to develop another evaluation tool for that competency.

In truth, many designers intuitively begin their design work at the Training Flow stage. They have an idea of what they want the training to be about, and they start thinking about ways to present the training. It is a natural temptation for some designers to rely unconsciously on their preferred thinking styles to begin their designs—either creatively, with "What are the possibilities here?" or pragmatically, with "How am I going to present this content?"

The SIM is built to hold off these considerations until you have established goals and objectives that directly support the desired behaviors and have identified the content essential for achieving those goals and objectives.

The work you have already done will help you in another significant way. In the previous two stages of the SIM, you have been encouraged to manage your design process with approaches that have balanced your preferred style of learning and information processing; by now, the products of this work are balanced in terms of learning style. This built-in balance will help you manage the temptation to select only the learning activities that fit best with your own preferences.

MACRODESIGN VERSUS MICRODESIGN

The macrodesign is a big-picture design; the microdesign is a detailed description of what will happen in the training. For example:

Macrodesign	*Microdesign*
Objective: Participants will identify five resources in the organization that they find most useful for responding to customer inquiries about new products.	*Objective:* Participants will identify five resources in the organization that they find most useful for responding to customer inquiries about new products.
Large-group discussion. (15 min.)	Large-group discussion. (15 min.) 1. Individuals jot down resources they use. (2 min.) 2. Report out to large group; instructor records on flip chart. (4 min.) 3. Q & A about unfamiliar resources. (5 min.) 4. Voting: individuals each stick three dots onto flip chart to indicate resources most useful in their experience; tally with large group; note top five overall. (3 min.) 5. Individuals record top five in own workbook. (1 min.)

Macrodesigns and Microdesigns

The Training Flow stage of the SIM has two phases. The macrodesign, or big-picture design, is the focus of this chapter. The microdesign, a detailed picture of the training design, is the focus of the next chapter. In the Macrodesign phase you will create a general outline of learning activities, with related content and times.

Do not waste your time designing any particular learning activity in detail at this point; there are sure to be further changes. Worse than wasted time is the danger that a learning activity will begin to take on a life of its own, and the designer will become so enamored of the activity that she will use it in her design no matter what. Do not let that happen to you. Stick with the SIM to produce the macrodesign. You will review it to see if the activities you have selected and sequenced are effective, efficient, and engaging—in terms of your learners and the other requirements established in your needs assessment. After you are satisfied that your design meets these criteria, then you can move confidently to the next step—fleshing out your design in detail (a microdesign).

CRITERIA FOR SELECTING ACTIVITIES

As you develop the macrodesign, you will consider everything that has gone into the design so far, and you will use that work as the basis for selecting learning activities. In selecting activities, there are several criteria to be considered:

CRITERIA FOR SELECTING LEARNING ACTIVITIES

- Support of objectives
- Fit with content
- Variety
- Adult learners and learning styles
- Transfer of learning
- Your participants
- Trainer competencies
- Logistical constraints
- Time

Support of Objectives

The learning activities you select must support the behaviors you described in your objectives. For example, if one of your objectives calls for participants to "demonstrate" a particular skill by the end of the training, then you must select an activity that will actually permit them to demonstrate the skill, not simply to describe or evaluate it. In addition—because the SIM is iterative—you may find, as you design learning activities, that some of the behaviors described in your objectives simply are not attainable within the constraints of your training situation. You may need to go back and modify your objectives, using the about, about-how-to, and how-to levels of objectives (Chapter Six). Remember, the SIM is iterative.

Fit with Content

The learning activities must fit well with the essential content you identified in the Key Topics stage of the SIM—and they must include all of it. In some cases, there will be a natural fit. For example, if the required content is very familiar to the group, you will select an activity that acknowledges that familiarity (perhaps a simple review game) rather than assigning reading or planning a lecturette. If the content is new and complex, you will select learning activities that segment the content into easily digestible "chunks," so that participants will be able to practice and build on earlier chunks as you add to the content.

Variety

You will not make a final decision about the sequence of learning activities until the microdesign phase (Chapter Nine), but be sure to plan a variety of learning activities—to avoid boredom for the participants and to appeal to different learning styles. For example, you may see a large-group discussion as the natural fit for a piece of content, but if it is likely to be sandwiched between two other large-group discussions, the repetition of the activity would decrease its value. In such a situation, you might adjust the sequence, select another activity, or do both.

Adult Learners and Learning Styles

Perhaps most important, you will plan all activities in light of what you know about how adults learn (Chapter Three). You will be asking yourself which activities create or reinforce a need to know. You will be looking for activities that acknowledge your learners' experience and that bridge the various experience levels that may be present in your group. Because you are always concerned about the learners' self-esteem, you will be looking for activities that help make the learning environment safe. And, because adults are independent and will pass judgment on whatever is presented, you will seek activities that invite the learners to assign personal meaning to what is being learned, to make judgments about it, and to evaluate its potency for their own needs and success.

You will balance your design so that it appeals to a variety of learning styles (Chapter Three). This is a challenging part of the design process: it involves creating and selecting activities that might not fit your own style of learning. It requires identifying learning activities that will engage a variety of styles. For example, you might notice that you usually select activities that focus on practical application and practice. A way to balance this preference would be to select an activity in which participants would reflect on *why* they are doing something a certain way or, if appropriate, one in which they would generate *alternate* ways to do the same thing. These activities would engage the more intuitive or conceptual learners.

Transfer of Learning

It is important to design activities so that, to the greatest extent possible, they mimic the participants' real world, in order to increase the potential for transfer of the learning. For example, if you are designing training in proofreading skills, the challenge is to structure activities so that you can mimic as closely as possible what it will be like to use the skills on the job with a variety of materials and many distractions; you might design an activity in which participants would proofread while being interrupted.

Your Participants

In the work you did to convert the needs assessment to design requirements (Chapter Five), you identified several characteristics of your learner group, all of which are critical to designing and selecting learning activities.

Participants' Preferences, Abilities, and Expectations. This is a very sensitive area of design. Naturally, you want to be responsive to these preferences, insofar as you can discover them; you may also choose to "stretch" the participants a bit.

For example, you might be working for an organization in which there is an expressed preference for quick lectures with no "touchy-feely stuff"—that is, application exercises. You might also know from your needs assessment that participants understand a certain policy but are not skilled at applying it, and you might have developed a training objective that states, "Participants will be able to demonstrate their ability to make coaching decisions based on X policy." A lecture will not satisfy the requirements of the objective; more important, a lecture will fail to address the real issue—performance, not understanding. You will need to design an activity that moves people away from lectures but does not threaten them so much that they become unwilling to participate.

Participants' Knowledge and Expertise. What participants already know—and do not know—is critical to consider in selecting learning activities. There is a widely held assumption that if participants don't know much about a certain subject then it is best to lecture first. We recommend that you question that assumption. While being sensitive to a lack of specific knowledge or expertise, you can still design activities that tap into participants' general knowledge or their strategies for knowing.

For example, you may be designing training for people who have no knowledge of a new company policy. The participants do have experience with other policies, however, and they have the ability to apply logic to the situation. In this case, you might design a discussion in which participants could brainstorm anticipated elements of the policy before they hear the new policy.

Number of Participants. Clearly, the size of the group is critical to training design. The number of participants will affect not only the types of activities you select but also the time you will allot for each one. Discussions, group reports, even participant introductions—all take more time with a larger number.

Differing Abilities. Your design will be affected by diverse abilities. With a group that has differing physical abilities, your design must accommodate those abilities—for example, minimizing participants' movement around the room. If your group has differing abilities with spoken and written language, you must take that into account in the activities you select and the time you allocate for them.

Cultural Diversity. The cultural backgrounds of your participants will affect the selection of activities. For example, participants from certain cultures may find it especially uncomfortable to assume a "role" during a role play or to "argue" during a structured debate. The designer must consider how best to address cultural norms and needs without compromising the program objectives.

Trainer Competencies

In order to design and select activities, the designer must determine how well the trainers know the content and how skilled they are at facilitating various learning activities. Selecting a learning activity that is beyond the competency of the trainer—no matter how effective, efficient, and engaging it might otherwise seem to be—is poor design. It will result in unsatisfactory training and possibly in embarrassment to the trainer. Having good information about the trainer's competence with content and facilitation will not only help you in your selection but it will also provide guidance concerning the level of detail to include in the trainer's guide (in terms of both content and process).

If you do not know about the competencies of the trainers, you will select learning activities that can be facilitated easily. In addition, your trainer's resources will need to include enough information on content and process to meet the anticipated minimum competencies.

Logistical Constraints

The amount of space, flexibility of layout, and availability of equipment are additional considerations in selecting appropriate learning activities. If your only option is a small conference room with a huge conference table, think twice about activities that require a lot of moving around.

Time

Concerns about the amount of time available for training are probably looming over your head every moment of the design process, but we have purposely positioned time limitations as the final consideration. Why? To begin with, if time is your first criterion, you will probably tend to select only low-interaction activities. Second, if you discard potential learning activities immediately because of time, you sacrifice the opportunity to fully consider activities that may help you refine your earlier design work.

Time is an essential consideration in selecting training activities. The careful designer makes the selection on the basis of *all* the criteria. Time is only one of them.

CHALLENGES IN MACRODESIGNING

This stage of the SIM presents rich opportunities and challenges—two of our favorite challenges, in fact. First, we relish the challenge of trying to stamp out the all-too-familiar lecture-process method. We search for approaches that are not based on "tell them, then let them practice," because we have seen time and again that adults know enough about how the world works to articulate principles and truths that will illuminate content—even unfamiliar content—as long as we ask questions that build on their existing knowledge and experience. Adults also have a variety of strategies for learning new content and skills.

Second, we see this as an opportunity to help participants "get it right" with minimal intervention or correction from the trainer. The design can minimize the probability that the trainer will have to correct participants' contributions to provide the right answer.

By avoiding the lecture-process approach, the designer does open the possibility that incorrect or partially correct data will come from the learners. Protecting the self-esteem of the learners and creating a safe place to learn are very important in design, of course; still, no one wants participants to end up with information that is incorrect, especially on key topics. So the designer's goal is twofold: to engage participants in generating and analyzing data and to minimize the possibility that the trainer will have to correct the data offered by participants. We will say more about how to do this in the next chapter.

In our work, we apply our best efforts to creating strategies for learning that will help participants obtain accurate information by building on and enhancing what they already bring to the learning event. They will not always be hearing the "right answers" from an expert; they will be embracing their own expertise and their ability to *discover* "right answers." Carl Rogers, in his classic work, *Freedom to Learn,* talks about learning as "self-initiated." He says, "Even when the impetus or stimulus comes from the outside, the sense of discovery, of reaching out, of grasping and comprehending, comes from within" (1969, p. 5). This is one of the greatest gifts a designer can give to learners—a learning event that fosters active discovery.

Yes, there is a lot involved. The Macrodesign phase of the Training Flow stage is one of those messy parts of the process. You will be playing with multiple ways to design learning activities, and the trick will be to hold the possibilities open until a clear picture for the entire training event begins to unfold as you work and rework the possibilities.

Yet most designers report that this stage of the SIM is fun and easy, that it emerges naturally from the first two stages. And why not? During the first two stages of the SIM, you have been formulating and reformulating the possibilities. You began by focusing on the end—the desired behaviors or outcomes. Then you considered content, double-checking your previous work at the same time, and you played with key topics to organize your content in ways that would have meaning for your learners. You also gave some consideration to possible organizational structures. Now it is time to turn on the creativity.

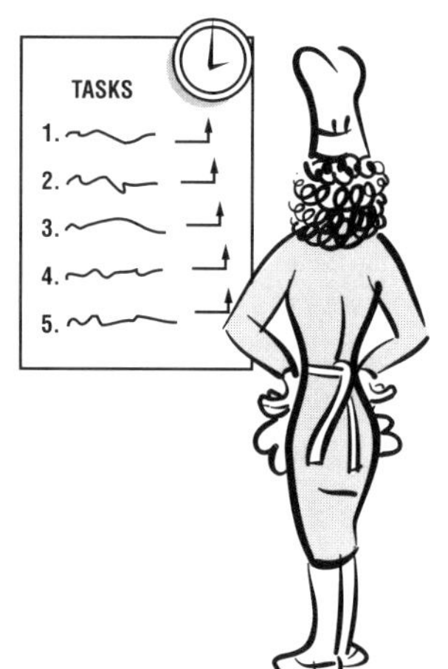

THE DESIGNER AND THE CATERER

Here is the caterer again. When she has finished the Macrodesign phase of her party plans, she will have a general list of the tasks that must be performed—a plan for preparing and presenting the meal. The plan includes when she will carry out each step, what she will have when she is finished with each major segment of the plan, what ingredients or supplies will be required, and roughly how long each step will take. She does not have a lot of detail in this plan yet, but she is confident of four factors: the sequence makes sense; she has included all essential ingredients; the plan will lead to the meal that has been described; and her time estimates seem reasonable.

HOW TO DEVELOP THE TRAINING FLOW—MACRODESIGN

Remember that the steps in this chapter guide you through the Macrodesign phase of the Training Flow stage. When you have completed this phase, you will microdesign your training flow. Because the microdesign is such a critical component of designing the training flow, we have dedicated the entire next chapter to it.

Your macrodesign will be a rough outline—at last! In it you will include all the learning activities, grouped into segments; most of the segments will have individual objectives. The outline will show an estimated time for each segment, plus information on the transitions within the design. It still will not include details of the design for individual activities; that comes later. For now, your focus is an overview of how the training session will go, built on a sequence of appropriate activities that will be effective, efficient, and engaging.

For example, the macrodesign for a two-and-a-half-hour workshop on formatting documents in a particular word-processing program might look something like this:

1. Lecturette: Objectives and Agenda. (10 min.)
2. Step-by-Step Demonstration and Practice. (30 min.)

   Objective. Participants will demonstrate ability to create headers and footers, access and use styles, and use the menus for columns and tables.

   A. Headers and footers.

   B. Accessing and using designated styles.

   C. Columns: menu and application.

   D. Tables: menu and application.
3. Individual Practice: Case Study with Sample Text. (35 min.)

   Objective. Participants will demonstrate ability to use approved letter style and to convert text to two-column format and tabular format.

   A. Approved style for letters.

   B. Two-column newsletter.

   C. Table.

Transition. Now that you've had a chance to try out these skills, but before you get started on your own individual work, what questions do you have?

4. Questions and Answers. (15 min.)
5. Individual Practice: Real Work. (35 min.)

   Objective. Participants will demonstrate ability to apply workshop information to their own work.

   A. Apply appropriate styles to own work (participants bring).

Transition. We all know that when we go back to the job, there will be many questions—maybe even a crisis or two. So before we leave, let's review the resources that are available for help outside this room.

6. Lecturette: Resources and Job Aids. (15 min.)

   Objective. Participants will identify useful resources.

   A. Examples: on-line help, keyboard template, manual, in-house tech support.

   B. Other suggestions from participants.

7. Interactive Summary. (10 min.)

THE NINE STEPS IN TRAINING FLOW—MACRODESIGN

1. Research existing activities.
2. Brainstorm activities.
3. Select possible activities.
4. Estimate time for possible activities.
5. Outline training design.
6. Articulate objectives for segments.
7. Sketch out transitions.
8. Review your macrodesign.
9. Check macrodesign with your client.

NINE STEPS IN TRAINING FLOW—MACRODESIGN

1. Research Existing Activities. You have already researched your subject matter. Now you will review available training activities. You will look for two things: ideas that might prompt your own creativity and activities that you might be able to use, either as they are or with slight modification. Here is what you will do:

______ Identify resources you might want to review:

______ Videos and video catalogs

______ Collections of activities

______ Professional journals or newsletters, such as *Creative Training Techniques*

______ Other training designs used in your organization

______ Notes from training programs you have attended

______ As you consider these activities, mentally check them against your key criteria:

______ Do the activities meet my objectives?

______ Do they cover the essential content identified in my key points?

______ Are they appropriate for my participants?

COPYRIGHT REMINDER

Remember that if you want to use someone else's work, you must honor copyrights. By this time in the design process, you know very well how many hours go into creating a workable learning activity. Copyrights ensure that authors and designers are fairly compensated for their work. Published learning activities usually provide information about obtaining permission to reprint; many even include limited rights to reproduce the materials with the purchase price. Just be sure to check.

2. Brainstorm Activities. Let your creative juices flow! You may have already had several ideas; now is the time to put them on your brainstorming list. At this stage, you may use either the key topics or the objectives as your starting point, because you have worked so hard in the previous two stages of the SIM to make the essential content congruent with the goals and objectives.

Throughout this stage, you may find yourself rethinking key topics or objectives. That's okay. Remember, the SIM is iterative, and an urge to reconsider previously developed elements of the design is a sign that the process is working well!

In order to brainstorm your list of potential learning activities, begin either with key topics or with objectives. Ask yourself, "What are some ways I could present this material or meet these objectives?" Here are some reminders and suggestions:

______ Just brainstorm possible activities; do not try to evaluate, categorize, or edit.

______ Try to come up with several optional learning activities to cover each of your key topics or objectives.

______ Avoid committing to the "right" activity during this brainstorming stage. As always, the brainstorming itself may lead to some other creative possibilities. Also, it will be to your advantage to have some backup activities or optional activities to include in the design.

______ Record your ideas without any judgment—just go for creativity. You may find that you will have several permutations on an idea.

______ Spend enough time with an idea to put some flesh on it (what kind of game or a discussion about what), but do not design it in detail. Your objective here is to generate possibilities.

______ As you brainstorm, you may find that an idea for one activity will include related activities—for example, a game followed by a discussion. That's great. Put the related activities on your brainstorming list, but do not spend time on details.

______ Get help if you need it—either by working with other people or by taking deliberate steps to boost your creativity.

______ Recognize that you may be most creative when you take some time away from the task; some of your best ideas may come in the shower a day or two later. If you have the luxury of time, why not make the most of your mind's natural desire to think creatively? Generate some options and then give them a chance to percolate. Use the intervening time to complete some of your research or to work with your client to plan for support of the training.

How does all this work in practice? For example, in the brainstorming you might initially say that you could use a game to help participants practice computational skills. That first idea might lead to several possible games—a *Jeopardy*-like game in which participants would generate questions to match answers, a competitive team game in which points would be won for correct problem solving, a physical activity in which teams would search for clues to find a buried treasure and the only way to solve the clues is by using computational skills. The list is probably endless. The point is to find lots of possibilities and avoid stopping the brainstorming process too soon. There is time for evaluation and reduction later.

3. Select Possible Activities. You will need to make some hard decisions at this point. You have probably generated several great ideas, and you would like to use all of them. You can't, of course. Now you must narrow them down to a few promising alternatives for each of your objectives or key topics. You will be tentatively playing with groupings and sequences, but you will hold off on your final decisions until a little later. Here are some suggestions for how to approach this step:

______ Analyze your potential activities, using the criteria detailed earlier in the chapter:

- ______ Support of objectives
- ______ Fit with content

- ______ Variety
- ______ Adult learners and learning styles
- ______ Transfer of learning
- ______ Your participants
- ______ Trainer competencies
- ______ Logistical constraints
- ______ Time

______ Trust your judgment as you eliminate unlikely activities and identify the ones that seem to be the most effective, efficient, and engaging.

About now, you may be seeing an appealing sequence starting to emerge—perhaps based on a particular activity, such as a case study. That's great. It may become the overarching framework for your design. Or you may have great activities in mind for different components of the training, and you might want to link them by means of a visual model that you created in the Key Topics stage. Hold that thought, but do not commit to it just yet. You will be considering sequence when you outline in Step 5.

At this point, it is usually a good idea to have a couple of possible activities for each objective or key topic. In addition, you may want to consider the advantages of having optional activities. For example, you might determine that the best approach for a particular aspect of writing memos would be skill practice on the computer, but you might hold in reserve a paper-and-pencil practice, in case computers are not available for all participants.

In any case, your task now is to choose the most promising possibilities from all the activities you brainstormed in the previous step.

4. Estimate Time for Possible Activities. You are still in the macrodesign phase, so it will be a bit of a challenge to estimate time—you will not know precisely how long some activities will take until you design them in detail. What you will do now is make your best estimate of time for each of the activities you selected in the last step—including all of the options you are still considering. This step will give you a general sense of whether the activities you select are likely to fit your overall time. In order to estimate times, try these suggestions:

______ Use your own experience of how long similar activities have taken in the past. Obviously, this personal resource will become much richer and more refined as you grow in design experience.

______ Look at predesigned activities that are similar to what you have in mind.

______ Ask your colleagues for their best guesses about time.

______ As you gain more design experience, you will know whether you tend to over- or underestimate times for activities, and you will adjust for that tendency.

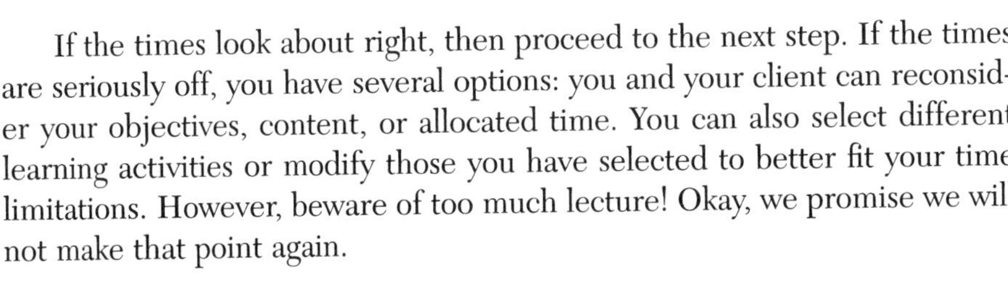

If the times look about right, then proceed to the next step. If the times are seriously off, you have several options: you and your client can reconsider your objectives, content, or allocated time. You can also select different learning activities or modify those you have selected to better fit your time limitations. However, beware of too much lecture! Okay, we promise we will not make that point again.

5. Outline Training Design. Until now we have said not to outline, but the time has finally come. In the earlier stages of the SIM, outlining might have locked you into a sequence too soon or reflected your own learning preferences rather than allowing you to consider a structure that would engage your participants. Through the work you have done on the earlier stages of the design, you have avoided both dangers; now it is time to make some final decisions about what learning activities you will include and how you will arrange them.

THE THREE E'S IN RELATION TO STRUCTURE

In selecting an organizational structure, remember that you are looking for an effective, efficient, and engaging way to organize this particular training.

- *Effective:* Because effective training must help participants to perform the desired behaviors, activities should mimic the world of application as closely as possible. If the job requires certain actions in a certain sequence, then that sequence must be a part of the learning activities in the training—even if it is not the overall structure of your design.
- *Efficient:* The structure must set a context for the learning. Select a structure that focuses the participants' energies on the desired behaviors and outcomes—not a structure that leaves participants wondering where they are going or why.
- *Engaging:* Look for a structure that might create a need to know and a desire to apply what is learned. In general, the most powerful way to create that desire is through the WIIFM ("What's in it for me?"). A second way to make a training structure engaging is to make sure it uses the actual experience of the people in the room.

By this point in some designs, the appropriate structure is obvious. For example, with a work process that has specific sequenced steps, the steps may form the basis for your training design. Or a visual model from the Key Topics stage may point the way. Or your brainstorming and selection of learning activities may have given birth to a natural structure. If you have not already seen a structure emerge, here is what to do next:

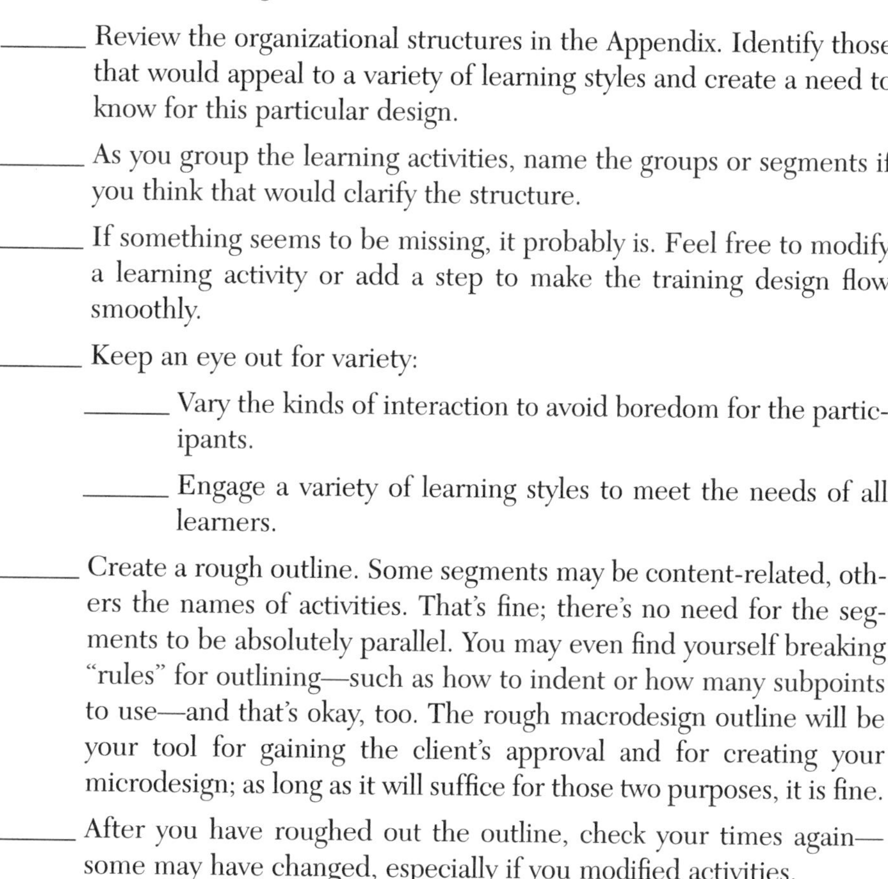

______ Review the organizational structures in the Appendix. Identify those that would appeal to a variety of learning styles and create a need to know for this particular design.

______ As you group the learning activities, name the groups or segments if you think that would clarify the structure.

______ If something seems to be missing, it probably is. Feel free to modify a learning activity or add a step to make the training design flow smoothly.

______ Keep an eye out for variety:

- ______ Vary the kinds of interaction to avoid boredom for the participants.
- ______ Engage a variety of learning styles to meet the needs of all learners.

______ Create a rough outline. Some segments may be content-related, others the names of activities. That's fine; there's no need for the segments to be absolutely parallel. You may even find yourself breaking "rules" for outlining—such as how to indent or how many subpoints to use—and that's okay, too. The rough macrodesign outline will be your tool for gaining the client's approval and for creating your microdesign; as long as it will suffice for those two purposes, it is fine.

______ After you have roughed out the outline, check your times again—some may have changed, especially if you modified activities.

Bear in mind that, whatever activities you select and however you arrange them, you must meet all of the objectives you have agreed to with your client.

6. Articulate Objectives for Segments. This is an exciting moment in the design process, because many things are coming together to confirm or clarify your work. You have just selected an organizational structure that arranges your essential content and learning activities into segments that will engage your learners and meet the training objectives. In this step, you will articulate one or more objectives for each appropriate segment of the training design—objectives that will clarify what participants will be able to do by the end of the segment. In order to articulate the segment objectives, here is what you will do:

______ Review the learning activities and content in the segment to clarify exactly what participants will be able to do by the end of that segment.

______ Recognize that in some segments objectives are not necessary. You can do without a segment objective when the participants' behaviors will not be measured—as in a question-and-answer segment or perhaps in a lecturette. You can also omit the segment objective when the activities do not relate directly to the training objectives—as in a segment that includes nothing more than participants' introductions, for example. When in doubt, however, go ahead and prepare an objective.

______ When articulating objectives, use the BAG 'M criteria:

 ______ *Behavioral:* About something that participants do, not about the instructional process

 ______ *Attainable:* Given the constraints of the training situation and the characteristics of your learners

 ______ *Goal-oriented:* Supports the overall goal of the training, plus the stated learning objectives

 ______ *Measurable:* Can be observed and assessed by trainer, participants, or both

______ You will probably find that for some segments the objectives are the same as the overall training objectives. In other segments, they may be enabling objectives—the kind that build participants' skills for performing the behaviors described in the training objectives (Chapter Six).

______ Compare the segment objectives with the training objectives.

 ______ By demonstrating all the behaviors articulated in the segment objectives, will participants fully meet the training objectives? If so, move on to the next step of the design process.

 ______ Even after demonstrating all the behaviors articulated in the segment objectives, will participants fall short of meeting the training objectives? If so, refine your design before moving to the next step. Identify which training objectives are not being met, and repeat the steps of the macrodesign process in order to meet them.

After you have clear objectives stating what participants will be able to do by the end of each segment of the training, you have an absolute checkpoint to determine whether your design truly enables participants to reach all of the training objectives. This is a critical step. If there is one central question in training design, it is *Does the design deliver on the objectives?* After you have affirmed that it does, you can move ahead with confidence.

7. Sketch Out Transitions. At this step, you are considering transitions in order to verify the integrity of your design. Some of these transitions may change when you microdesign, but the purpose of developing them now is to ensure that the flow of the design will be apparent to both the trainer and the participants. If the transitions feel forced or unnatural, take another look at your sequence of activities. In order to sketch out the transitions, here is what you will do:

______ Think through or write out what you want the trainer to say in moving from one segment of the training to the next.

______ Within each segment, identify where specific transition points will be necessary, so that the trainer can manage the relationships between the activities in a way that will fulfill the intent of your design.

______ For each transition, you may take one of three approaches:

  ______ Write it out in full—especially for transitions that may be complex or not obvious.

  ______ Make notes of key points to include—just enough to help the trainer make the transition effectively.

  ______ Leave the simpler transitions to the trainer's discretion.

Throughout this process, bear in mind that your transitions may refer to a core reference point that you want all of your activities to support, or they may simply link what has just happened in the training to what is coming next.

8. Review Your Macrodesign. You have created a training flow, or training outline, that incorporates all of your key content into sequenced learning activities, grouped into segments. You have assigned time estimates. You have developed transitions wherever necessary to ensure internal integrity. Before you begin developing the microdesign, review your macrodesign against the following criteria:

______ Does the design support my training goals and objectives?

  ______ Do the learning activities allow participants—during the training—to perform the behaviors described in the objectives?

  ______ Is there anything in the design that is not essential to meeting objectives?

______ Does the design embrace all the essential content I identified in the Key Topics stage?

______ Is the design appropriate for the participants?

  ______ Is it responsive to the general characteristics of adult learners?

  ______ Does it engage a variety of learning styles?

  ______ Does it meet the needs, abilities, and expectations of my particular learners?

______ Do the learning activities simulate, as much as possible, the world of application?

______ Does the macrodesign appear to fit with my logistical requirements?

9. Check Macrodesign with Your Client. You have an outline of the proposed training, and this is a great time to hear feedback from your client. Because you have been working collaboratively with your client to develop objectives and key topics, the client is now in the ideal position to offer feedback on how your proposed design will fit with the participants, as well as with the organizational culture.

Assuming that your client approves, you now have a macrodesign that provides an overall picture of your training plan. But your training flow is not finished. The next thing is to flesh out the activities you have selected. That is what you will be doing in Chapter Nine, Training Flow—Microdesign.

Question: Can't I just use prepared activities from other training instead of designing original ones?

Answer: On rare occasions, you may find a predesigned activity that fits your needs exactly. Be sure to check the copyright restrictions; it is your ethical and legal responsibility to make certain that you have permission to use the materials.

More often, however, you will find that an activity requires some tailoring. Again, you are responsible for adhering to all copyright limitations on the use of materials.

Question: I find that really interesting and engaging activities take more training time than I have available. Does this mean that I'm stuck with lectures or less interesting activities?

Answer: We agree that interesting and engaging activities can sometimes take more training time than is available—though not always. The real trick is to avoid all-or-nothing thinking. Even if you find that you simply cannot use a particular activity in a certain learning event because of time, space, or resource limitations, you still may not need to revert to lecture. Spend some time brainstorming alternative activities, and you will often be able to come up with a more interesting, engaging activity.

Question: For a variety of organizational reasons, I frequently have to use lectures when I would prefer to use a more interactive activity. Should I accept this restriction, or is there any other approach I can take?

Answer: First, question the idea that a lecture is your only option. If it really is, there still are many things you can do to move from a one-way transmission of information to an interactive training activity based on a lecture—thereby increasing comprehension and retention while still adhering to an organizational preference for lecture.

To have participants interact with one another or with the facilitator, build in some short pauses for questions (from the facilitator or the participants) or some brief opportunities for participants to interact with the people sitting near them.

Another possibility, less often thought of as interaction, is to help participants interact with the content—instead of just passively receiving it. For example, you might present a case problem at the beginning of a lecture and stop at various points in the lecture to let participants apply the lecture content to the case problem. This problem solving engages learners with the content, thereby increasing comprehension and retention. It may be followed by some form of sharing or reporting—but it does not have to be.

RESOURCES FOR ENLIVENING LECTURES

For the times when only a lecture will do, there are still a number of steps a designer can take to increase interaction. Here are two resources we recommend:

Silberman, M. (1990). *Active training.* San Francisco: Jossey-Bass/Pfeiffer.
Eitington, J. E. (1996). *The winning trainer* (3rd ed.). Houston, TX: Gulf.

Question: You mentioned that it is sometimes the job of the designer to "stretch" participants a bit. I work in an organization in which participants and clients say they are not at all comfortable with interactive training. They prefer to listen during the training and apply afterward. How do I stretch them, while still being responsive to their discomfort?

Answer: Your question brings up a couple of very interesting points. One is about the role of the designer—as an expert who makes determinations about the training product or, to use Peter Block's term (1981), as a "pair of hands" who does what the client asks. The other point is about balancing the needs of the learners and clients with the organizational mandate to empower learners to perform the desired behaviors. The bind is that if the learners do not perform the task in the training situation, they have no opportunity for feedback during the training, and there is no way to evaluate their performance of the new skills until everyone is back on the job.

Our feeling is that the best way to deal with this situation is to discard the all-or-nothing mind-set. The "all" part is demonstration of the skills. You know that demonstrating the skills during the training is the closest to actual application, but your client says that demonstrating will make people too uncomfortable—and you do not want the discomfort to inhibit learning. At the opposite end of the spectrum is "nothing"—simply hearing about the skills. This seems to be what your client is requesting, but you know that it will not provide any measurable outcomes during the training—for the trainer, the client, or the learners.

One good approach is to look at the issue in terms of the level of the objectives. You would prefer an objective on the how-to level, such as, "By the end of this session, participants will be able to demonstrate their ability to respond to customer questions about the new policy." At the other end of the spectrum would be an about objective, such as, "By the end of this session, participants will be able to describe the major points of the new policy." What about trying for something in the middle? Use an about-how-to objective, such as, "By the end of this session, participants will be able to describe how they will interpret the new policy to respond to customer questions." Such an approach could involve individual or group work, or both, during the training. It would be less passive than having learners simply listen, but it would not require a level of interaction that would cause them undue discomfort.

Taking the long view, you would hope that, as you gradually introduce interaction into the learning environment with successive training events, participants will become more comfortable with it and might even want more opportunities for interaction.

Question: How do I "sell" my client on an activity that is stretching her own comfort level?

Answer: First, before you do any selling, be sure that the activity will in fact be effective, efficient, and engaging. Also, have some contingency plans in case your client is not convinced—one reason for brainstorming a variety of activities and not just stopping at the first one you think of.

In terms of persuading your client to try the stretch, there are several things you can do to help strengthen your case: first, present the entire design and show how the activity you are trying to sell is simply part of an overall design. Second, be honest about why you have selected the activity, and reinforce your decision by relating it to the desired outcomes, which your client has already approved. Almost all clients are interested in the relationship between what will be going on in training and the desired outcomes back on the job. Third, be open. Hearing the client's reservations may help you improve the fit between your design and the needs of your participants.

Question: Sometimes I sense a tension between "logical" and "interesting" ways to sequence the training activities. Should I go for the logical or the interesting sequence?

Answer: Try not to make it an either/or choice. First, question what criteria you are using to determine what is "logical"—does that mean it reflects your preferred learning style? If so, the approach that you call "interesting" may be perfectly "logical" to someone with a different learning preference.

The most powerful designs are both interesting and logical. Designs that are simply interesting are usually engaging for participants, but they are not necessarily effective or efficient ways to reach desired behaviors. Designs that are merely logical may leave learners with good information but without much motivation to change behaviors. For example, presenting basic supervisory skills in a categorical structure is very logical; but opting for a problem-resolution structure may help participants to link the skills with personal needs.

Question: I'm just not very creative, so I never seem to come up with much when I brainstorm. Any suggestions?

Answer: Many designers who are pragmatic in their approach to design, who are concrete thinkers, or who really like closure may find brainstorming possible activities to be very frustrating. Some participants in our design workshops have told us that, once they have an idea that seems workable, it is very difficult for them to generate others. They see the value in the creativity, especially after a few tries at it, but it simply does not come naturally. We believe that everyone has the potential for creativity. Granted, it may come more easily and naturally to some people than to others, but creativity is a skill that can be developed.

We have found three powerful ways to come up with more creative designs. The first is to do this step of the design process with other people—even if you only bring a group together for ten or fifteen minutes to generate some ideas. Brainstorming and creativity seem to come much more readily when one person's wild idea becomes the basis for several other people's ideas.

The second way is to make the most of available resources so that you can become familiar with a broad variety of learning activities. During the research step of each stage of the SIM, ask colleagues for suggested resources. Or check with your professional associations; some of them, such as the American Society for Training and Development, provide members with library searches.

Finally, make a point of developing your own creativity. Simple techniques, such as thinking about your topic or desired objectives as if they were something else, often prompt creativity. For example, in designing a workshop to help employees enter data correctly into a particular automated system, the designer might think of the system as a hot-air balloon. (Stick with us here. The purpose is to stimulate creativity—right?) That metaphor might suggest possible learning activities: a discussion about how users overload the system with too much weight (data), a skill practice of making the thing crash and then getting it back up without any damage, a game during which participants would review sample data-entry screens to decide which ones would "fly" and which would not.

At this point, you may be smiling and thinking that this sounds like fun. Or you may be smiling in a different way—confident in your sanity and concerned about ours. The point is this: creativity comes from thinking and doing things in different ways. Thinking about a familiar topic in an entirely new way is a technique for stimulating creativity.

RESOURCES FOR CREATIVITY

Creativity is, at least in part, a skill—and it can be learned. Here are some excellent resources:

DeBono, E. (1994). *DeBono's thinking course* (rev. ed.). New York: Facts on File.
DeBono, E. (1990). *Master thinker's handbook.* Larchmont, NY: International Center for Creative Thinking.
DeBono, E. (1990). *Thinking: Skills for success.* St. Paul, MN: Paradigm.
Von Oech, R. (1993). *A whack on the side of the head.* New York: Warner.
Von Oech, R. (1986). *A kick in the seat of the pants.* New York: HarperCollins.

Question: I find that most of my designs tend to look pretty much the same. I feel as though I'm in a rut. What can I do?

Answer: The first step is to identify what organizational structure you tend to use (see Appendix). Next time you design, make a point of trying a different organizational structure. A new structure will guarantee a different approach to your training.

The second is to try some of the suggestions for boosting creativity outlined in the answer to the previous question.

Question: Sometimes an activity has seemed like a great idea to me, but in practice it has not worked very well. What can I do?

Answer: It is sad but true: ideas that look great on paper are not always so great in practice. However, you do have four powerful resources to help you judge more accurately during the design stage: first, you have your client and participants. If you are wondering about an idea, ask for their reactions. Second, you have your colleagues. Ask for feedback about the strengths and weaknesses of any activity you select. Third, friends or likely participants can help you do a dry run and test out new activities. Fourth, your own experience is a vital resource. The more you design, the more confident you will be in your ability to determine what is a reasonable risk in terms of potential learning activities.

Question: As I do the Training Flow stage of the SIM, I have the feeling that some of my objectives are more important than others; I see that some objectives will take a long time to meet, whereas others are quite short. If I'm short on time, can I sacrifice the less-important objectives?

Answer: On the basis of the time estimates in your macrodesign, you may indeed have to modify objectives to allow the proper emphasis for the most important ones. This is an example of the iterative nature of the SIM and of training design. Such changes would require collaboration with your client, of course.

However, remember that the time needed to meet a particular objective is not a measure of that objective's importance. For example, in training for a word-processing program, it might not take much time to have participants demonstrate their ability to save a document; but the objective still is an absolutely critical one. In the same training, it might take much longer for participants to demonstrate their ability to format a document; but that does not make formatting more important. In order to determine how important an objective is, you must go back to your needs assessment data and your list of essential skills from the Goals and Objectives stage of the SIM.

Question: I find that the transitions I prepare at this stage feel a bit forced. Is the problem with my transitions or my design?

Answer: It could be either, but probably the problem is with the sequence of learning activities. Of course, even in a solid design, there are times when you must present two unrelated pieces of content or skill. In these circumstances, it is best to make an honest and explicit transition such as, "At this point, we have completed our work on X and are ready to move on to Y. Before we do, what questions or comments do you have on what we have done?"

When the transition problem is not simply that the pieces are unrelated, but that they really do not fit well, it is time to rework some of your design. You might go back to the Key Topics stage and play again with categories for your essential content. Do any models or visuals emerge that might offer a point of reference for transitions? Might a different organizational structure (see Appendix) help you arrange your content better? For example, when you can use a problem-resolution structure, the transitions can refer to specific problems that will be addressed by the learning activities. Also, you might wish to select different activities, change your sequence, or add a core reference point to make smoother transitions.

Here is an example of how the addition of a simple training activity can provide the core reference point that will tie together an entire learning event. Imagine that you are designing a review of personnel policies. You have a lot of content, and your design will be moving from one policy to another frequently. You might decide to begin with a fun quiz or game that tests participants' existing knowledge. Each time you finish a topic area, your transition can refer participants back to the quiz or game to check their answers and then point out where you will be moving next.

Question: Where do I find ideas for learning activities and training designs?

Answer: There are many kinds of predesigned training events that you can review, such as the three volumes of Mel Silberman's *20 Active Training Programs* (1997, 1993, 1992). You can also find collections of training activities that can be used as parts of a design, such as those found in the Jossey-Bass/Pfeiffer *Annual* series. If you combine these resources with the design approach of the SIM, you will find that your ability to design strategically and creatively will continue to develop. Also, simply talking to other designers will give you many ideas.

BEFORE YOU MOVE ON

At last you have an overall flow for your training event. Because it is based closely on the work you have done in the earlier stages of the SIM, you can be confident that it supports your goals and objectives, includes your key topics, and addresses the needs of your adult learners. You will be adding more detail in the next phase.

Before you move on to the Microdesign phase of the Training Flow stage, it is time to look again in your imaginary computer files to see what you have created. Your first file, Goals and Objectives, still contains an umbrella—the goal that describes why the organization is doing this training. Under that umbrella are the objectives (training outcomes) and the associated essential skills. You may have made some modifications to the objectives or the skills on the basis of your continuing design work. The second file, Key Topics, is now empty. You have moved all of your content into your Training Flow. The third file, Training Flow—Macrodesign, has an outline in it. The outline is

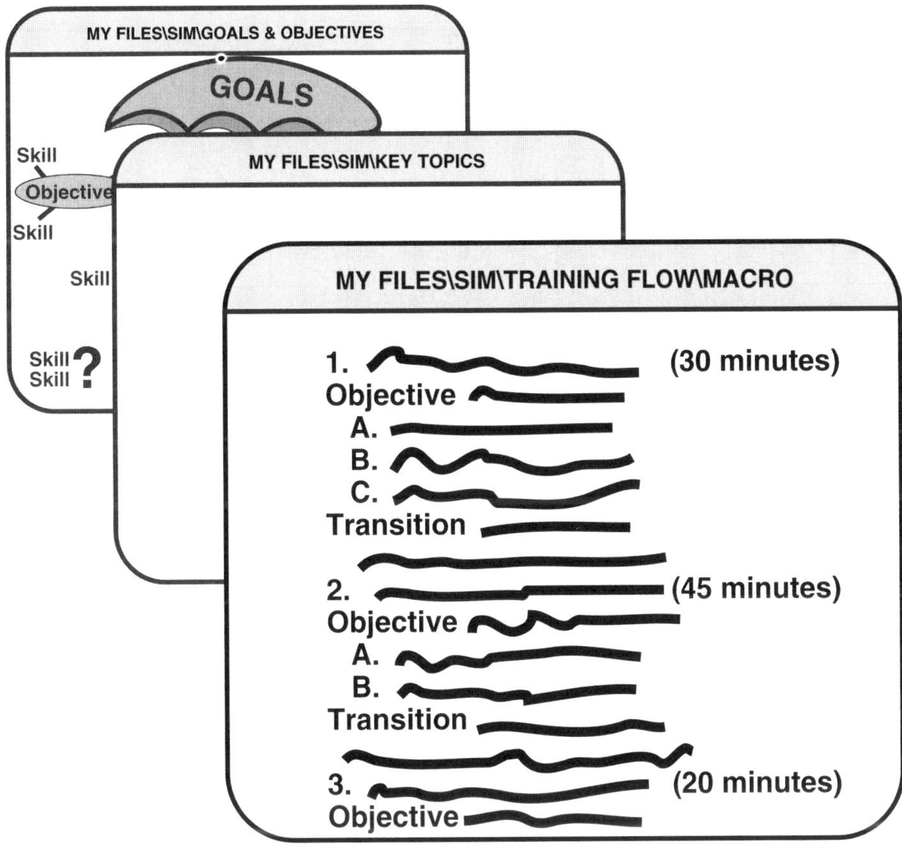

still fluid and open to modification, but it contains these essential elements: sequenced learning activities in segments, objectives for the segments, related key points, time estimates for learning activities, and probably some transitions. Now you are ready to put flesh on this training flow. It is time to microdesign.

Looking Back

Here is the SIM process to this point:

Goals and Objectives

1. Review design requirements.
2. Establish a goal statement.
3. Brainstorm the skills for reaching the desired behaviors.
4. Edit: determine essential versus nonessential skills for reaching the desired behaviors.
5. Consolidate: cluster related skills together.
6. Draft objectives.
7. Review and edit the proposed goals and objectives.
8. Review the goals and objectives with your client.

Key Topics

1. Research the subject.
2. Brainstorm possible key points.
3. Determine essential versus nonessential points.
4. Group key points into key topics.
5. Identify additional points for key topics.
6. Consider possible organizational structures.
7. Review and edit key topics.
8. Check work with your client.

Training Flow—Macrodesign

1. Research existing activities.
2. Brainstorm activities.
3. Select possible activities.
4. Estimate time for possible activities.

5. Outline training design.
6. Articulate objectives for segments.
7. Sketch out transitions.
8. Review your macrodesign.
9. Check macrodesign with your client.

Running Example: Training Flow—Macrodesign

Building on the approved goals, objectives, and key topics, Simone begins the first phase of developing her training flow—creating a macrodesign.

1. Research Existing Activities

Simone's research takes two main avenues:

- First, she continues in the direction of the needs assessment by reviewing Jexon policies on performance appraisals. Also, in collaboration with the key client on the senior management team and the director of employee relations, Simone selects examples of appraisals—both well-written and not.
- Second, Simone reviews other training programs on performance appraisals. Colleagues in other companies permit her to look at programs they have developed, and she also examines some packaged training programs. She looks for appropriate videos but finds none.

NOTE TO READER

Shown here are two samples of brainstorming, one for each of the possible approaches. Sample 1 is based on an objective; Sample 2 is based on a key topic. (Remember that at this stage of the SIM, you may use either the objectives or the key topics as your starting point.)

Naturally, in real life the designer does brainstorming for all objectives or all key topics, not just for one. Here, we have shown just one of each for purposes of illustration.

During the research, she notes that most prepared programs focus on a much broader range of topics, going beyond appraisals to performance management. However, she does find some activities about describing performance in behavioral terms; they confirm her earlier thinking that it will be easy to design exercises on this point.

2. Brainstorm Activities

Because she has done so much work already to make sure that her objectives and key topics are congruent, Simone can base her brainstorming on either one.

Sample 1: Brainstorming Starting with Objective

Objective. By the end of this session, you will be able to translate what is in your gut into language that is clear to both you and the employee and that reduces the possibilities of misunderstandings.

Possible activities

- Written description of employee performance; individuals or small groups will translate first into gut reactions and then into behavioral language.

- Individuals jot a word or two to describe overall performance of one of their employees, then translate that into specific statements that (a) could be written in an appraisal and (b) meet the criteria for behavioral statements.
- Individuals or small groups read prepared appraisal and identify statements that sound like gut reactions and those that are behavioral.
- A game (to be developed); points earned for translating gut reactions into behavioral descriptions.
- Small groups do brief skits to demonstrate interpersonal communication skills; other groups then have a limited time to come up with a gut name for the performance and then list as many specific behaviors as possible (from the skit) to support their gut names.
- Large-group discussion of a public figure, generating words/phrases to describe that person's work; small groups write statement converting them into behavioral language.

Sample 2: Brainstorming Starting with Key Topic

Key Topic. Why it is important to summarize performance.

Key points within this key topic

- Legal requirements
- Your time
- Meaningful feedback to employee
- Length of appraisal
- Summary of discussions you have had throughout the year
- Importance of performance trends
- Sample summary statements
- Sample summary formulas

Possible activities

- Large-group discussion: why it is important to summarize performance, especially in terms of saving time for supervisor or manager.
- Instructor provides list of reasons; group (large or small) adds more; individuals or small groups select three or four most important to them.

- Brief lecturette on legal requirements, with questions and answers
- Written statement of legal requirements, including two or three deliberate errors; small groups identify and correct errors.
- Distribute sample statements from appraisals and processes for summarizing; large group discusses; small groups use one of the processes to summarize a statement.
- Individuals select a process they want to try, then draft summary statement on one of their employees; review with small group.
- Large group discusses appraisal samples and processes for summarizing; small groups use one of the processes to summarize a statement from sample.

Simone repeats the brainstorming process for every objective or every key topic, generating as many ideas as possible for activities that she might use in this training. Part of what she is trying to do is to trigger her own creativity for ways to present the training.

3. Select Possible Activities

As with earlier brainstormed steps, Simone reduces the list. This time, her goal is to select the activities that seem likely to work. She will probably start seeing sequences that seem reasonable. However, she keeps her options open until she is ready to make decisions about sequencing the activities and grouping them into segments, and that is still a few steps away.

To make this first cut, Simone reviews the criteria for activities. Four stand out as especially important for this particular training design:

- *Support of objectives:* Two of the three objectives for the training call for participants to demonstrate skills. For those objectives, Simone wants to make certain that the activities will actually permit participants to practice and apply the skills—not just to discuss, analyze, or evaluate the skills.
- *Variety:* Because there is a high emphasis on application of skills, she will be careful that her activities are not too repetitive.
- *Adult learners and learning styles:* Simone wants to ensure a balance of learning styles. Jexon is a pragmatic place, but still she wants to include enough "why" information to engage intuitive learners. She also wants to balance analytical thinking with the opportunity for fun and helping one another—again, to appeal to various learning styles. Finally, for this

hands-on workshop, with its emphasis on application of skills, she wants to provide adequate opportunity for observation, reflection, and synthesis to meet all learners' needs.

- *Participants:* Knowing Jexon, Simone suspects that many of the participants will want to move into application as quickly as possible. The design must address this tendency. Since the very beginning, the overall focus has been on practical application and tools that will make the task of writing the appraisal easier and more objective. It will be important to use learning activities that focus on practical, job-related applications, that move quickly, and that permit people to share experiences rather than leave them feeling that the information is being presented as if it is all new.

  In addition, Simone knows that supervisors and managers from diverse cultures will attend the training. All are quite good at written English, but a few have mentioned in focus groups their discomfort speaking in front of groups, especially when they have to come up with answers on the spot. There will need to be time for personal reflection and sharing in small groups, where the comfort level will be higher.

With these concerns in mind, here are the activities Simone tentatively selects:

NOTE TO READER

Again, the example shows two alternate approaches—based on an objective and on a key topic. The real-life designer would have chosen one of these two approaches and would select the most promising of the brainstormed activities. For convenience, we have shortened the descriptions of the activities.

Sample 1: Selecting Activities Starting with Objective

Objective. By the end of this session, you will be able to translate what is in your gut into language that is clear to both you and the employee and that reduces the possibilities of misunderstandings.

Tentatively Selected Activities	*Simone's Thoughts*
• Read appraisal; identify gut and behavioral language.	Will help participants identify language that is not behavioral.
• Game: translating gut reactions into behavioral descriptions.	Will develop skill of translating.
• Jot a description of employee performance; translate into behavioral language for appraisal.	Will allow practice in realistic application.

Activities Not Selected	*Simone's Thoughts*
• Written description, to be translated into gut reactions and then into behavioral language.	Keeping open for now; may add later as part of another activity.
• Skits; others describe in gut language, then list behaviors.	Eliminated; too lengthy.
• Discuss public figure; convert descriptions into behavioral language.	An intriguing possibility; will keep open for now.

Overall, the activities Simone has tentatively selected fall into a sequence that seems promising to her. It will give participants a chance to practice the skills first in a generic setting and then in a simulation that is much closer to real-world application. She believes it will work well; but all the same, she is keeping a few other possibilities in mind. She stops here for now and does not go on to design the activities in detail just yet.

Sample 2: Selecting Activities Starting with Key Topic

Key Topic. Why it is important to summarize performance.

Tentatively Selected Activities	*Simone's Thoughts*
• Large group discusses why important, especially for saving time.	Will generate a list of reasons.
• Lecturette on legal requirements; Q & A.	Essential material. Method fits the Jexon culture of transmitting information quickly and efficiently.
• Sample statements and processes for summarizing; discuss; small groups use process to summarize statement.	Will give trainer a chance to clarify any misconceptions.

• Individuals select a process to try; draft summary; review with small group.	Will allow participants to choose own approach to practice.
Activities Not Selected	*Simone's Thoughts*
• Instructor provides reasons; group adds; individuals/groups select 3–4 most important to them.	Eliminated; prefer to use a "known-to-unknown" structure with these participants whenever possible.
• Legal requirements; small groups identify and correct errors.	Will keep this as an optional activity to add if time.
• Appraise samples and processes; groups use process to summarize sample statement.	Keeps as an alternative possibility, in case the related activity selected doesn't work out.

In this series of tentatively selected activities, the first two help show why it is important to summarize performance. The third and fourth focus on how to summarize, so the structure for this piece of the training is beginning to look like theoretical to practical (see Appendix), which Simone thinks will be appropriate for this group of participants.

She stops here for now. She has identified learning activities that look likely to work, and she has some possibilities in reserve. She won't make final decisions or design the activities in detail until she is confident about the entire macrodesign.

4. Estimate Time for Possible Activities

Simone uses her past experience to come up with time estimates.

Sample 1: Times for Activities Starting with Objective

Objective. By the end of this session, you will be able to translate what is in your gut into language that is clear to both you and the employee and that reduces the possibilities of misunderstandings.

NOTE TO READER

The example shows times for the two alternate approaches—based on an objective and on a key topic. Here, too, the real-life designer would have chosen one of these two approaches and would estimate times for all tentatively selected activities and all alternate possible activities. For convenience, we have again used the shortened descriptions of the activities.

Tentatively Selected Activities	*Time Estimate*
• Read appraisal; identify gut and behavioral language.	10 minutes for selecting; 10 minutes for reporting
• Game: translating gut reactions into behavioral descriptions.	15 minutes
• Jot a description of employee performance; translate into behavioral language for appraisal.	10 minutes

Alternate Possible Activities	*Time Estimate*
• Written description, to be translated into gut reactions and then into behavioral language.	15 minutes
• Discuss public figure; convert descriptions into behavioral language.	5 minutes for discussion; 10 minutes for small-group work

Sample 2: Times for Activities Starting with Key Topic

Key Topic. Why it is important to summarize performance.

Tentatively Selected Activities	*Time Estimate*
• Large group discusses why important, especially for saving time.	5–8 minutes
• Lecturette on legal requirements; Q & A.	8–10 minutes
• Sample statements and processes for	10 minutes

summarizing; discuss; small groups use process to summarize statement.	
• Individuals select a process to try; draft summary; review with small group.	20 minutes

Alternate Possible Activities	*Time Estimate*
• Legal requirements; small groups identify and correct errors.	5 minutes for reading; 10 minutes for small-group work
• Appraise samples and processes; groups use process to summarize sample statement.	10 minutes for discussion; 15 minutes for small-group work

Simone estimates times for every activity she has selected, and then she checks the total. The figures look pretty good, so she proceeds.

5. Outline Training Design

It is time to outline at last. Simone has reviewed objectives, key topics, and possible learning activities. She now has a sense of how much time various activities and groups of activities will take. She has also looked at possible organizational structures and discussed them with some colleagues.

In this instance, Simone decides on an overall categorical structure that allows the participants to discuss the characteristics of well-written appraisals and what's in it for them to do such appraisals, before addressing the three major challenges that came up in the needs assessment. By selecting the major challenges, she has also decided on a problem-resolution structure within the overall categorical structure. To bring it all full circle, she will return to the categorical structure with a final segment that goes back to the WIIFMs.

Simone decides to use a shorthand format for her outline. Here is how it looks, with times included for all major segments and the details shown for Segment 4:

NOTE TO READER

Here, the example shows only Segment 4 at the level of detail appropriate for this step. The other segments are shown with name and time only, to provide an overall context. In real life, the designer would outline the entire design.

The completed macrodesign for the Jexon training, which is based on this outline, appears on pages 197–200.

1. Introductions and Challenges. (10 min.)
2. Workshop Focus. (15 min.)
3. WIIFM. (12 min.)
4. Challenge #1: Translating What's in the Gut to Behavioral Language. (45 min.)
   - A. Demonstration with large group.
     - (1) Gut language: vague/judgmental.
     - (2) Behavioral language: descriptive/objective.
   - B. Working with real appraisals: Identify gut language.
     - (1) Individuals read, identify gut language.
     - (2) Large-group sharing; vote on a few examples.
   - C. Game: Translating gut language.
     - (1) Small groups fix gut language from above exercise.
     - (2) Large group compares and refines results.
   - D. Application with real employee.
     - (1) Individual work: gut to behavioral.
     - (2) Triad feedback.
5. Challenge #2: Summarizing Year's Performance. (50 min.)
6. Challenge #3: Using Appraisal to Look Forward and for Performance Improvement. (50 min.)
7. Summary Debrief: Return to WIIFM. (12 min.)

Estimated Versus Available Time

Total time available: 3.5 hours, or 210 minutes

Breaks: one 15-minute break or two 10-minute breaks (instructor decides)

Training time available: 190–195 minutes

Time estimate for activities: 194 minutes

During the outlining phase, Simone has grouped the selected activities, changed a few of them somewhat, and started to modify times. Overall, at this point, these are her best estimates of times, based on her experience with similar designs. She will be doing more detailed, realistic time estimates in the next phase of the training flow—the microdesign. Simone does suspect that some cutting may be necessary, but she decides that she is close enough on the estimates that she can proceed with the next step in the macrodesign.

6. Articulate Objectives for Segments

Looking at the activities and the content selected for each segment, Simone asks herself, "What will participants be able to do by the end of this segment?" She articulates an objective for each of the seven segments of the design. Here's the objective for Segment 4:

4. Challenge #1: Translating What's in the Gut to Behavioral Language.

   Objective. Participants will demonstrate their ability to identify vague language and translate it into behavioral language.

After Simone has articulated the segment objectives, she compares them with the objectives for the training. The question she asks at this point is "If participants perform the segment objectives, will they be meeting the overall training objectives?" Here are the overall training objectives, determined earlier:

Objectives. By the end of this session, you will be able to

- Translate what is in your gut into language that is clear to both you and the employee and that reduces the possibilities of misunderstandings
- Describe some quick steps you can use to reduce an entire year's performance into brief and meaningful summaries without missing any critical performance data
- Demonstrate your ability to include in the appraisal the impact of the employee's performance, exactly what you expect, and suggestions for getting there
- Describe what's in it for you to write more effective appraisals

As Simone compares the two sets of objectives, she addresses a pair of possible concerns. One concern is that several of the segment objectives say "identify" or "describe"; the other concern is that the segment objective on benefits does not match the overall WIIFM objective that she added during the Key Topics stage.

On considering these concerns, Simone decides that the objectives with "identify" and "describe" are just fine. They are enabling objectives; they help link the training with the needs assessment; and the related activities are brief. In addition, the heart of the workshop is in the activities relating to the three major challenges; two of them are "to demonstrate," and the third has participants working directly on their own needs. (See pp. 197–200.)

The concern about the WIIFM is even more easily addressed. It is an advantage, not a problem, that the segment objectives express benefits in terms of Jexon and the employees. The addition is a useful one, so she rewrites the WIIFM training objective: "You will be able to describe what's in it for you, for Jexon, and for employees when you write first-class appraisals."

Now that she is confident about the objectives in the macrodesign, Simone is ready to proceed.

7. Sketch Out Transitions

The task here is to think through the transitions at each segment of the macrodesign in order to check the logical sequence of the design. In this case, Simone sketches out all the transitions for her major segments, as well as for some elements within segments; some of them she writes out in full, and for others she just does bullet points. Here are the transitions before, during, and after Segment 4:

Transition Points [after Segment 3, WIIFM]

- *Let's look at first challenge on list* [refer to objectives].
- *Will come up with practical techniques to manage this challenge.*

4. Challenge #1: Translating What's in the Gut to Behavioral Language. (45 min.)

   Objective. Participants will demonstrate their ability to identify vague language and translate it into behavioral language.

   A. Demonstration with large group.
      (1) Gut language: vague/judgmental.
      (2) Behavioral language: descriptive/objective.
   B. Working with real appraisals: Identify gut language.
      (1) Individuals read, identify gut language.
      (2) Large-group sharing: vote on a few examples.

Transition. Great! You've found language that needs to be fixed. Now let's have a little fun fixing it.

   C. Game: translating gut language.
      (1) Small groups fix gut language from above activity.
      (2) Large group compares and refines results.

Transition Points

- *Have come up with ways to fix appraisal language.*
- *Now practice on a real-life situation, get feedback.*

  D. Application with real employee.
    (1) Individual work: gut to behavioral.
    (2) Triad feedback.

Transition [into Segment 5, Summarizing]. I hope you feel that you have some practical ways to translate gut feelings into descriptive, objective, behavioral language. We saw some great examples of how to do it during the last few minutes, and now I'd like us to move on to the second challenge: summarizing a year's performance on the appraisal [refer to objective]. *It is, as we all know, no small challenge! Let's begin by discussing why it is important to do.*

After she has sketched out the transitions, Simone is ready to take a good look at her macrodesign as a whole.

8. Review Your Macrodesign

As Simone goes back to look at her macrodesign, she asks herself the following questions:

- *Does the design support my training goals and objectives?* Yes. During this workshop, participants will identify what's in it for them to write effective appraisals; translate judgments about performance into behavioral descriptors of performance; describe the process they will use to summarize performance; describe performance impacts; clarify performance expectations; and develop suggestions for performance improvement strategies. Simone does, however, have one concern about supporting the goals and objectives: because most of the activities are to be done in small groups, it will be a challenge for the trainer to ensure that individuals actually are meeting the objectives. There also are significant time constraints, so she cannot add training time for individual evaluation here. Instead, Simone is now thinking that she would like to develop a coaching tool (to be used after the training) to facilitate transfer of learning. That way, those who manage the participants can help ensure that they have learned the skills and can adapt them to the real-life work environment. She puts a note into the Materials file.
- *Does the design embrace all the essential content I identified in the Key Topics stage?* Yes. Simone has selected activities and sequenced them in

an outline, so the items are in a different order from how she listed them when she was determining key topics. But it is clear that the major segments do address the WIIFM (Segment 3 and Segment 7), First-Class Appraisals (Segment 2 and throughout), Looking Back (Segments 4 and 5), and Looking Forward (Segment 6). Simone is confident that she will be able to incorporate the details of content (the key points) when she does the microdesign.

- *Is the design appropriate for the participants?* Yes. It addresses the general characteristics of adult learners (Chapter Three):
  - It recognizes and builds upon what they already do well.
  - Because the three major challenges addressed in the training were identified through the needs assessment, the training responds to an identified need to know.
  - Individuals will determine their own strategies for summarizing, so they will be making independent judgments.
  - Most sharing of personal work is done in small groups of two or three, with very little risk to participants' self-esteem.

    In addition, the design appeals to a variety of learning styles—balancing "why" and "how" discussions and activities. It does lean toward the practical, somewhat at the expense of the theoretical, but that emphasis is perfectly in keeping with the Jexon culture. Beyond that, the design is particularly appropriate for Jexon supervisors and managers in a couple of other ways:
    - All examples will come from Jexon.
    - Participants will leave with strategies and tools that they will be able to use in the next two months for the appraisals that are coming up soon.
- *Do the learning activities simulate, as much as possible, the world of application?* Absolutely. Participants will be working with real appraisals actually written at Jexon; in addition, each participant will be choosing a real employee on whom to focus in one of the exercises.
- *Does the macrodesign appear to fit with my logistical requirements?* In general, yes. It is okay that further adjustments in timing may be required during the next phase; after all, the SIM is iterative.

What Simone has at this point is a large-scale flow of the training, in rough outline form. There is enough detail for her to determine whether the proposed plan will meet the key criteria outlined in the five questions above.

There is not yet enough detail—intentionally—to describe exactly what is happening during each activity (such as specific directions for small-group activities); that detail will come in the next phase.

9. Check Macrodesign with Your Client

Simone takes her macrodesign to the key client on the senior management team and talks through it with her. Because the client has been closely involved in the process from the beginning, she approves nearly all of it. She does express a concern about confidentiality with regard to the exercise in which participants will talk about a specific employee. Though acknowledging and sharing her concern, Simone points out the need to make the application as realistic as possible. They agree to include two cautions in the directions for this exercise: participants should pick a situation for which others in the group will not be able to recognize the employee, and no names should be used.

With that adjustment, things are looking good. Simone is ready to move on to the Microdesign phase of the Training Flow stage.

Complete Macrodesign for Jexon Training

1. Introductions and Challenges (10 min.)

   Objective. Participants will identify key problems with written appraisals at Jexon.

   A. Welcome and introductions.

      (1) Participants guess at problems with Jexon appraisals.

   B. Compare with needs assessment list of problems.

Transition Points

- *Acknowledge common themes.*
- *Will develop concrete sense of first-class appraisal.*
- *Jexon always striving to be "first-class."*

2. Workshop Focus. (15 min.)

   Objective. Participants will identify characteristics of effective appraisals.

   A. First-Class Appraisals.

      (1) Dyads: 2–3 characteristics.

      (2) Report to large group.

HOW SEQUENCE AFFECTS ACTIVITIES

Simone had thought of doing this activity in a large group, an approach that seemed time-efficient. As she starts to outline and put activities into a sequence, however, she realizes that the rest of the design relies heavily on large-group and small-group activities. She decides that using dyads here will help provide variety.

B. Lecturette: Objectives and Agenda.

(1) Link to needs assessment: what they do well.

(2) Focus on 3 challenges (objectives).

(3) Agenda.

Transition Points

- *Have reached agreement on well-written appraisal.*
- *Have revisited challenges you raised in needs assessment.*
- *Objectives of workshop relate to those challenges.*
- *Now, what's in it for you to meet the challenges and write first-class appraisals?*

3. WIIFM. (12 min.)

Objective. Participants will identify 2–3 personal benefits of striving to write effective appraisals.

A. Individuals identify.

B. Small-group sharing.

Transition Points

- *Let's look at first challenge on list* [refer to objectives].
- *Will come up with practical techniques to manage this challenge.*

4. Challenge #1: Translating What's in the Gut to Behavioral Language. (45 min.)

Objective. Participants will demonstrate their ability to identify vague language and translate it into behavioral language.

A. Demonstration with large group.

(1) Gut language: vague/judgmental.

(2) Behavioral language: descriptive/objective.

B. Working with real appraisals: identify gut language.

(1) Individuals read, identify gut language.

(2) Large-group sharing; vote on a few examples.

Transition. Great! You've found language that needs to be fixed. Now let's have a little fun fixing it.

ADDING ACTIVITIES

As Simone works on the sequence for this segment, she realizes that participants will need some introduction before they read the samples. She decides to add a quick demonstration, followed by a large-group discussion.

C. Game: translating gut language.

(1) Small groups fix gut language from above activity.

(2) Large group compares and refines results.

Transition Points

- *Have come up with ways to fix appraisal language.*
- *Now practice on a real-life situation, get feedback.*

D. Application with real employee.

(1) Individual work: gut to behavioral.

(2) Triad feedback.

Transition. I hope you feel that you have some practical ways to translate gut feelings into descriptive, objective, behavioral language. We saw some great examples of how to do it during the last few minutes, and now I'd like us to move on to the second challenge: summarizing a year's performance on the appraisal [refer to objective]. *It is, as we all know, no small challenge! Let's begin by discussing why it is important to do.*

5. Challenge #2: Summarizing Year's Performance. (50 min.)

Objective. Participants will individually describe the process they will use to ensure that they are summarizing performance patterns and trends as well as including critical performance events that are not part of the performance trends.

A. Why

(1) Large-group discussion: why important

a. Trainer adds legal information as necessary

(2) Lecturette: performance trends

B. How

(1) Individuals list key ideas for how to summarize.

a. Share with small group.

b. Small groups report to create composite list for large group.

(2) Individuals write out own process for how to summarize.

a. Dyads/triads share processes, give feedback.

Transition Points

- *Have tools to meet two challenges.*
- *Move to last challenge* [refer to objectives].

6. Challenge #3: Using the Appraisal to Look Forward and for Performance Improvement. (50 min.)

   Objective. Participants will demonstrate ability to use behavioral language in describing current performance, performance expectations, and recommendations for performance improvement.

   A. Large-group discussion: why/when to include performance impacts

   B. Small-group game: How

      (1) Small groups each fix 2–4 samples by articulating:

         a. Behavioral description: present performance.

         b. Behavioral description: desired performance.

         c. Strategy for achieving desired performance.

      (2) Points given for each reasonable response.

Transition. We have packed a lot into a very brief time. We have covered (ask participants to name one thing that stands out for them). I'd like to close by going back to a question we asked at the beginning of this workshop: What's in it for you to do what we have discussed? But I'd like to expand the question a bit, and talk about what's in it for Jexon and for employees as well as for you.

7. Summary Debrief: Return to WIIFM. (12 min.)

   Objective. Participants will identify personal benefits of writing effective appraisals, as well as benefits to Jexon and to employees.

   A. Large-group discussion: benefits for Jexon, employees, and participants

9 The SIM

Training Flow—Microdesign

Welcome to the second and more detailed phase of the Training Flow stage of the SIM: the Microdesign phase. In the Macrodesign phase of the Training Flow stage, you produced a big-picture outline of the training. It gave you enough detail to make some reasonable time estimates for learning activities and to determine whether the overall design was sound enough to continue with it. In the Microdesign phase, you are fleshing out the design. This phase will give you additional information; as a result, you will confirm your previous decisions or reconsider some of them.

The completed microdesign is a detailed plan for the learning activities in all the segments of the macrodesign outline. It specifies the steps within each activity, identifies the products of each step, and lays out the training processes. Not only is this phase of design essential for developing the trainer's guide, but it also allows you to reexamine the training methods and refine the time estimates.

PRODUCT OF THE TRAINING FLOW—MICRODESIGN PHASE

When you have completed this stage of the SIM, your new product will take the place of the previous product. The macrodesign, which you completed in the last phase, will have been transformed into a detailed plan for meeting your objectives.

- *Training Flow—Microdesign:* The flesh on the bones of the macrodesign. The microdesign goes beyond the macrodesign to lay out exactly what is to happen at each step of every learning activity. The microdesign includes what the participants will produce in each step, how they will do it, and how long it will take; it also provides specific objectives for each learning activity, additional transitions, and information about how to initiate various activities within the training. In the microdesign, the times are precise enough to allow for such details as moving participants into and out of groups.

Because the microdesign grows directly out of the macrodesign, it has the same firm foundation in the training event's goals and objectives. At the completion of the microdesign phase, your training flow is complete.

In the training on listening skills for medical professionals, here's how the microdesign for the first part of "What makes it hard to listen and really hear" might look:

3. What Makes It Hard to Listen and Really Hear. (40 min.)

   Objective. Participants will identify delivery characteristics that are challenges to listening and hearing.

   A. Large group: briefly revisit list of personal habits from intro. (3 min.)

   B. Identifying challenges to delivery. (20 min.)

   Initiator. As you watch these brief video vignettes, please make notes about specific things the speaker does that make it challenging to listen to and really hear what is being said.

      (1) Individual work: notes during videos. (5 min.)

      (2) Small-group work. (5 min.)

         - Share notes.
         - Make composite list of challenges.

      (3) Large-group reporting: develop composite list of challenges. (10 min.)

The microdesign would go on with details on remaining learning activities: the next seventeen minutes of this segment, as well as all the rest of the training event. For each part of the training, the microdesign would show process, content, times, and significant transitions. At this level of detail, the designer is planning and directing the flow of the training.

From the microdesign will come everything the designer needs in order to create—in the next stage of the SIM—training materials for participants, for trainers, and for the learning environment itself.

TRAINING FLOW—MICRODESIGN: WHY? AND WHY NOW?

Many participants in our workshops ask why they need this level of detail, especially if they are not only the designer but also the trainer. Admittedly, this phase of design can be a challenge for designers for whom detail is not a particular talent. Nevertheless, we believe it is a critical part of the process because

- The microdesign is the basis of your trainer's guide. It contains detailed information so that someone who has not created the design will be able to replicate your intentions and manage the details of the learning event.

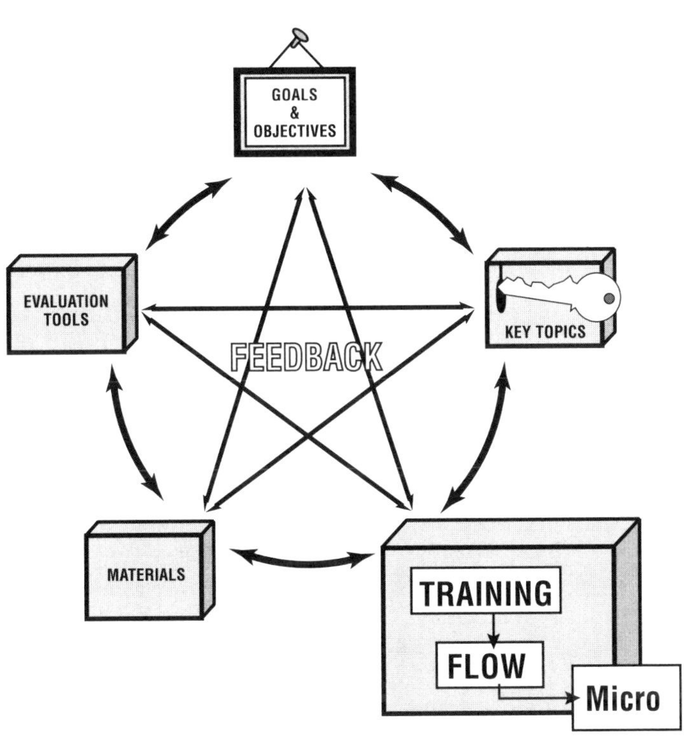

- This level of detail will also give you enough information for accurate time estimates. For example, you may need to account for how long it will take participants to move into groups. Or you may realize that your macrodesign allocated ten minutes for small-group reports, but that with five groups you would have only two minutes per group and no time for questions or discussion.
- Explicit directions can be developed easily at this level of detail. Surely you have seen training events in which the directions for an activity were not clear, so time was wasted trying to figure out what was supposed to be going on in the small groups. By developing a microdesign, you avoid such problems.
- You will determine products for each activity, correlated with the enabling objectives (Chapter Six). These products are the outcomes of each activity; usually, in an effective and efficient design, products developed in one part of the training are used in the next part.
- This level of detail will either confirm or challenge your earlier conclusion that the selected learning activities truly support the training objectives.
- You will be able to determine which activities require high trainer control and which do not. For example, a discussion about opinions could work well in small groups, with no trainer control. An interpretation of policy could begin in small groups, but you would want to design a way for the trainer to check the interpretations so that only the correct ones would be reinforced.
- At this level of detail, you will see clearly where you want to design alternate activities. For example, your macrodesign might call for a game to cover a certain area. If you know from your needs assessment that the number of participants will be unpredictable, and if you realize during microdesign that the game needs at least twelve people, you will design an alternate activity for smaller sessions.
- The microdesign process will show you where you need materials—such as audio or visual aids, a handout with directions for an activity, or trainer's resources.

- The microdesign process will allow you to consider which activities can serve as evaluation points. For example, a particular skill practice might be an opportunity for participants and the trainer to stop and assess the participants' demonstrated abilities in relation to the training objectives.
- For us, the greatest benefit of microdesigning is that it helps us create learning events that are powerfully responsive to adult learners (Chapter Three). It does this in a very specific way: a good microdesign minimizes the possibility that the trainer will have to intervene at the end of an activity and give the "right" answer. Occasionally, of course, a small group may report incorrect responses to the large group, and they must be corrected. Still, the design should do everything possible to reduce the probability, and microdesigning allows the designer to think at this level of detail.

Some designers, especially those whose talents are best expressed in concrete details (Chapter Four), begin their design process at this level. Don't! You will waste time designing details of activities that may never make it to the training. Worse yet, you may include activities that are not effective, efficient, or engaging—because you have spent so much time on them that your ability to make clear-headed decisions is diminished.

If you have been following the SIM rigorously, you will see that now is the perfect time to microdesign. You have done great work to come up with a macrodesign that truly supports the goals and objectives for the training and that will include all the essential content. The macrodesign is a road map that promises to be a solid way to reach your destination, and now is the time to add the fine lines to the map. As you do so, you may find that some of your earlier choices must be reconsidered. That's okay. Remember that this is an iterative process.

You are going to complete your microdesign before you develop materials for participants or for the trainer, and that is another way to save time. You do not want to bother designing and formatting an engaging worksheet, for example, until you are certain that you will actually need it.

ONE DESIGNER'S CONFESSION

I have always been careful about the first steps of the SIM—goals and objectives, key topics, and macrodesign—but I used to create participant materials before I had fleshed out all the details of the design. Here's what almost always happened: I would have the participant materials finished, or so I thought; sometimes they would even have been photocopied for distribution. Then, as I immersed myself in the details of preparing the trainer's guide, I would suddenly realize that I needed another worksheet or that the steps of an activity would work better in a different order.

It was always a scramble, and sometimes the effectiveness and efficiency of the training were compromised. So finally I got smart and started taking the time to microdesign before working on my participant materials. It has made all the difference in the world, and it saves me time.

As in the earlier stages of the SIM, you will probably come up with some great ideas for materials and evaluation tools as you are microdesigning. Record those ideas for later, but do not waste any effort on them now.

CHALLENGES IN MICRODESIGNING

The microdesign phase is challenging and time-consuming. For some designers, it is a real stretch; for others, it comes more easily. Either way, it is an essential part of creating training that will be effective, efficient, and engaging.

Finding Your Best Way

Because of the level of detail at the microdesign phase, it will be helpful for you to experiment to find tools and approaches that fit your own preferences. Some designers prefer to work with words. Others prefer to use graphic techniques so that they can *see* the details. The how-to steps for the SIM will guide you through the process, no matter what tools or approaches you prefer.

Just to illustrate some of the possibilities, here are examples of how two different designers, Vicki Verbal and Geoff Graphic, might work out the microdesign for the same learning activity:

Designer. Vicki Verbal

Learning Activity Objective. Participants will demonstrate ability to identify and correct errors in a Standard Form 1A.

1. Individuals review completed form and identify errors.
2. Large group: share errors and reach agreement when there are differences of opinion.
3. Dyads work together to correct errors on form.
4. Large group: report out, get confirmation or correction of responses.

Designer. Geoff Graphic

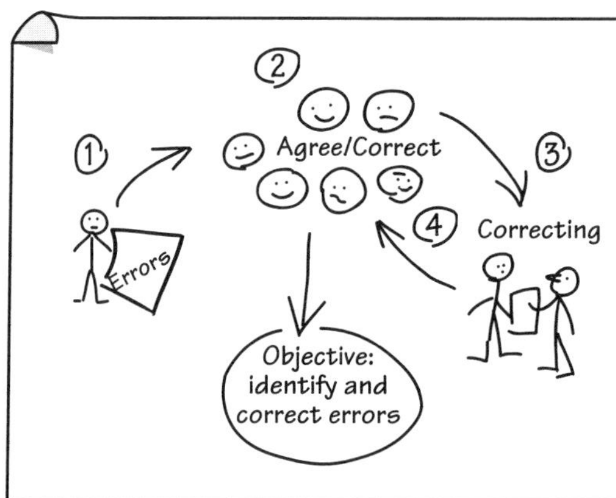

Defining the Universe of Acceptable Responses

Part of the microdesign process is to define the universe of responses for each learning activity. Every learning activity has a set of acceptable responses, ranging from one to infinite. Defining the range is a powerful tool for avoiding designs that waste time or that make participants feel set up. For example, when there is only one correct response, participants may well feel manipulated if they are asked to engage in a time-consuming large-group discussion that generates multiple responses.

If you make the effort, during the microdesign phase, to define the universe of acceptable responses, you will be rendering your design more efficient, guiding the trainer, and helping participants accomplish the objectives without undue expenditures of time or energy.

The Possibilities. Some activities have only *one acceptable response.* For example, imagine a workshop on sexual harassment in an organization that has a clearly articulated policy: "Any complaint or allegation of sexual harassment is to be referred directly to the Manager of Employee Relations." In this organization, when you are designing a learning activity—perhaps a discussion or a skill practice—about how a supervisor should respond to an employee's complaint, there is only one acceptable response.

Some activities have a *small number of acceptable responses.* For example, say you are designing an activity on the three ways to copy text in a particular word-processing system. You might have participants play the role of a technical assistant for the software company to explain to users how to copy on this system. Before the role play, you might have a quick discussion on copying. A good opening question for this discussion would be "What are the various ways you can copy on this system?" This question would cue learners that there is more than one correct answer.

Some activities have a *large set of acceptable responses* but also some unacceptable ones. For example, for a career-management workshop you might design a learning activity on how to describe job experience in a résumé. There are many acceptable ways, each with some advantages and disadvantages; but some ways, such as lying, are unacceptable. Similarly, if you are designing a workshop on managing difficult people, there are many acceptable ways to manage certain situations, but physical violence is not one of them; the design would have to support the trainer in clarifying that point if it came up.

Some learning activities have an *infinite number of acceptable responses* and no wrong responses. In any discussion of opinions or personal reflections, all responses are acceptable; that fact makes a big difference to both the designer and the trainer in terms of do's and don'ts. If you are designing such an activity, here are some guidelines:

- The initiating question should be open-ended.
- The design should tell the trainer to record either all of the responses or none of them.
- There should be no reduction of the list (such as the "ten best"), because reduction implies that some responses are "more correct" than others.

USING THE UNIVERSE OF ACCEPTABLE RESPONSES

Karla is designing a coaching-skills workshop for supervisors and managers. Her macrodesign calls for small groups to generate possible resolutions to a situation described in a case study, then report out to the large group. As she is defining the universe of acceptable responses for the small-group activity, she realizes that there are several possible acceptable resolutions (large universe) but also that the groups might generate resolutions that would be unacceptable in light of organizational policy.

Karla does not want to put participants' self-esteem on the line. Also, she would like to keep the trainer from having to provide the "right" answers. In addition, because the training will include various supervisory and management levels—and some participants might even be attending along with their own bosses—she is sensitive to the possibility of embarrassing participants.

So in the microdesign phase, Karla makes three refinements to the design:

- All participants will read the case study; then, in a large-group discussion, participants will generate unacceptable resolutions and analyze what makes them unacceptable.

- For the small-group work, participants will be directed to indicate with a question mark any proposed resolutions of which they are uncertain.
- The trainer will circulate during the small-group work to make any necessary corrections before reports are made to the large group.

Karla's design does not completely eliminate the possibility that corrections might have to be made in front of the large group, but it greatly reduces the probability of such an intervention.

Making the Determination. What makes a response acceptable or unacceptable? The distinction is a challenging one to make. It is not about whether the designer or the trainer agrees with the response. Rather, it is about what is appropriate and useful—within organizational policy, within the law, within the context of the subject. For example, in a workshop on effective communications, it would not be acceptable for a participant to say, "I just tell them once. If they don't get it, that's their problem."

Some new designers wonder why they should bother distinguishing acceptable from unacceptable responses during the design process. This distinction is incredibly important in both design and presentation, as confusion often results from activities in which it is not clear what the "correct answer" was—or whether there was one at all. The confusion may be particularly distressing for participants with certain learning styles (Chapter Three). Difficult participant behaviors may often arise when participants think they are being asked for an opinion but are later told, directly or indirectly, that they were wrong. In addition, the trainer may feel uncomfortable needing to correct unacceptable responses while trying to protect the self-esteem of the learners. Of course, this is part of being a good trainer; but good designs can minimize the problem by defining the universe of acceptable responses and building in appropriate process steps to lead to these responses.

THE DESIGNER AND THE CATERER

The caterer might prepare something like a microdesign, too. At this stage, she will have all the details of meal preparation and serving mapped out. Her plan will specify which steps of preparation need to be done before other steps, which ingredients will be needed at each step, and which steps could be modified at the last minute if necessary. Her time estimates will be quite precise, and she will be confident that she can have the meal prepared and served according to the schedule and format agreed to with her client.

HOW TO DEVELOP THE TRAINING FLOW—MICRODESIGN

You will be working from your macrodesign during this phase of training flow design, and the details that you produce will give you new insights into your overall training flow. You will likely find that you want to adjust the macrodesign. That's fine. Do it. In fact, the impulse to go back is a sign that you are doing a great job.

What is the difference between a macrodesign and a microdesign? The difference is the level of detail. For example, if you have a macrodesign calling for a twenty-minute small-group discussion after a training video, the microdesign for the same twenty minutes might look something like this:

Activity. Discuss video. (20 min.)

Objective. Participants will identify management strengths and weaknesses.

1. Small groups list, on flip-chart paper, three strengths and three weaknesses of the management style of the supervisor in the video. (10 min.)
2. Groups report. (5 min.)
   - Alternate, reporting one strength at a time, until all are reported.
   - Trainer records.
   - Trainer encourages questions for clarification and checks for agreement before listing strength.
   - Trainer keeps separate list of contributions about which there is lack of agreement, to be discussed later.
3. Repeat step 2 for weaknesses. (5 minutes)

The microdesign gives a more vivid, specific picture of exactly what is going on during the twenty minutes—what is being discussed and how the discussion process is to be managed. To do your own microdesign, you will follow the steps described below.

THE TEN STEPS IN TRAINING FLOW—MICRODESIGN

1. Identify specific objective for each activity.
2. Define the universe of acceptable responses.
3. Develop the steps and the processes for each activity.
4. Refine time estimates.
5. Develop initiators.
6. Develop transitions.
7. Check time estimates one final time.

8. Review microdesign.
9. Complete outline of the training design.
10. Determine whether to check the microdesign with your client.

TEN STEPS IN TRAINING FLOW—MICRODESIGN

1. Identify Specific Objective for Each Activity. Ask yourself exactly what participants will be able to do as a result of this particular activity. For a segment that has only one learning activity, the objective for the activity is the one you have already articulated for the segment. Here is what you will do:

_____ State the exact objective—it may be an enabling objective, supporting the segment objective—for this particular activity.

_____ Whenever possible, express the objective so that it meets the BAG 'M criteria:

- _____ *Behavioral:* About something that participants do, not about the instructional process
- _____ *Attainable:* Given the constraints of the training situation and the characteristics of your learners
- _____ *Goal-oriented:* Supports the overall goal of the training, plus the stated learning objectives
- _____ *Measurable:* Can be observed and assessed by trainer, participants, or both

Even though the objectives in your microdesign are small, they are essential. The designer and the trainer must know exactly why each learning activity is taking place at its particular time in the training and what the desired outcomes are. Communicating the objective to the trainer enables him to make adjustments on the spot, without sacrificing the integrity or intention of the learning activity.

UNIVERSE OF ACCEPTABLE RESPONSES

One acceptable response

Small number of acceptable responses

Large set of acceptable responses

Infinite number of acceptable responses

2. Define the Universe of Acceptable Responses. By yourself, with your design team, or with a subject-matter expert, determine the universe of acceptable responses for each particular learning activity. Doing so will enable you to design methods to reach the desired response without undue confusion or frustration for participants—and with a minimum of direct trainer control. Defining the universe of acceptable responses is the best way a designer can reduce the probability that the trainer will have to correct participants. Here is how to go about it:

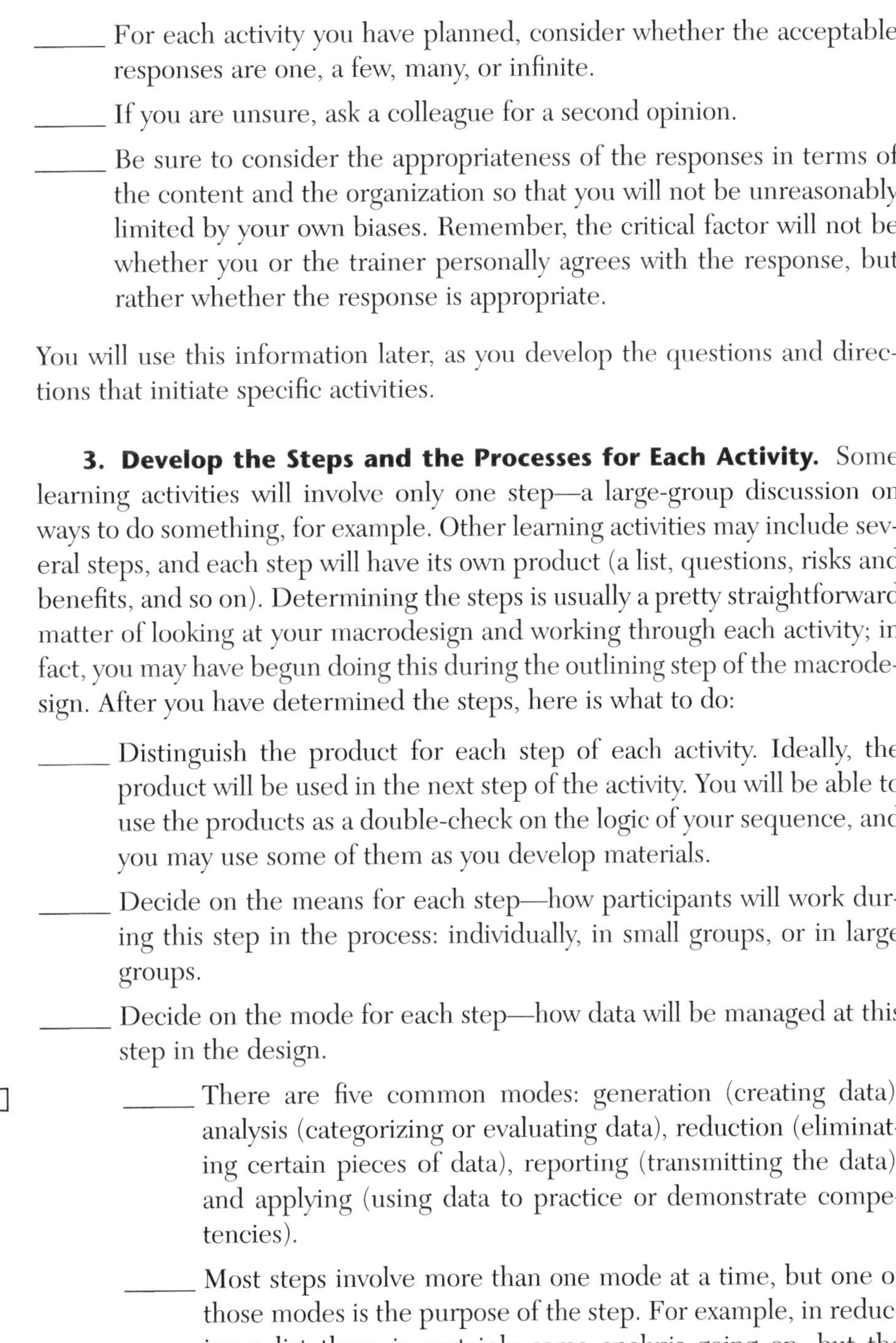

_____ For each activity you have planned, consider whether the acceptable responses are one, a few, many, or infinite.

_____ If you are unsure, ask a colleague for a second opinion.

_____ Be sure to consider the appropriateness of the responses in terms of the content and the organization so that you will not be unreasonably limited by your own biases. Remember, the critical factor will not be whether you or the trainer personally agrees with the response, but rather whether the response is appropriate.

You will use this information later, as you develop the questions and directions that initiate specific activities.

3. Develop the Steps and the Processes for Each Activity. Some learning activities will involve only one step—a large-group discussion on ways to do something, for example. Other learning activities may include several steps, and each step will have its own product (a list, questions, risks and benefits, and so on). Determining the steps is usually a pretty straightforward matter of looking at your macrodesign and working through each activity; in fact, you may have begun doing this during the outlining step of the macrodesign. After you have determined the steps, here is what to do:

_____ Distinguish the product for each step of each activity. Ideally, the product will be used in the next step of the activity. You will be able to use the products as a double-check on the logic of your sequence, and you may use some of them as you develop materials.

_____ Decide on the means for each step—how participants will work during this step in the process: individually, in small groups, or in large groups.

_____ Decide on the mode for each step—how data will be managed at this step in the design.

  _____ There are five common modes: generation (creating data), analysis (categorizing or evaluating data), reduction (eliminating certain pieces of data), reporting (transmitting the data), and applying (using data to practice or demonstrate competencies).

  _____ Most steps involve more than one mode at a time, but one of those modes is the purpose of the step. For example, in reducing a list there is certainly some analysis going on, but the

Modes

Generation

Analysis

Reduction

Reporting

Applying

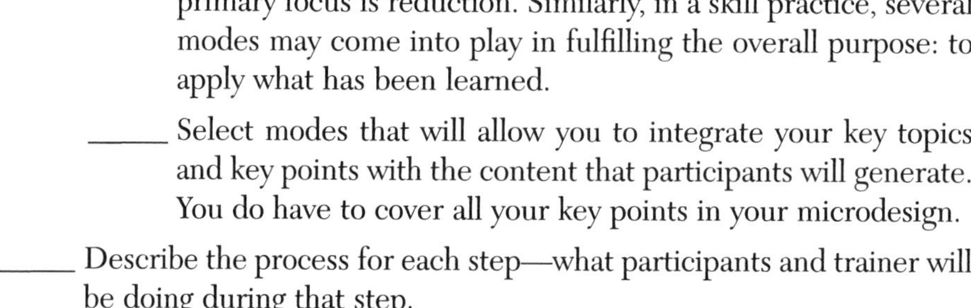

primary focus is reduction. Similarly, in a skill practice, several modes may come into play in fulfilling the overall purpose: to apply what has been learned.

_____ Select modes that will allow you to integrate your key topics and key points with the content that participants will generate. You do have to cover all your key points in your microdesign.

_____ Describe the process for each step—what participants and trainer will be doing during that step.

For most designers, the concepts of "product," "means," and "process" are fairly familiar. "Mode" may be less familiar, but it is critical. Your determination about modes will do two things for your design: first, it will ensure that you are selecting efficient ways to manage data in order to reach objectives. For example, if a subject has only one acceptable response, it makes good sense to have a discussion that focuses on analyzing that response, to help participants comprehend and retain why it is correct. If you are dealing with a subject that has many acceptable responses, it probably does not make sense to reduce the responses simply for the sake of a briefer list.

Second, clarifying the mode will help you to write the initiating question or direction for each step of the process—and you will need to do that soon. In a situation in which the mode is generation—especially if you want to generate a lot of data—the initiating question or direction needs to be open-ended to encourage diverse responses. If the mode is analysis, the initiating question or direction must cue participants as to the type of analysis you want, in order to lead logically to the product for the step. Identifying the mode is a critical part of your preparation for writing the initiators.

PROCESS STEPS, WITH PRODUCTS

Imagine the training flow for a workshop on telephone techniques. The macrodesign has "Creating a call message" as its third major learning activity. The overall objective for the activity is "Participants will demonstrate their ability to create an accurate and legible call message."

At the microdesign phase, the designer breaks the activity into process steps, determining the product, means, and mode for each one. So within this learning activity, the steps would be developed something like this:

A. Large-group discussion: list components of a call message (generation).

Product. Components of call message.

B. Small groups examine sample call messages, identify problems/errors (analysis).

Product. Identified errors.

C. Small groups develop rules to follow in creating call message.

Product. Rules for completing call messages accurately.

- Small groups list possible rules (generation).
- Report to large group (reporting).
- Compare results with prepared list presented by trainer (analysis).

D. Individuals practice skill.

Product (final). Demonstrated ability to create a call message.

- Each person creates two call messages from simulated phone calls (applying).
- Dyads give feedback according to rules from Step C (analysis).

Another way to approach this same task is by way of a chart. If the microdesign for this activity were charted according to all four components, it might look like this:

Process Step	*Product*	*Means*	*Mode*
A. Discussion	Components of call message	Large group	Generation
B. Discussion	Identified errors	Small groups	Analysis
C. Discussion, then reading	Rules for completing call message accurately	Small groups, then large group	Generation, reporting, and analysis
D. Practice, then feedback	Demonstrated ability to create a call message	Individual, then dyads	Applying, then analysis

4. Refine Time Estimates. Now you are in the great position of having a clear picture of what is going on at each step of your learning activity, and you can check to make sure that your planned activities will fit into the available time. Here is what to do:

_____ Calculate the time for each step (including time to put people into groups and time for them to move around, if needed).

_____ Compare the results with your original time estimate. If you find that the times are very different, rethink your macrodesign, your microdesign, or both. You may even go all the way back to objectives to reconsider whether they are attainable within the time limitations.

_____ Beware of the possible temptation to simply adjust the time estimates. It is nearly always a better idea to reconsider your activities, your objectives, or both.

To calculate times, use your own experience, any information you can glean from published resources (especially if you are using predesigned activities), and the input of colleagues. When in doubt, it is usually wise to allow more time for an activity rather than less.

5. Develop Initiators. Now that you are clear on what you want to happen in each step of your process (the product and mode) and how you want participants to do it (the means), you are ready to develop initiators. You will need an initiator for any activity that requires either directions for a process or a well-phrased question to focus a discussion. You may decide to write out the initiators or simply to list the essential points.

WHY INITIATORS MATTER

Imagine a training session on listening skills. The macrodesign might call for a demonstration skill practice, followed by a large-group debrief of the skill practice. If the designer has the trainer ask, "What were the things Jane did to demonstrate that she was listening to the employee?" the question will set the stage for a nicely focused generation of data—because it prompts the participants for concrete actions that demonstrate listening. In contrast, simply asking, "What did you think about Jane's approach?" could easily lead to a rambling discussion. It might also subject Jane to unnecessary criticism, whereas the first question would help protect her.

All in all, the first question is more efficient and more effective, because it directs participants along the most likely route toward the desired product: a list of concrete behaviors that demonstrate listening.

Many designers leave the initiators to the trainer, but we think it is better to make them—at least the critical ones—part of the design. If you want a discussion to lead to a particular product, then as the designer you are in a position to determine the most engaging and effective way to ask the question or give the directions. As you develop initiators, here's what to keep an eye out for:

_____ Make sure that questions or directions are focused enough to start participants thinking about the specific thing that you want them to think about.

_____ Questions may be closed-ended or open-ended to whatever degree is appropriate for your determined universe of acceptable responses.

_____ If your initiator will include directions for an activity, consider including the following elements:

- _____ What participants are to do.
- _____ How they are to do it.
- _____ By when (time frame).
- _____ Who has what responsibilities (if working in groups).
- _____ Why they are doing the activity.

Of course, you cannot control whether the trainer will use the exact questions and directions you develop—nor should you. Skilled trainers adjust to the needs of the participants. But by providing guidance on initiators, you give trainers concrete information that makes it easier for them to make their on-the-spot changes appropriately.

During this stage of microdesign, you will also make decisions about which directions and instructions need to be visual and which can simply be spoken. For example, if your design calls for a cost-benefit analysis of suggested recommendations in a case study, you might choose to have a flip chart prepared with a line down the middle—"costs" over one column and "benefits" over the other. This simple visual would help keep participants focused on the categories (products) for the discussion. You would not design the flip chart now, but it would be a good idea to make a note in your Materials file.

6. Develop Transitions. You already sketched out transitions at the macrodesign stage to ensure a logical flow from one segment of the training to another and between some of your learning activities. At this point, you may wish to develop some of them in greater detail. Your main focus now is transitions from one step in an activity to another. In order to develop the transitions, here is what you will do:

_____ Examine the process and product of each step.

_____ Think through or jot down a brief statement, question, or activity to link that step with what comes next.

_____ If the transitions feel forced, reexamine the sequence and the products of the steps. You will probably find that you can add or eliminate a product or perhaps modify the sequence slightly.

_____ Determine which of the transitions need to be written out or bulleted to help the trainer and the participants get what you intend. Do those now.

Many of the transitions will probably never be spoken in exactly the way you develop them; that would be too much detail for any trainer to follow. However, the process of developing them is a great double-check on your microdesign. It will tell you whether there is logic in the movement from one step to the next. It will also tell you whether the product of one step is useful for the next step or whether it is a tangent that can be eliminated.

Sometimes participants can become so involved in learning activities that they lose sight of the objectives. Strategically placed transitions can continually refocus participants while highlighting the relationships among activities and their bearing on the objectives.

7. Check Time Estimates One Final Time. Some of your initiators or transitions may add time to the design. For instance, you may plan to develop a flip chart for small-group directions and decide to allocate a few minutes for questions about the directions. Also, you may decide that in order to highlight some key transitions you want to make them interactive—for example, asking participants what they see as the relationship between the activity they have just completed and the one you are introducing. This type of interactive transition will require some time for discussion, so add it to your microdesign. To accomplish this step, here is what you will do:

_____ Add the total time for initiators, process, and transitions.

_____ Remember to include time for breaks and meals, if appropriate.

_____ Compare your results with the total time available.

You will probably want to round most of your time estimates to five-minute increments; in most cases, neither the designer nor the trainer wants to fine-tune more precisely than that.

8. Review Microdesign. Your microdesign is a detailed and concrete description of the training plan you have designed. You have designed activities that incorporate all the key content you selected and that meet all the objectives for the training. You have a clear sense of the time required for the training.

Before you create the materials for participants and trainers that will make this training real, review your microdesign by asking yourself some critical questions. Most of the questions are the same as the ones you asked at the end of the macrodesign phase. You ask them again now because you have more detailed information and can consider them more fully; in fact, the question about content is actually more detailed than the question you asked about content before. Here is what to ask:

_____ Does the design support my training goals and objectives?

  _____ Do the learning activities allow participants to perform —during the training—the behaviors described in the objectives?

  _____ Is there anything in the design that is not essential for meeting the objectives?

_____ Does the design now specifically include all of the key content—each of the key points I identified in the Key Topics stage?

_____ Is the design appropriate for the participants?

  _____ Is it responsive to the general characteristics of adult learners?

  _____ Does it engage a variety of learning styles?

  _____ Does it meet the needs, abilities, and expectations of my particular learners?

_____ Do the learning activities simulate, as much as possible, the world of application?

_____ Does the microdesign appear to fit with my logistical requirements?

_____ Does it fit with the learning context for the organization?

9. Complete Outline of the Training Design. By the end of the Microdesign phase, you have made nearly all the decisions about your training design. You have completed the Training Flow stage of the SIM. Now you will transfer the results of all this work into your outline. Here is what you will be doing:

_____ Look again at what your outline already contains: sequenced learning activities, an objective for each activity, and time estimates for activities or segments. Verify that all of those still seem right.

_____ Include these additional elements in the microdesign outline:

- _____ Products for activities where desired.
- _____ A process description for each step of each activity.
- _____ Key initiators and transitions—either as points or as sentences, whichever is required.
- _____ Fairly precise times for each activity and step.

_____ If you know that your trainers will need a detailed trainer's guide, be sure to include at least that level of detail in your outline.

10. Determine Whether to Check the Microdesign with Your Client. Because you have already reached agreement on the macrodesign, you probably will not need the client's input on the microdesign. However, there are two situations in which you might want client feedback now:

- If the client enjoys working at this level of detail, doing this step together may be important in building or maintaining your relationship.
- If the microdesign has led to significant changes in the design, you need the client's approval.

Check with the client if appropriate, and negotiate whatever adjustments are needed. If you do not need to check the microdesign with the client, you are ready to move ahead to the next stage of the SIM, Materials.

Question: I don't think this way. My mind just doesn't work at this level of detail. What should I do?

Answer: It's true that thinking at this level of detail is quite a stretch for some people. It is not a natural fit with their information-processing preferences. One helpful approach is to work with others who are more comfortable with this level of detail. They will balance your preferences, and you will most likely have preferences that will balance theirs. If the concreteness of this activity is stressful or unappealing to you, then do it more creatively. Try to play out the training event as a video or a storyboard in your head, and imagine at each step in the microdesign what you are seeing and hearing.

For some people, it helps to microdesign visually rather than verbally. You can use drawings, mind-maps, or whatever you are comfortable with (recall Geoff Graphic's design). The point of this process is to delve into the detail. You may simply have to experiment for a while until you find a way that is comfortable for you. We guarantee that the results will be more than worth the effort.

Question: Doesn't this take a lot of time?

Answer: Yes, it does. However, the process is time-efficient in several ways: first, you are engaging in this level of detail only when you have good reason to believe that your macrodesign is sound, so no time is wasted by investigating possibilities at this micro level. Second, working at this level of detail will make creating materials for the trainer and participants much easier; often, you will be able to lift materials almost directly from the microdesign. Third, consider your level of effort against the outcome. If you spend two hours refining the detail on fifteen minutes' worth of training, that effort produces fifteen minutes of powerful training—multiplied by the number of people who will benefit from it.

Question: How much detail is right?

Answer: This is a difficult question. You need enough detail to picture what is going on in the training. You also need enough detail to make refined time estimates and to make sure that the activities are aligned with your objectives. Beyond that, the correct level of detail depends on several factors:

- Are you going to be the trainer, or will others facilitate your design? Other people will usually need more detail than the designer would.
- What level of detail will you need for your trainer's guides, to meet the content skills and facilitation skills of your trainers? We will be talking more specifically about developing trainer materials in the next chapter. For now, if you have some idea of the level of detail you will be required to include in the trainer's materials, then your microdesign should provide at least that level.
- What is the particular learning activity? Some activities are so simple that they don't require much detail in the microdesign. For example, your design may include a written test that has straightforward directions; you won't need much detail to describe the activity. In contrast, some activities require several steps and combine individual, small-group, and large-group work, plus lecturettes. Such complex activities require considerable detail to clarify the products of each step and to establish how each product supports the succeeding steps.

Question: What about when I am really under pressure and don't have time to microdesign?

Answer: If you have done careful work on objectives, content, and macrodesign, you have good reason to believe that your work is fairly sound. If time is very short, we recommend that you review your macrodesign and identify those learning activities with which you have strong experience; you can be confident that they will work and that you will be able to provide sufficient guidance for managing them in the trainer's materials, so you need not spend much time on microdesigning them. Then identify those activities that are new to you or that feel like the risky or complex parts of your design; focus your limited time on microdesigning those activities.

Question: Isn't this like creating a script? It seems to lack flexibility.

Answer: We agree that scripts for training should be used only when absolutely necessary. Scripted learning events do not fit well with what we have said about adult learners and the experience and needs they bring to the training event.

However, we are talking about a fairly detailed map, not a script. Imagine that you are taking a two-thousand-mile trip by car. A macrodesigned map would have major routes, cities, and stops on your journey; a microdesigned map would have specific directions for changing routes, points of interest, and maybe some visual cues to show you where you were. When you were driving, the microdesigned map would not limit your ability to take a small side trip or consider an alternate route that looked more interesting. Similarly, the microdesigned training gives you enough detail so that you can make decisions with the assurance that you can go where you want to go and that you can get back on track if you lose your way.

Question: How can I write transitions? I don't know what participants will say or do in a learning activity, and I want the trainer's transition to refer to what's going on in the training.

Answer: You will be including written transitions in your trainer's guide only when there is a compelling reason to do so. Your goal is to help the trainer make the training event work as well as possible. Often, the link between two steps of an activity is so obvious that you can leave the transition entirely to the trainer. Sometimes you may want to emphasize a few specific elements; you can present them as bulleted "transition points" for the trainer to cover in whatever way feels comfortable. Occasionally, you will write out a complete transition to help the trainer understand what you see as the link between the steps—not because it needs to be said exactly that way.

You are right, of course, that the designer wants the trainer to be able to use participants' comments and specific examples of previous learning in his transitions. Planning the transitions during the microdesign phase does not prevent the trainer from doing that.

Question: Isn't it true that there will always be times when the trainer will have to provide the "right" answer? Although you have made the point that one of the goals of design is to reduce the probability that people's answers will require correction, isn't it going to happen quite of bit of the time?

Answer: Yes. The aim is to reduce the probability, not eliminate all possibility. The trainer's job is to decide which answers require correction and how to make corrections while maintaining the self-esteem of the participants who gave the answers. The designer's job is to help the trainer manage the training in ways that reduce the probability of having to correct a participant's responses. Sometimes the way to do that is simply to phrase a question carefully; sometimes the designer may choose to develop a quick additional activity to point the participants in the right direction. The process is not fail-safe, but it is integral to respecting adult learners' self-esteem.

Question: No matter how I try to adjust my microdesign, I still cannot fit everything into the time allocated by my client. What should I do?

Answer: There are several options. You can revisit your objectives and see whether you can eliminate or change the level of any. For example, you might choose to adjust down from "demonstrating" a skill to "describing" how to do that skill—with the awareness that making such an adjustment will affect the transfer of learning. Also, review your key topics to see if there is any content that is really not essential in order for participants to meet the objectives.

You may also want to consider reopening the time issue with the client. By this point in the design process, you have already worked with him to agree on essential objectives and content, so you are in a good position to demonstrate clearly that you cannot meet the requirements within the time allocated. Sometimes, engaging your client in a discussion about which objectives or content can be adjusted will lead him to the conclusion that everything is important and that more time is needed.

Unless your client is fairly sophisticated about adult learning and training methods, we recommend that you avoid discussing the training methods in detail—because the inclination of many clients is to sacrifice interactive training methods for the sake of time.

BEFORE YOU MOVE ON

Give yourself another big pat on the back! Microdesign is a complex and detailed phase, and it takes considerable time, effort, and skill. This is where much of the magic you created in the macrodesign will really take shape. Sometimes, just by altering a few words in an initiator, you change what could have been a rambling, pointless discussion into one that will be focused and engaging. It is your attention to detail as you are microdesigning that makes the difference.

When you return to your imaginary computer screen at the completion of the Microdesign phase of the Training Flow stage, here is what you will see: the Goals and Objectives file still has that umbrella, with clusters of objectives and skills beneath it. There should be no stray skills left at this stage; some may have been transferred to the existing clusters, and others have been dropped. The second file, which once held your content, is empty; everything in it has been moved into the Training Flow—Macrodesign folder, which contains your rough big-picture outline.

The new folder, your fourth, is Training Flow—Microdesign. In that folder, you will see a detailed outline for the training—including activities with their related content, times, and critical initiators and transitions. By this time, you have made a lot of decisions about the process and sequence for the training, so what is in this folder is now less fluid than anything you have seen before—although it still is not completely fixed. You may still make changes as you work through the final two stages of the SIM.

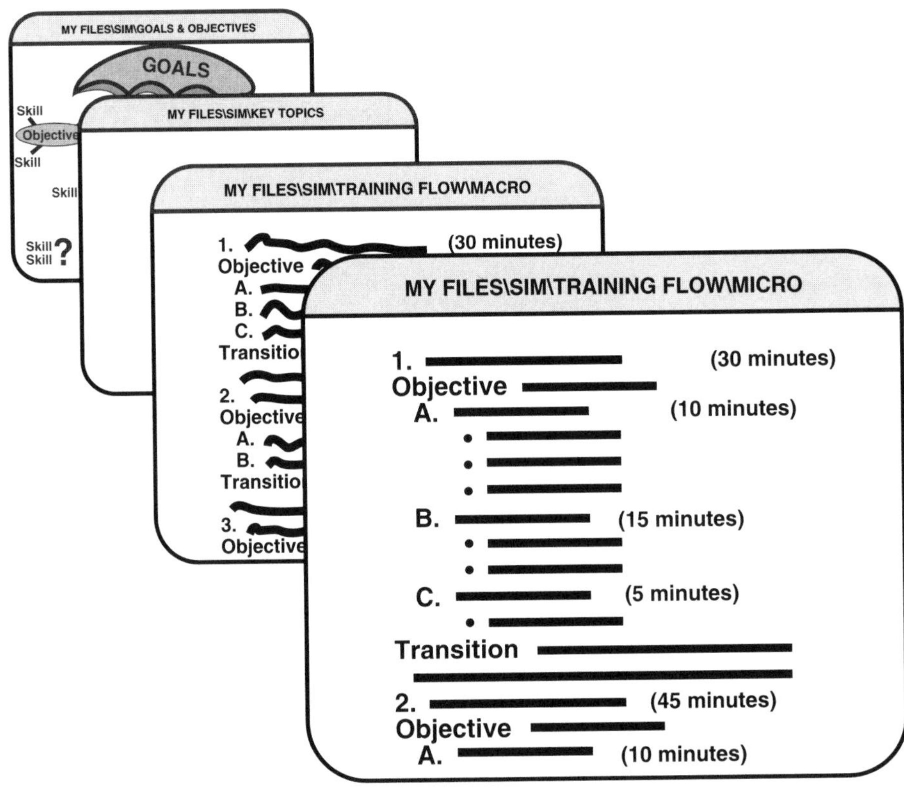

Looking Back

Here is the SIM process up to this point:

Goals and Objectives

1. Review design requirements.
2. Establish a goal statement.
3. Brainstorm the skills for reaching the desired behaviors.
4. Edit: determine essential versus nonessential skills for reaching the desired behaviors.
5. Consolidate: cluster related skills together.
6. Draft objectives.
7. Review and edit the proposed goals and objectives.
8. Review the goals and objectives with your client.

Key Topics

1. Research the subject.
2. Brainstorm possible key points.
3. Determine essential versus nonessential points.
4. Group key points into key topics.
5. Identify additional points for key topics.
6. Consider possible organizational structures.
7. Review and edit key topics.
8. Check work with your client.

Training Flow—Macrodesign

1. Research existing activities.
2. Brainstorm activities.
3. Select possible activities.
4. Estimate time for possible activities.
5. Outline training design.
6. Articulate objectives for segments.
7. Sketch out transitions.
8. Review your macrodesign.
9. Check macrodesign with your client.

Training Flow—Microdesign

1. Identify specific objective for each activity.
2. Define the universe of acceptable responses.
3. Develop the steps and the processes for each activity.
4. Refine time estimates.
5. Develop initiators.
6. Develop transitions.
7. Check time estimates one final time.
8. Review microdesign.
9. Complete outline of the training design.
10. Determine whether to check the microdesign with your client.

Running Example: Training Flow—Microdesign

Building on the macrodesign she created, Simone now moves through another series of steps to create the microdesign.

NOTE TO READER

For the training on performance appraisals at Jexon, the steps of the Running Example illustrate the designer's work with Segment 4, Part C, of the macrodesign: the game on translating gut language.

Existing Macrodesign for Segment 4

4. Challenge #1: Translating What's in the Gut to Behavioral Language. (45 min.)

   Objective. Participants will demonstrate their ability to identify vague language and translate it into behavioral language.

   A. Demonstration with large group.
      (1) Gut language: vague/judgmental.
      (2) Behavioral language: descriptive/objective.

   B. Working with real appraisals: identify gut language.
      (1) Individuals read, identify gut language.
      (2) Large-group sharing: vote on a few examples.

Transition. Great! You've found language that needs to be fixed. Now let's have a little fun fixing it.

   C. Game: translating gut language.
      (1) Small groups fix gut language from above activity.
      (2) Large group compares and refines results.

Transition Points

- *Have come up with ways to fix appraisal language.*
- *Now practice on a real-life situation, get feedback.*

   D. Application with real employee.
      (1) Individual work: gut to behavioral.
      (2) Triad feedback.

Transition. I hope you feel that you have some practical ways to translate gut feelings into descriptive, objective, behavioral language. We saw some great examples of how to do it during the last few minutes, and now I'd like us to move on to the second challenge: summarizing a year's performance on the appraisal [refer to objective]. *It is, as we all know, no small challenge! Let's begin by discussing why it is important to do.*

NOTE TO READER

Although the steps of the Running Example illustrate the detailed microdesign only for Segment 4, Part C, you will find the complete microdesign on pages 231–239.

1. Identify Specific Objective for Each Activity

The segment objective is "Participants will demonstrate their ability to identify vague language and translate it into behavioral language." The earlier parts of this segment have enabled participants to identify the language. For the game itself, here is what Simone comes up with:

> *Objective.* Participants will translate gut language into behavioral language.

Because this objective is one of the overall training objectives, the activity will allow participants and the trainer to measure success.

2. Define the Universe of Acceptable Responses

In considering the acceptable responses, here is what Simone decides for the game activity:

> *Acceptable Responses.* Large universe; there are many correct ways to word the translations, but there are some unacceptable answers—such as translations that are not behavioral.

Simone anticipates that the preceding activity with the large group will minimize the possibility that the trainer will have to correct participants' responses in the game. In addition, she will have the trainer circulate to coach participants further during the game.

3. Develop the Steps and the Processes for Each Activity

Within this activity, Simone has already determined in the macrodesign that there are two main steps: the game itself and the large-group processing that follows it. Now she determines product, means, mode, and process for each of those steps.

Before the game, participants have already identified and practiced fixing gut language, and then the group has agreed on several examples of vague or judgmental language from sample appraisals; those agreed-on examples, shown on an overhead transparency, provide the material for the game.

C. Game. (20 min.)

(1) Small-group game: fix as many as possible in limited time. (5 min.)

Product: Translations into descriptive/behavioral language.

Means: Small groups.

Mode: Applying.

Process:

- Put participants into triads (some random method—count off by 3s, birthdays, colors, and so forth).
- Overhead transparency remains visible to highlight vague/judgmental statements.
- Give directions for game; solicit questions about directions.
- Trainer circulates and helps correct statements when appropriate.
- Remind when there are 2 minutes and 1 minute remaining.

(2) Large group compares and refines results (prizes for each group in some category). (15 min.)

Product: Correct and approved translations of vague/judgmental language into behavioral language.

Means: Large group.

Mode: Applying.

Process:

- Review point system for game.
- For each group, review each translated statement.
- Determine whether behavioral; if not, lead a brief discussion on what it would take to make it behavioral.
- Assign points on groups' flip charts.
- Award prizes (different categories—most points, most creative, most humorous—a prize to each group).

4. Refine Time Estimates

Now that Simone has worked through each of the steps in this activity, she is able to be more specific about her estimates of how much time to allow. The original estimate was twenty minutes, but here is what she determines now:

C. Game. (25 min.)

(1) Small-group game: fix as many as possible in limited time. (10 min.)

a. Directions and group movement. (5 min.)

b. Timed work in small groups. (5 min.)

(2) Large group compares and refines results (prizes for each group in some category). (15 min.)

Simone decides on some extra time to allow for the trainer to give directions and for participants to move into their groups; she estimates three minutes and rounds it to five minutes. For the large-group processing, the fifteen-minute limit will require the trainer to keep the groups focused, but Simone decides that keeping this portion fast-paced will add to the excitement of the game and will not detract from the usefulness of the activity.

5. Develop Initiators

The critical initiator will be the directions for the game. They will be most useful as bullet points, so that is how Simone develops them:

Initiator Points

- 5 minutes to fix as many of the statements as possible.
- "Fixing" means translating into descriptive and behavioral language, as we did earlier.
- Record translations on flip chart; there's one for each team.
- If you finish all the statements, go back and develop additional translations.
- Team receives 1 point for each correct translation.
- Prize for winning team or teams.

As Simone develops this initiator, she puts a note into her Materials file about needing prizes for this activity.

6. Develop Transitions

Moving into the game is fairly simple, so Simone decides she does not need to include a transition there, even though she had sketched it out in her macrodesign. Moving into the next activity, however, seems a bit more complex, so Simone retains the points for that transition.

Transition Points After Game

- *Have come up with ways to fix appraisal language.*
- *Now practice on real-life situation, receive feedback.*

7. Check Time Estimates One Final Time

After Simone has completed Steps 1 through 6 for all of the activities, she will look at times again to make sure that she has allowed for each step of the activity (including initiators and transitions)—as well as enough time for any necessary movement and time for required breaks. Simone must make sure that the microdesign will fit the half-day that is allotted for this training.

8. Review Microdesign

After Simone has completed Steps 1 through 7, her microdesign is ready for review. She asks herself the following critical questions:

- *Does the design support my training goals and objectives?* It does. There are a variety of activities that will help participants use their existing coaching skills to prepare better written appraisals. In the segment on using the appraisal to look forward, the activity has been reworked (adding some prereading and a discussion that had not been included in the macrodesign) to better support the objectives.
    - *Do the learning activities allow participants to perform—during the training—the behaviors described in the objectives?* Yes. Specifically, during the WIIFM exercise, participants will articulate how they personally will benefit. They will also practice the essential skill of translating gut responses into behavioral language (in the activity illustrated above); then they will apply that skill to the bigger picture in terms of describing the impacts of their employees' performance, clarifying performance expectations, and identifying strategies for performance improvement. Finally, participants will have the chance to clarify and write down the steps in the process that they will use individually for summarizing information in the yearly appraisal.
    - *Is there anything in the design that is not essential for meeting the objectives?* No. One of the questionable content points, "ways to balance the appraisal (between positive and corrective feedback)," has been eliminated as not essential.
- *Does the design now specifically include all of the key content—each of the key points I identified in the Key Topics stage?* It's all here, double-checked against the notes from the Key Topics stage.
- *Is the design appropriate for the participants?* It seems to be. Simone has taken special care to make sure.
    - *Is it responsive to the general characteristics of adult learners?* Yes. There is time at several points for individual judgment and reflection, and the design builds on participants' existing knowledge and experience.

- *Does it engage a variety of learning styles?* Yes. There is a balance of individual work with group work, quiet reflection with discussion, and "why" with "how" content.
- *Does it meet the needs, abilities, and expectations of my particular learners?* Yes indeed. The language throughout is appropriate to the Jexon culture, and the design is based closely on the findings of the needs assessment.

- *Do the learning activities simulate, as much as possible, the world of application?* Yes. Participants will be working with real-life materials—the sample appraisals and information about their own staff members.
- *Does the design appear to fit with my logistical requirements?* It's looking good. As usual, having more time would be great—but what has been designed will fit nicely in the time allowed.
- *Does it fit with the learning context for the organization?* Quite well, as supported by a quick review of the three factors of people, structures, and culture (Chapter Five).

9. Complete Outline of the Training Design

Having completed her review of the microdesign, Simone cleans up her work and puts it into outline form. She knows that she need not specify means, mode, or universe of acceptable responses in the outline; those decisions have shaped the work and are now embedded in it. She does include objectives, products, processes, and key points, plus guidance for the trainer on transitions and initiators. Simone has selected an outline format that will position her well to develop the trainer's guide, which she will be working on in the next stage of the SIM.

10. Determine Whether to Check the Microdesign with Your Client

Because Simone has a sound relationship with the key client on the senior management team, and because there are no significant changes since the macrodesign, she probably does not need to check the microdesign with the client. Just to be sure, Simone makes a quick call to find out whether she particularly wants to see it. The client says no, and so Simone is ready to move ahead.

Complete Microdesign for Jexon Training

Revised Time.

Revised Method. Using flip chart will save time.

1. Introductions and Challenges. (15 min.)

   Objective. Participants will identify key problems with written appraisals at Jexon.

   As they enter room, participants jot on flip chart their guess at one key problem.

   A. Trainer introduction and welcome. (1 min.)

   B. Participant introductions. (8 min.)

   - Name.
   - Department.
   - Key problem guess (refer to flip chart).

Transition Points

- *Acknowledge common themes.*
- *Will develop concrete sense of first-class appraisal.*
- *Jexon always striving to be "first-class."*

   C. Solicit comments from large group, comparing participant list with needs assessment data. (6 min.)

2. Workshop Focus. (15 min.)

   Objective. Participants will identify characteristics of effective appraisals.

   A. First-class appraisals. (8 min.)

   (1) Dyads generate 2 or 3 characteristics. (2 min.)

   (2) Each dyad reports 1 characteristic to create list; repeat until all suggestions are recorded. (6 min.)

Transition. The characteristics of an effective appraisal that you have listed are exactly where Jexon wants to go. Let's take a moment to review what you already do well and the three challenges to creating effective appraisals that are the focus of this workshop.

   B. Lecturette: Objectives and Agenda. (7 min.)

   (1) Display list of what participants already do well (from needs assessment).

(2) Explain objectives, including three key challenge areas to be addressed during workshop.

- Translating gut to behavioral.
- Summarizing a year's performance.
- Looking forward and improving performance.

(3) Briefly review agenda.

Transition Points

- *Have reached agreement on well-written appraisals.*
- *Have revisited challenges raised in needs assessment.*
- *Objectives of workshop relate to those challenges.*
- *Now, what's in it for you to meet the challenges and write first-class appraisals?*

Revised Time.

3. WIIFM. (10 min.)

Objective. Participants will identify 2 or 3 personal benefits of striving to write effective appraisals.

Added Method. Demonstration will help.

A. Large-group demonstration. (2 min.)

(1) Trainer gives personal example of benefit.

Initiator. For me, one of the personal benefits of writing first-class appraisals is [insert appropriate example]. *Let's come up with 2 or 3 examples of personal benefits as a large group, and then I'll give you time to think on your own.*

(2) Trainer solicits examples of personal benefits.

(3) Trainer records sample benefits; will become wall chart for future reference.

Transition Points

- *Some benefits may feel more or less meaningful to individuals.*
- *Focus on benefits that matter to you personally.*

B. Individual: identify personal benefits. (3 min.)

Initiator. I'd like you to think about 2 or 3 personal benefits. In just a few minutes, you'll have the opportunity to share them with a few colleagues and listen to their benefits. Of course, you need only share the ones you wish to. Jot yours down on the worksheet.

- Individuals record personal benefits on worksheet.

C. Small group: share personal benefits. (5 min.)

- Group in triads.
- 1 minute per person.
- Participants record as they wish.

Transition Points

- *Let's look at the first challenge on list* [refer to objectives].
- *Will come up with practical techniques to manage this challenge.*

Revised Time.

4. Challenge #1: Translating What's in the Gut to Behavioral Language. (60 min.)

Objective. Participants will demonstrate their ability to identify vague language and translate it into behavioral language.

A. Demonstration with large group: identifying and translating. (10 min.)

(1) Gut language. (5 min.)

- Show sample gut language.
- Ask what makes it gut language.
- Record on flip chart.

Transition. Let's try to fix it by translating it into more behavioral language. The two key characteristics of behavioral language are that it is objective and descriptive.

(2) Behavioral language. (5 min.)

- Refer back to sample gut language.
- Solicit help fixing it.
- Record suggestions on flip chart.
- In suggestions, ask what words/phrases are behavioral.
- Emphasize: behavioral language is descriptive/objective.

B. Working with real appraisals: identify gut language. (15 min.)

(1) Individuals read section of sample appraisal, underline vague or judgmental (gut) language. (7 min.)

Transition. Let's hear what you found in your individual work. This will be an area in which we will have different opinions on what is and isn't a gut feeling. The key here is to become more sensitive to such language, so we will highlight all the sections that you considered gut language, and then work on ones the majority of you agree are too subjective.

(2) Large-group sharing. (8 min.)

- Trainer solicits examples of gut language from samples.
- Underline on overhead transparency.
- When all are taken, ask for show of hands on each one: Do people think it is gut language?
- Circle where majority agrees (5 items or more, preferably).

Transition. Great! You've found language that needs to be fixed. Now let's have a little fun fixing it.

C. Game: translating gut language. (25 min.)

(1) Small-group game: fix gut language from above activities—as many as possible in limited time. (10 min.)

a. Setup. (5 min.)

- Put participants into triads (some random method—count off by 3s, birthdays, colors, and so forth).
- Overhead transparency remains visible to highlight vague/judgmental statements.

Initiator Points

- *5 minutes to fix as many of the statements as possible.*
- *"Fixing" means translating into descriptive and behavioral language, as we did earlier.*
- *Record translations on flip chart; there's one for each team.*
- *If you finish all the statements, go back and develop additional translations.*
- *Team receives 1 point for each correct translation.*
- *Prize for winning team or teams.*
- *Solicit questions about directions.*

b. Small-group game. (5 min.)

- Trainer circulates and helps correct statements as appropriate.
- Remind when there are 2 minutes and 1 minute remaining.

(2) Large group compares and refines results (prizes for each group in some category). (15 min.)

- Review point system for game.
- For each group, review each translated statement.
- Determine whether behavioral; if not, lead a brief discussion on what it would take to make it behavioral.
- Assign points on groups' flip charts.
- Award prizes (different categories—most points, most creative, most humorous—a prize to each group).

Transition Points

- *Have come up with ways to fix appraisal language.*
- *Now practice on real-life situation, receive feedback.*

D. Application with real employee. (10 min.)

Initiator. Think of a gut feeling you have about the performance of one of your employees—either positive performance or problem performance. We'll be working with that for the next 10 minutes. We need to be sensitive to confidentiality here, and in a little while you'll be sharing some of this information with colleagues. So choose a situation that other people in the room today won't be familiar with, and please don't use the employee's name. I'll be available if you would like any help.

- Review instructions.
  - 5 minutes to work.
  - Choose employee.
  - Write out a gut feeling.
  - Translate into behavioral language that you could write on an appraisal.
  - If finished before time, try a second one.

(1) Participants work alone. (5 min.)

(2) Dyad consulting: share individual work; obtain feedback. (5 min.)

Revised Method. Had planned to use triads, but dyads will be quicker.

Initiator. Each person will have 2 minutes at center stage in your pair. Remember confidentiality, and please don't use any names.

- Arrange into dyads.

- Review directions.
  - 2 minutes per person.
  - Share gut feeling, behaviors, and translation.
  - Peer feedback: what makes translation descriptive/behavioral; suggestions.

Transition. I hope you feel that you have some practical ways to translate gut feelings into descriptive, objective, behavioral language. We saw some great examples of how to do it during the last few minutes, and now I'd like us to move on to the second challenge: summarizing a year's performance on the appraisal [refer to objective]. *It is, as we all know, no small challenge! Let's begin by discussing why it is important to do.*

Revised Time.

5. Challenge #2: Summarizing Year's Performance. (35 min.)

   Objective. Participants will individually describe the process they will use to ensure that they are summarizing performance patterns and trends as well as including critical performance events that are not part of the performance trends.

   A. Why. (10 min.)

      Initiator. In our list of challenges, we listed this as a major one. Before we talk about how to do it, let's focus on why it's important to do.

      (1) Large-group discussion: why it's important. (5 min.)
      - Solicit and record responses from large group.
      - Add legal reasons if not provided by participants.

Transition. Summarizing is even more challenging than simply reducing performance data to summary statements. It involves some very strategic management decisions about what performance data need to be included in the written appraisal.

      (2) Lecturette: performance trends. (5 min.)
      - Why we want to focus on trends.
      - Leaving out unimportant details.
      - Determining critical events.

Transition. So our task is to decide what to include, identify and describe trends when we can, and write this all in a summary format. Rather than my providing the "how to do this," I'd like to start with the experience in this group.

Revised Method. Had planned to distribute tips for summarizing. More effective and engaging to let participants offer ideas.

B. How. (25 min.)

(1) Individuals list key ideas they have for summarizing a year's worth of performance data. (7 min.)

Initiator. On page XX of your workbook, you will find a place to jot down the key steps you already take or want to take in order to achieve what we have just discussed: a yearly performance summary that clarifies performance trends and critical performance events [display flip chart]. *Identify those steps, and then we'll share what you've come up with.*

- Review worksheet. (1 min.)
- Individual work. (6 min.)
- Trainer circulates to assist and refine responses before they are shared with large group.

Revised Method. Deleted small-group reporting.

(2) Large group creates composite list. (10 min.)

- Record key steps as participants mention.
- Make necessary additions.

Transition. Okay, we have lots of experience in this room and many ways to go about summarizing performance. I'd like you to leave with a way that will work well for you and that you can implement on your upcoming appraisals, so I will give you some time to decide on and write down the steps you want to take to summarize performance.

Revised Method. To save time, deleted feedback on process. Will address process in coaching tool instead.

(3) Individuals write the steps in their own process. (8 min.)

Transition Points

- *Have tools to meet two challenges.*
- *Now move to the last challenge* [refer to objectives].

Revised Time.

6. Challenge #3: Using the Appraisal to Look Forward and for Performance Improvement. (40 min.)

Objective. Participants will demonstrate ability to use behavioral language in describing current performance, performance expectations, and recommendations for performance improvement.

New Step. Added large-group discussion, with prereading. Macrodesign did not meet objectives: not enough attention to describing expectations and suggestions. Also changed "why and when" to "why and how."

A. Large-group discussion: why and how to use appraisal for performance improvement—reactions to prereading. (10 min.)

(1) Review and discuss each question from prereading.

(2) Discuss suggested improvements for sample statement given in prereading.

Transition. It's time to try it out by putting together the tools we have developed today. In this exercise, you will have the opportunity to change vague descriptions of performance into objective behavioral descriptions, describe the desired performance in behavioral terms, and give a brief strategy for development. You will be working in small groups.

Revised Method. Had seen as a game; really an application exercise. Simplified: just one vague statement, but still three tasks.

B. How. (30 min.)

(1) Small-group application exercise. (15 min.)

a. Setup. (5 min.)

- Arrange participants into new teams, groups of 4 or 5.

Initiator. This will be your chance to put together the work of the entire session, using samples from real appraisals. Each team will receive a vague statement of a performance problem from an appraisal, along with some brief background information. You have 10 minutes to complete three tasks [refer to flip chart].

- *Translate the vague, gut-feeling statement of present performance into one that is descriptive and behavioral.*
- *Write a statement of expectations, also in behavioral terms, for desired performance. You may want to refer to the samples on page XX.*
- *Write one or two suggestions for performance improvement. You may want to refer to the samples on page XX.*

b. Small-group work. (10 min.)

- Trainer checks in and consults as necessary.
- Remind groups 2 or 3 times of remaining time.

Transition Points

- *Final reporting out: a chance to see opportunity for creativity and individuality in writing appraisals.*
- *Each group started with same performance appraisal statement.*
- *Note to yourself what you like about each presentation.*
- *This will help you find a style that works well for you.*

(2) Group Reports. (15 min.)

- First group presents statements.
- Quick debrief.
- Ask rest of group, "What's one thing you like about the way they approached this?"
- Solicit 2 or 3 responses, depending on time.
- Encourage participants to jot down ideas they like.
- Repeat process for remaining groups.

Revised Transition and Method. Focus on connection between WIIFMs and objectives.

Transition. We've covered a lot, and our time together is just about over. Before we go, let's revisit the objectives and at the same time take a look at the benefits that you identified at the beginning of the session. This time, I'll ask you to refocus your thinking about benefits—now we're going to talk about the benefits to Jexon and your employees.

7. Summary Debrief: Return to WIIFM. (15 min.)

   Initiator. To the extent that we are successful meeting the three challenges that are stated in today's objectives [refer to wall chart], *what is one thing that is in it for Jexon or for employees?*

   A. Provide time for individual reflection.

   B. Large group shares responses.

   C. What's in it for Jexon?

   D. What's in it for employees?

   E. Thank participants.

10 The SIM

Materials

You have created a training flow—a solid plan for engaging participants in the learning, focusing their energies efficiently on meeting the agreed-on learning objectives, and effectively enabling them to develop the skills that will help them be more successful. During the Materials stage of the SIM, you will focus on designing or selecting appropriate materials to make the plan come to life as a learning event: materials for the trainer (trainer's guide and resources), the participants (handouts, job aids, workbooks, computer-assisted learning activities), and the learning environment (audio and visual aids).

By this time in the design process, you have probably recorded several ideas in your Materials file. Now is the time to decide whether they are really a good fit for your design and, if so, to make them happen. You will again be applying the analytical and creative skills you have been using throughout the design process. The Materials stage of the SIM focuses especially on the auditory and visual senses, as you are creating materials that not only must contain essential information but also must engage the senses of the learner.

PRODUCTS OF THE MATERIALS STAGE

When you have completed this stage of the SIM, you will have a big bundle of new products:

- *Materials:* Most of the tangible, physical things needed for the learning event, grouped into three categories:
    - *Participant Materials:* Everything that learners need in order to prepare for the learning event, to participate fully in the event, and to use as resources after the event. Essentially, participant materials include whatever the participants will hold in their hands.

- *Trainer's Materials:* Also called facilitator's materials or leader's materials, the trainer's materials include all the resources that you create or acquire to help the trainer prepare for and facilitate the training event.
- *Learning Aids:* Learning aids, often called audiovisual aids, are all the resources needed to create a positive learning environment and accompany learning activities.

For the training session on listening skills for medical professionals, one of the participant materials might be a feedback form for participants to use in the final skill practice.

The form that the designer prepares for this skill practice has two purposes: to focus the attention and note taking of the observers and to provide the agenda for the discussion after the skill practice. It might look like this:

Interviewer's Name ______________________ Date ____________
Observer's Name ______________________

Directions. In both categories below, jot down specific questions the interviewer asks.

Gathering Information | Checking Your Understanding

One suggestion for development:

I was most impressed when you . . .

The designer may be responsible only for drafting the materials and turning them over to someone else for production; may handle the materials all the way from concept to finished product; or may do some and collaborate on others. In any case, the designer ensures that all participant materials, trainer's materials, and learning aids will meet the requirements for this particular training event.

MATERIALS: WHY? AND WHY NOW?

The time is right. You have articulated clearly why you are doing this training and what participants will be able to do by the end of it. You know exactly what content they must comprehend in order to meet the training objectives. You have built a detailed training flow that describes precisely what learning activities participants will engage in to reach the objectives. Now it is time to create all the tools that the participants and the trainer need to make this

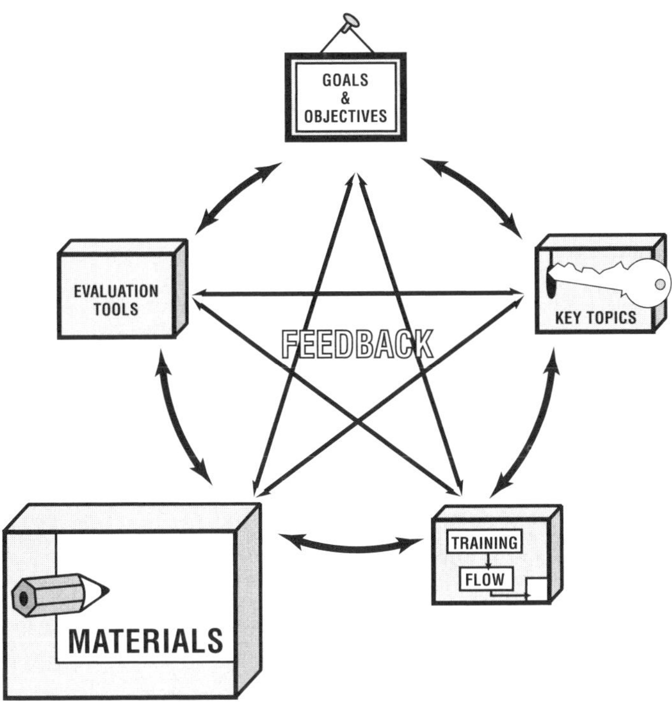

learning event happen—preparation tools, materials for use during the training, and job aids or resources to help participants transfer the learning.

Even though you may already have had some great ideas for materials, we have encouraged you to wait until now to design them. Why? To save you time and keep you from falling so in love with an idea that you would be reluctant to let go of it even if it were not the best idea. Until you have every possible confidence that your detailed training plan is thoroughly effective, efficient, and engaging, creating any training materials is a waste of time. It would be like buying furniture for a new home before you had selected the home and knew the dimensions of the rooms. You would choose pieces that you loved. With luck, some of them would fit well; others, though appealing in and of themselves, would not be right for the space. Similarly, if you had created training materials before this stage of the design process, they might be fine materials but not a very good fit for your design.

The iterative nature of the SIM is important to keep in mind during this stage of the design process. At this stage, you are creating and selecting materials that people will hold in their hands and absorb through their senses, so you may find yourself reevaluating earlier stages of the design. For example, as you prepare a worksheet for debriefing a learning activity, you may realize suddenly that the objective for the activity is not clearly worded. Or you may realize as you create supporting materials for a learning activity that there is additional essential content to be mastered before participants can successfully perform the learning activity. That iterative quality is the nature of design.

CONSIDERATIONS FOR MATERIALS

In the how-to section of this chapter, we describe the decisions you will make about your training materials to ensure that they support and enhance your design. However, producing materials is complex and demanding and may require specialized skills, such as graphics and layout, camera skills, or multimedia authoring. All of those specific skills are very important, and their particulars are beyond the scope of this book. Our intention is to focus on the key considerations that will help you make your training materials match all the good work you have already put into the training design in the earlier stages of the SIM—no matter what form your training materials may take.

TRAINER'S MATERIALS

According to the needs of the trainers and of the design, trainer's materials may include items such as these:

- Trainer's guide
- Supplemental resources (articles, videos, computer disks, and so on)
- Bibliographies

Trainer's Materials

The question always is "How much detail should the trainer's materials contain?" There is no hard-and-fast answer. Some trainers—and some training designs—require more detail, some less. Designing materials is a big responsibility. If your trainer's materials do not include enough detail, the trainers may just "wing it" on content or on process more than you or the organization would like. But if you go to the other extreme by including massive amounts of detail, the trainer's guide may be perceived as overwhelming or restrictive—and may well be ignored. Either way, the materials will not support the trainer in re-creating your intended design.

Still, even without hard-and-fast answers, you can find guidance in the needs assessment and elsewhere. For example, you already have information on the trainers; when you were converting your needs assessment data to design requirements, you considered the expertise of the trainers. There are two critical issues:

- What is their content expertise?
- What is their expertise with processing or facilitating the kinds of learning activities you have selected?

Even beyond the expertise of the trainers, there may be organizational reasons for including additional information in the trainer's materials. For example, portions of content may need to be delivered verbatim each time the training is offered, for legal reasons. If so, that content must be included—or at least referred to—in the trainer's materials.

In general, designers who create materials for a number of trainers encounter a wide range of content and process expertise. We find that it helps to consider a spectrum of detail that we might include in the trainer's materials and then to establish some standards to guide the development of materials.

Minimum Detail. The minimum level of detail for trainer's materials is a macrodesign including the following for each learning activity:

- Objectives for the activity
- Key topics and, as needed, supporting key points
- Overall description of the learning activity (for example, "large-group discussion: risks and benefits of the three ways of doing X")
- References to required participant materials and learning aids
- Estimated times for activities

This level of detail is appropriate for seasoned trainers who have high levels of expertise in content and facilitation. If you are delivering the training yourself, you will probably use this level of detail in your own trainer's guide, especially if you are a content expert; you need only a reminder of the key components of each activity.

Maximum Detail. The maximum level of detail would be a scripted trainer's guide that tells the trainer exactly what to say and do. Such guides are often used in situations in which large numbers of instructors with little or varying degrees of experience will be presenting the training and in which it is essential that training events be consistent in content and execution. Even so, there are grave risks in scripting trainer's materials. One is that trainers may abandon the guide for their own plans, which seem simpler to them. Another is that trainers may just read the script rather than facilitate the training. All the same, occasionally a designer or an organization may judge these risks preferable to inaccurate information or poorly facilitated training methods.

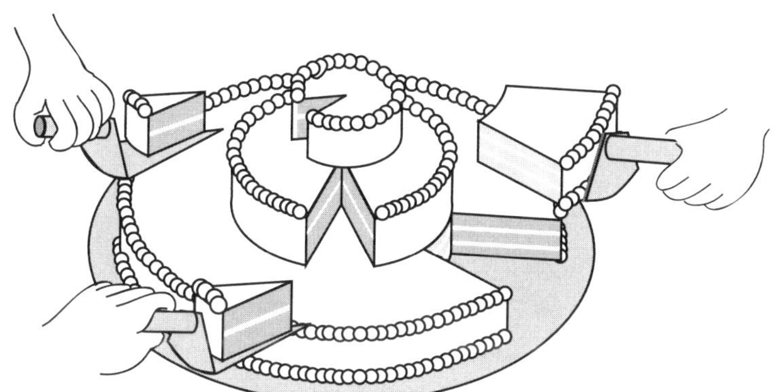

A Middle Range and Some Options. Between these two extremes lie innumerable possibilities. For example, training materials may include a lot of detail on how to facilitate each activity, while listing only the key topics for content. Such a trainer's guide is appropriate for subject-matter experts who are not professional facilitators.

When you are designing trainer's materials for a varied group of trainers, consider using layers of detail so that each trainer can access whatever she needs as she prepares for and facilitates the training. For example, the first layer might be very much like a macrodesign: an outline of sequenced learning activities with related key content and times. A second layer might provide more detailed information (content, process, or both), close to the microdesign level; it would be of use to trainers who need guidance on content or process. The third layer would go beyond the second; it might even include suggested scripts for some of the key learning activities and additional resources on content and process.

By designing a layered guide, you meet the needs of a variety of expertise levels among your trainers; you also provide a resource that an individual trainer might use in one way when doing initial preparation for the training and in quite a different way the third or fourth time she is facilitating the training.

PARTICIPANT MATERIALS

Depending on the specific learning event, participant materials might include such items as

- Prework assignments
- Reading materials: a book, an article, a computer disk
- A workbook
- Worksheets for skill practices or role plays
- Feedback forms for skill practices or role plays
- Case studies
- Directions for activities
- Forms for guided note taking
- Materials for games or other activities
- Additional worksheets or handouts
- Job aids
- Bibliographies

Participant Materials

In planning and creating participant materials, the designer will again be guided by the design requirements as well as the earlier steps of the SIM. Here are some of the key questions:

- *What do you know about the culture of the organization, or about any particular patterns of learning-style preferences among the participants?* For example, a group of technical workers might be more comfortable with specific, detailed written material than would a group of marketing people who spend most of their workday creating new product campaigns.

- *What are the reading and language competencies of the participants?* For example, materials prepared for a group of clergy members would probably need to be at a different reading level from those prepared for assembly-line workers.
- *Are there specific layout or formatting standards that will best enhance the learning process?* For example, older learners may need a larger print size, or a particular group of participants may need materials in two languages.
- *What amount of written material seems to fit with the subject matter and the objectives?* For example, it is probably reasonable to plan on a greater volume of printed materials for a workshop on writing skills than for one on public speaking.
- *What is the most efficient way to present participant materials?* For example, the designer or the organization may wish to minimize the number of separate handouts and prefer to include materials in a single workbook.
- *What are the organizational expectations about the format of the training materials?* For example, one organization might request that prework and job aids be provided in an electronic format; another might require a particularly high level of graphic sophistication.

These criteria will be useful to guide your work as well as to communicate to anyone who assists you in the design of participant materials.

LEARNING AIDS

To create the appropriate learning environment, here are some of the kinds of materials that might be needed:

- Wall charts
- Flip charts
- Overhead transparencies
- 35mm slides
- Computer-displayed images
- Three-dimensional models
- Visual/auditory cues (pictures, flowers, sounds)
- Videos/films
- Audiotapes
- Music

Learning Aids

This category of training materials used to be called audiovisual aids, but now it includes a variety of electronic learning aids far beyond traditional notions of audiovisual materials. Developing or selecting learning aids demands not only creativity but decision making as well, because there are so many possibilities. As a designer, you are always aiming to support the learning process, never to detract from it. Surely you have attended training events in which the visual aids were entertaining but overshadowed the learning objectives, and you do not want that to be the case for your event.

As you make decisions about learning aids, keep in mind their key functions:

- To focus learners on objectives
- To reinforce key points
- To provide illustrations or directions
- To provide a common experience for reflection or analysis
- To stimulate thinking
- To provide a visual or auditory reference point or model
- To meet the needs of various learning styles
- To simulate the real world of application as closely as possible

It is also important to consider that learning aids assist the trainer as well as the participant. For example, effective visual aids can remind the trainer of what is to be emphasized, serve as reference points, and provide visual cues about the training flow.

THE DESIGNER AND THE CATERER

Remember our caterer? By the time she has completed this stage of her work, she has all the pots, pans, and cooking utensils necessary to prepare the meal (trainer's materials). She also has all the materials guests will need to eat the meal, such as dinnerware, flatware, crystal, and table linens (participant materials). In addition, she has all the decorations and serving materials she will need—such as platters, soup tureens, pitchers, and baskets (learning aids). In short, she has all the materials needed to translate her menu into a wonderful meal that will carry out the theme she and her client agreed on. You, as a training designer, have done the same by creating a plan and materials to nourish learners in ways that empower them to grow and succeed in their work.

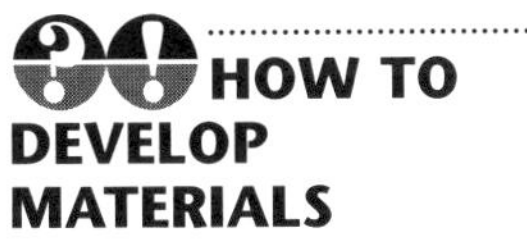

HOW TO DEVELOP MATERIALS

Rather than focusing on the technical aspects of producing materials, the how-to steps will focus on helping you make decisions about creating materials that will render your design more effective, efficient, and engaging.

Effective materials for supporting a training design are those that help participants reach the desired objectives. For example, if an objective is "to describe X," then you will need to produce a worksheet or activity that allows participants to do that—and not just take notes on a lecture.

Materials that are *efficient* help ensure that participants will reach the objectives without undue expenditures of energy. For example, a wall chart is often used to maintain the focus on the objectives. In addition, efficient materials do not overwhelm the participants with unreasonable amounts of optional reading, especially right in the middle of a workbook.

Engaging materials help draw the participants into the learning experience. Materials need to be targeted carefully in their language level, use of graphics, and appeal to a variety of learning styles.

THE SEVEN STEPS IN DEVELOPING TRAINING MATERIALS

1. Establish requirements for materials.
2. Identify what training materials are required and what materials are optional.
3. Draft required materials.
4. Review drafts of required materials.
5. Select, draft, and review optional materials.
6. Have others review the materials.
7. Finalize the materials.

1. Establish Requirements for Materials. For each of the three areas in which you will develop materials, begin by establishing requirements. They will guide your design work, direct the work of others who may assist in developing materials (such as subject-matter experts, a subcontractor, or a graphics team), and serve as criteria against which to evaluate the materials after they have been drafted. Here is how to establish requirements for training materials:

_____ Interview your client(s) to identify their requirements and preferences. You may wish to show your clients a variety of materials to clarify the discussion.

_____ Review your needs assessment data to identify pertinent information about participants, such as reading and language abilities.

_____ Examine a variety of formats for materials to help you see what will work and what will not in your situation.

_____ Review existing training materials in the organization to identify any standard formatting requirements.

When you have completed this step, you will have three lists of requirements—one for each category of training materials.

SAMPLE: REQUIREMENTS FOR PARTICIPANT MATERIALS

Sarel, an external consultant who is designing a workshop on grassroots organizing for a large nonprofit association, works with her client and reviews her needs assessment data to establish the following requirements for participant materials:

- Number all pages for easy reference.
- Space for taking notes on each page.
- Some graphic element at least every other page.
- Language and graphics must be gender-balanced and racially and culturally diverse.
- High school reading level.
- Include glossary of unusual or technical terms.
- Include reference materials for those who wish to learn more.
- Keep individual handouts to a minimum; include materials in workbook if at all possible.

2. Identify What Training Materials Are Required and What Materials Are Optional. There are materials you simply have to design, without which the training cannot work. For example, if participants are to give one another written feedback on a skill practice, they need a feedback form that focuses on key learning points. Other materials are more discretionary. For example, you might ideally prefer to prepare stacks of colorful individual cue cards for a particular group activity, even though you realize that a single utilitarian flip chart would do the job well enough.

The reason for distinguishing between required and optional training materials is purely practical: most designers and most organizations are limited by money and time—but they still want to create the best possible learning experience. The idea is to set priorities. After you are certain that you have the time and money to design and produce the required materials, then you can confidently go on to create and produce any optional materials that will make the learning event even more effective, efficient, and engaging. Here is how to go about determining the required and the optional materials:

_____ Review your microdesign and identify points at which training materials are essential.

- _____ For participant materials, note what materials are necessary for learners to prepare for the event, participate in an activity, or ensure the transfer of learning.
- _____ For trainer materials, assume that a trainer's guide is needed for the entire training event. Identify the points at which specific process instructions or content resources will be required for trainers to manage the learning event properly.
- _____ For learning aids, identify every activity or concept that cannot be communicated effectively without an audio or visual aid. Remember to plan learning aids for goals and objectives, agendas, and any core reference point that integrates the training.

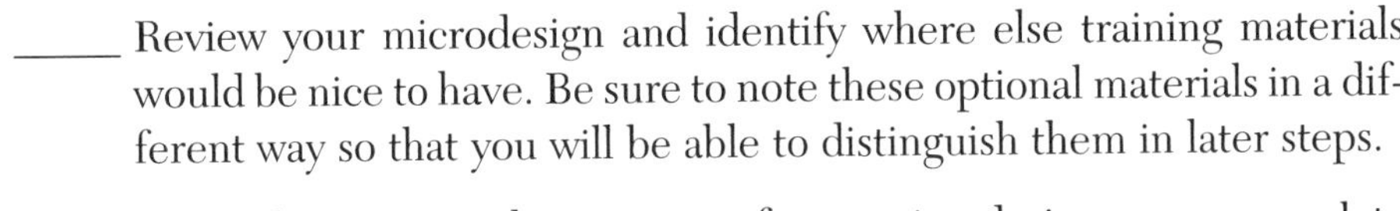

_____ Review your microdesign and identify where else training materials would be nice to have. Be sure to note these optional materials in a different way so that you will be able to distinguish them in later steps.

You may choose to mark up a copy of your microdesign as you complete this step, or you may prefer to make a separate list. Use whatever approach is comfortable for you.

3. Draft Required Materials. This is a step you may carry out personally, or you may work with others who will draft the materials. Whether you are executing or managing the drafting process, here is what you will do:

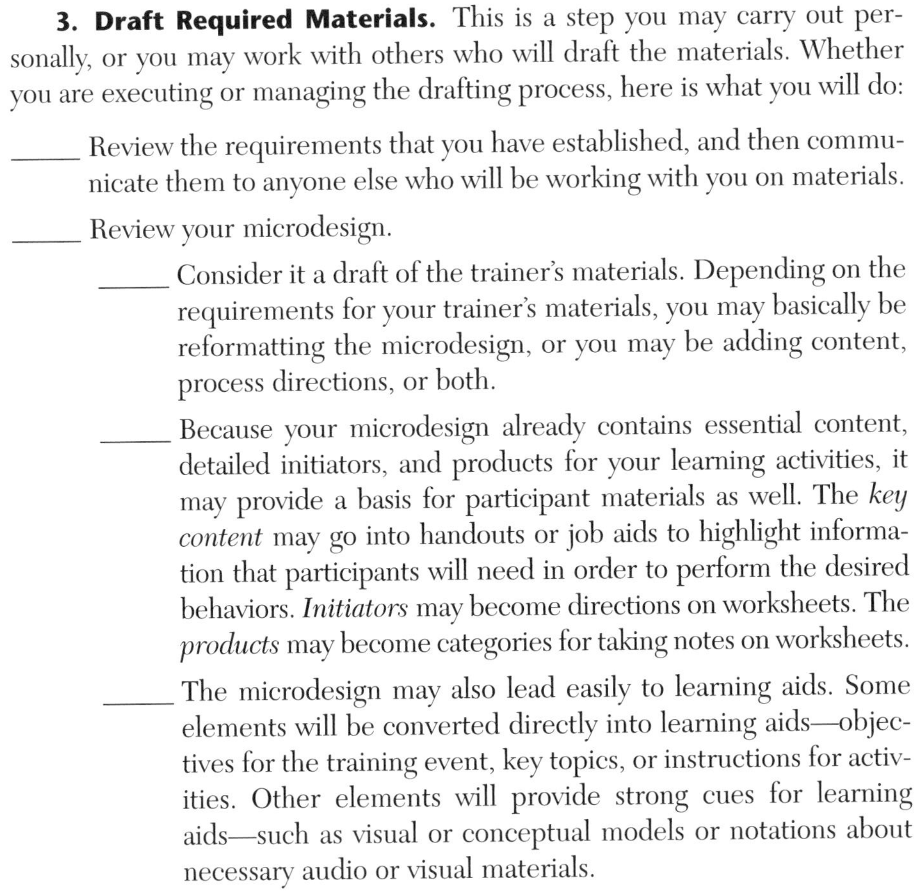

_____ Review the requirements that you have established, and then communicate them to anyone else who will be working with you on materials.

_____ Review your microdesign.

- _____ Consider it a draft of the trainer's materials. Depending on the requirements for your trainer's materials, you may basically be reformatting the microdesign, or you may be adding content, process directions, or both.
- _____ Because your microdesign already contains essential content, detailed initiators, and products for your learning activities, it may provide a basis for participant materials as well. The *key content* may go into handouts or job aids to highlight information that participants will need in order to perform the desired behaviors. *Initiators* may become directions on worksheets. The *products* may become categories for taking notes on worksheets.
- _____ The microdesign may also lead easily to learning aids. Some elements will be converted directly into learning aids—objectives for the training event, key topics, or instructions for activities. Other elements will provide strong cues for learning aids—such as visual or conceptual models or notations about necessary audio or visual materials.

After your review is complete, sit down and start drafting—or turn the task over to the person or persons who will.

4. Review Drafts of Required Materials. You have worked very hard to create the most effective, efficient, and engaging design that you can. The materials will largely determine how that powerful design is translated into a learning event. It is worth the time to step back from the details for a moment now to review and edit your materials. Here is what to do:

_____ Review the materials in each category to see if they meet the requirements that you established for the category.

_____ Be open to modifying requirements at this stage; the process is iterative. Sometimes, no matter how well you have planned, the draft will prompt a new realization about the requirements. For example, you might be reviewing participant materials and realize that you did not establish a requirement for color-coding handouts but that it is critical for your participants. Do it now.

_____ Check for alignment with the overall learning objectives. Because your work in the Goals and Objectives stage of the SIM has carefully anchored your goals and objectives in desired performance, this check of materials against objectives will ensure that the materials you have developed will mirror your participants' real world of application.

_____ Review your materials in relation to your learners. Especially with participant materials, consider the following:

- _____ How well do your materials fit with the ways adults learn? Do the materials acknowledge and incorporate the experience your learners bring to the learning event? Do they encourage the learners to make judgments about what is being learned? Do they highlight immediate application and the need to know?
- _____ Are the materials written and formatted in ways that appeal to a variety of learning styles?
- _____ Do they fit well with your particular group of learners? Are the reading level and language appropriate for your learners? Do they match organizational norms—in terms of writing style, format, and delivery system?

5. Select, Draft, and Review Optional Materials. If time and resources are still available, celebrate! You are in the enviable position of being able to enhance your design and make the learning event even better. Take these actions as you create your optional materials:

_____ Set priorities within the optional materials. Aim first for those that will add the greatest value to the training design and that you have time and resources to produce.

_____ Draft those materials.

_____ Review the drafts.

It can be tempting at this step to continue creating and producing materials, but bear in mind a couple of significant factors: first, there is still more work to do in terms of obtaining feedback and polishing the materials, so be sure to allow enough time; second, remember that even the most beautifully produced materials are useful only insofar as they assist the learners in accomplishing the desired objectives and support the trainer in facilitating the learning process. In other words, stay grounded in your goals and objectives and in your appreciation for the needs of the adult learner.

6. Have Others Review the Materials. This is the first design step of the SIM that requires a review by your users—or at least by reviewers who will represent your users. At the end of each stage of the SIM design process, we have recommended soliciting feedback from your client. Now you are developing the pieces of the training that will literally be in the hands of your learners and trainers and that translate your design into a learning event. At this point, you need the perspective of one or more reviewers who are not intimately familiar with the design. Here are a few guidelines:

_____ Select reviewers who are representative of your learners and trainers or who can at least be advocates for their interests.

_____ Especially for participant materials, select reviewers who represent a variety of learning preferences.

_____ Provide the reviewers with a checklist of specific things to look for (such as ease of following directions and appropriateness of language).

_____ Provide a brief overview of the training flow with participant materials, to help reviewers evaluate specific learning materials.

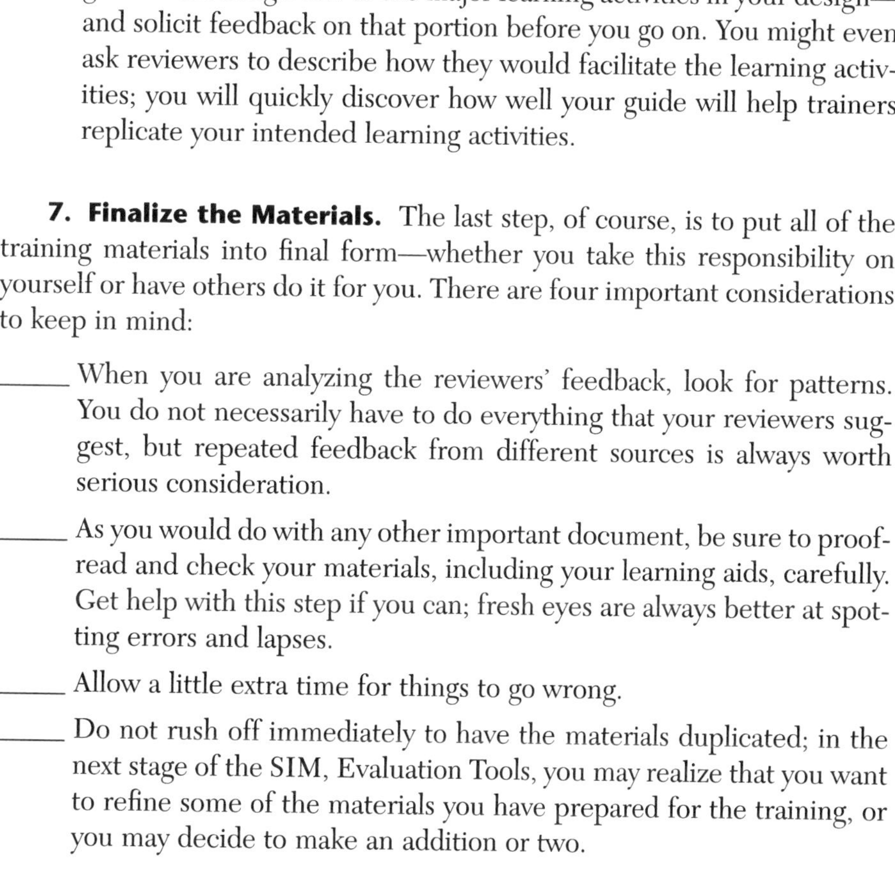

_____ You may want to start by drafting just a portion of your trainer's guide—covering a few of the major learning activities in your design—and solicit feedback on that portion before you go on. You might even ask reviewers to describe how they would facilitate the learning activities; you will quickly discover how well your guide will help trainers replicate your intended learning activities.

7. Finalize the Materials. The last step, of course, is to put all of the training materials into final form—whether you take this responsibility on yourself or have others do it for you. There are four important considerations to keep in mind:

_____ When you are analyzing the reviewers' feedback, look for patterns. You do not necessarily have to do everything that your reviewers suggest, but repeated feedback from different sources is always worth serious consideration.

_____ As you would do with any other important document, be sure to proofread and check your materials, including your learning aids, carefully. Get help with this step if you can; fresh eyes are always better at spotting errors and lapses.

_____ Allow a little extra time for things to go wrong.

_____ Do not rush off immediately to have the materials duplicated; in the next stage of the SIM, Evaluation Tools, you may realize that you want to refine some of the materials you have prepared for the training, or you may decide to make an addition or two.

COMMON QUESTIONS

Question: I'm confused about how much to include in the participant materials. On the one hand, I've seen materials that are little more than an outline of the training. On the other, I've seen extensive narrative workbooks that include every word of the training, or even more. How do I determine the appropriate level of detail for participant materials?

Answer: It depends on your requirements and what you and your client are trying to achieve. For one design, participant materials might be primarily for the purpose of helping participants engage in the learning activities; in this case, you would keep materials to a minimum. For another design, you might determine that the materials must help participants apply the new learning after they are back on the job. In this case, the workbook might have a lot of content so that participants can use it as a resource after the learning event.

Or you might want both: participant materials for facilitating the learning process during the training and reference materials to assist in the transfer process after the learning event.

Also, what you identified as essential content in the Key Topics stage of your design work will help guide your decisions about what to include in participant materials. If you are including nice-to-know resources, be sure to label them in some distinctive way.

Question: You keep saying to make certain that the participant materials appeal to a variety of learning styles. Considering that we are talking mostly about written materials, how can this be?

Answer: Participant materials can and should be formatted in ways that engage a variety of learning styles. One useful approach is to balance visual and verbal presentation in your materials. Charts and graphs, icons, illustrations, even borders, are all ways to balance the verbal presentation.

You can also appeal to a variety of learning styles by the content you select for participant materials as well as the way you present the materials. Here are some tips that coincide with Silver and Hanson's four learning styles (Chapter Three):

_____ Balance "why" and "how" materials.

_____ Balance facts with people stories, anecdotes with statistics.

_____ Balance the words "think" and "feel."

_____ Balance practical and creative content, the present with future possibilities.

_____ Leave room for participants to take notes, record key words, or draw pictures to remember key learning points; they will do so in their own style.

_____ Ask learners to summarize content areas in a variety of ways, such as:

    _____ What I will do with this material (appeals to S-T preference)

    _____ How it can be used to help others (S-F)

    _____ How it supports organizational goals and objectives (N-T)

    _____ What it means to me (N-F)

Question: I don't have the resources to do high-end desktop publishing. Is it okay to create my participant materials on a word processor as long as they are neat and attractive?

Answer: Of course. We all have to work with what is available. However, the designer's task is to engage adult learners, no matter what tools are used. If you are using a word-processing package, learn how to enliven your pages with graphics, even if they are only borders and boxes, or find a graphics package that can be integrated with your word-processing software. In addition, do not forget hand drawings. You may not be an artist, but you may be able to enlist the help of someone who is. We find that hand-drawn illustrations offer a warm balance to the more high-tech computer-generated graphics.

Finally, be sure to consider your participants and the environment in which the training will be delivered. If the training will be delivered in an organization in which sophisticated graphic presentations are the norm, then you must find ways to meet that expectation—perhaps by partnering with your client for formatting and graphics.

Question: I've never developed a trainer's guide before, and I have to learn how. The part I find most challenging is writing the guide so that someone else can re-create the design I have in mind. Any tips?

Answer: "Challenging" is a word people often use to describe the task of developing a trainer's guide. Your primary resource is your microdesign. When you were creating that, you were doing something akin to creating a mental storyboard or videotape of the training event. The more attention you paid to details then, the better position you are in now to convert that microdesign to a trainer's guide that someone else will be able to use in preparing for and managing the learning event. Your second resource is feedback—from the actual trainers if possible, otherwise from other colleagues.

Writing trainer's guides is an art, and you may need some time to become fully competent at it. Stay close to your microdesign, and be sure to solicit and use feedback. Those are the best ways to develop your skills and to ensure that what you develop will meet your objectives.

Question: I design training that has quite a bit of content. Some of the trainers who will deliver the training are content experts, and others are not. I'm struggling with a way to meet everyone's content needs. Aside from the "layered" approach that you've described, is there something else I can do?

Answer: Another good approach is to provide resources for the trainer (articles, background information, sample lecturettes) at the back of the trainer's guide and simply refer to those resources in the body of the guide. That way, all levels of trainers can use the guide to prepare for training; resources are available for those trainers who need assistance with the content, but they are conveniently out of the way for trainers who are already familiar with it. A similar format can be used to provide process resources for trainers who might need assistance managing specific learning activities.

Question: I find that developing the trainer's guide sometimes takes more time than designing the training. What am I doing wrong?

Answer: You may not be doing anything wrong. Developing really good trainer's guides does take a lot of time. We generally allocate at least as much time for the development of the trainer's guide as we do for the training design—sometimes more.

There are some things you can do to save time as you develop trainer's guides. You may wish to think through your requirements for trainer's materials before you do the outlining step of your microdesign so that you can be certain to provide in the microdesign itself the level of detail the materials will require. Another way to save some time is in the actual setup and formatting of the guide. If you use the layered approach we have described, begin with the simplest layer and refine it to a complete product before you begin working on the next layer; that way, you can just copy the first layer and add details. Use your word-processing program to help you with this task, and be sure to set up all your formatting and style requirements early in the process so that you can make additions without reconfiguring the style each time.

Question: My favorite type of trainer's guide has the trainer's material on one side and the participant material on the facing page. Isn't this the best format?

Answer: There certainly are some great advantages to this format. Both during preparation for the training and during delivery, the trainer can look at her materials and the participant materials at the same time. When these guides work, they can make the trainer's job much easier; there is simply less paper to juggle. However, such guides can be very difficult to develop and should be used only when they will work well.

The obvious challenge is that the volume of material required to describe a learning activity is not always equal to the volume of related participant materials. For example, a simulation that is very complex to manage and requires several pages of directions for the trainer may involve only one worksheet for participants. That presents the problem of matching pages in the participant workbook with those in the trainer's guide.

If matching pages is not a problem in your design and you like this format, then use it. Our main caveat is to avoid letting the format become the main requirement—at the expense of developing materials for participants or trainers that are the most effective, efficient, and engaging.

Question: I have a very hard time finding videos that work well with my training programs, but I know that they can be a powerful training tool with adults who are used to television and movies. Any suggestions?

Answer: We share your concern. Videos and films can be powerful tools to engage learners; but with limited time in learning events, no designer wants to select inefficient activities. It can be difficult to find videos that efficiently support the content identified in the Key Topics stage of the design. For example, in designing a workshop on public speaking, you might find a video that is very engaging but that uses language different from the language in a core model you have developed for the training, or one that includes preparation steps you have decided are not essential for your participants. In addition, other requirements (such as gender balance, racial/cultural diversity, or an organizational environment similar to your own) may cause you to reject videos that are, on a content level, highly compatible with your design.

There are some ways to manage this dilemma. One is to produce your own videos. Though expensive and time-consuming, video production does ensure direct alignment with your training objectives—and it may be cost-effective for training programs that will be offered many times.

Another design option is to include a learning activity in which participants make quick videos of their own to reinforce key learning points, then show the videos to other participants. It can be either a synergetic learning activity (in which groups are dealing with different content or skills) or an activity in which all groups are dealing with the same key content and have the advantage of seeing several interpretations of it.

Yet another design approach is to look at existing videos as a part of your research during the Key Topics stage. That way, if you find something that directly supports the desired performance for which the training is being designed, the content of the video will become key topics and key points in your design. Of course, be sure to honor copyright requirements.

Question: Aren't purely audio learning aids a thing of the past?

Answer: No, they are integral parts of some training designs. They are particularly useful for training that focuses on telephone skills or any oral communication situations that do not involve face-to-face communication. Audiotapes can easily be used to simulate questions and complaints or to demonstrate skills and evaluate performance for telephone training.

Also, music can be an aid to the learning process: to set a mood or theme in the training room, to signal the beginning or end of breaks, or to engender creativity and facilitate the learning process during specific activities (Rylatt & Lohan, 1997, pp. 183–187). Again, be careful of copyright limitations; for information regarding the use of recorded music, contact ASCAP (American Society of Composers, Artists, and Publishers, telephone: 212–621–6160; Internet: http://ascap.com.).

Question: The technology for visual aids advances and changes continually. I am an independent consultant and simply cannot afford high-end electronic equipment. What do I do?

Answer: This question is often asked. Independent consultants often find equipment costs to be prohibitive. First, remember to view your visual aids as aids to learning, not ends in themselves. If you are designing training about using electronic technology, then you cannot avoid using it. However, if the technology is just one possible way to enhance learning, then you will have to assess the learning environment, the expectations and needs of your participants, and your own expertise and capabilities. As we said earlier, this may be a place to collaborate with your clients. If they have access or expertise that is beyond yours, a collaboration may provide the best possible training for their learners—and, after all, that's the primary goal.

Question: From a design point of view, what are some of the criteria I should use to determine which is the most appropriate medium to use for a particular learning aid? For example, some of the visuals I consider essential for the training could just as easily be produced on a wall chart, a flip chart, an overhead transparency, or a multimedia projection system.

Answer: Here are some criteria we find useful for making such decisions:

_____ *Does one medium more closely reflect the real-world application?* For example, if you are planning a visual that participants will find on a computer screen in their work, then it is best to display it from the screen during the training.

_____ *Do some media display the necessary content better?* For example, if you wish to reveal a flowchart one step at a time, then use an overhead transparency or a multimedia projection system rather than the more static medium of a wall chart.

_____ *How will the visual be used in the training?* If you are designing a model that will be a core reference point throughout the training, use a medium that will keep it visible throughout the training—such as a wall chart or a three-dimensional model.

_____ *What is the physical learning environment, and which media will best work in that environment?* It may be difficult to use electronic media in a room that cannot be darkened sufficiently. Or if the room has very limited wall space, using a lot of wall charts may not work very well.

_____ *How portable do the visuals need to be?* If you are designing training that will be presented at many sites, select media that are easy to transport. A bundle of overhead transparencies is easier to carry than several pads of prepared flip charts.

_____ *What equipment will be available, and are the trainers skilled in the use of the equipment you are considering?* Do not count on using fancy electronic equipment if you will be training out-of-doors, for example, or if your trainers have never used the equipment before.

Let's see what is happening in your SIM computer files. You have four existing files, and they are very closely related. The first file, Goals and Objectives, still has the umbrella that answers the question "Why are we doing this training?" Clustered beneath that goal are the objectives and the skills related to them. The second file, Key Topics, is empty; all its contents have been moved to the next file. The third file is Training Flow—Macrodesign, with your big-picture outline. The fourth is Training Flow—Microdesign, which contains a

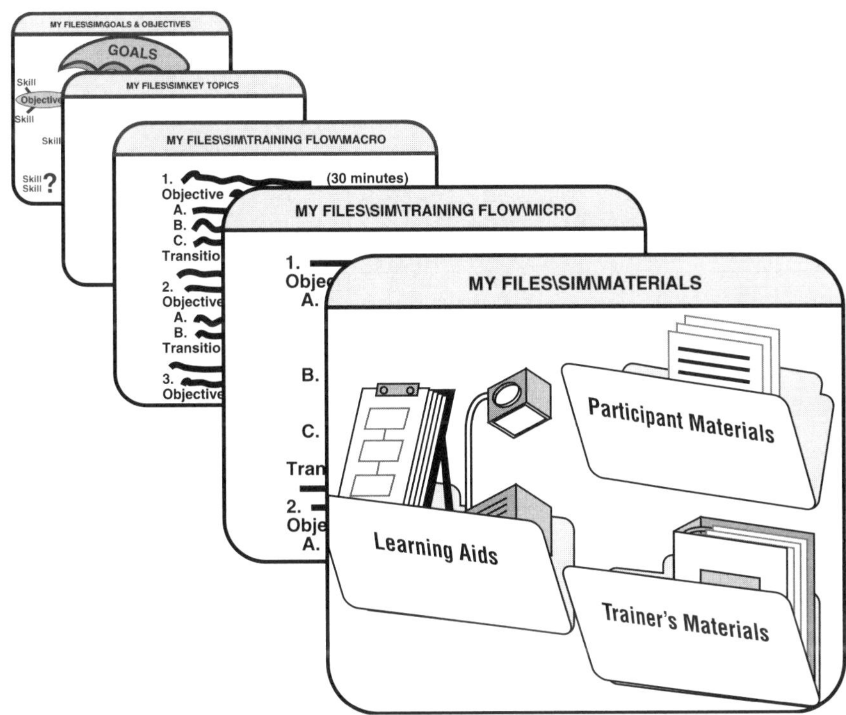

detailed outline of the training with all the sequenced learning activities, their related content and objectives, the times for each activity, and critical transitions. This file absolutely supports the goals and objectives in the first file.

The new file, Materials, includes three subfiles: Participant Materials, Trainer's Materials, and Learning Aids. These files contain all of the materials that will be used during the training event to translate your design into a learning event. They contain the workbooks, references, handouts, and other materials that participants will use. They contain materials to support the trainer in managing and facilitating the training. They also contain audio and visual learning aids that will be used as parts of learning activities or as cues in the training environment to stimulate and reinforce learning.

You are nearly there. The final design step in the SIM, Evaluation Tools, lies just ahead.

Looking Back

Here is the SIM process up to this point:

Goals and Objectives

1. Review design requirements.
2. Establish a goal statement.
3. Brainstorm the skills for reaching the desired behaviors.
4. Edit: determine essential versus nonessential skills for reaching the desired behaviors.
5. Consolidate: cluster related skills together.
6. Draft objectives.
7. Review and edit the proposed goals and objectives.
8. Review the goals and objectives with your client.

Key Topics

1. Research the subject.
2. Brainstorm possible key points.
3. Determine essential versus nonessential points.
4. Group key points into key topics.
5. Identify additional points for key topics.
6. Consider possible organizational structures.
7. Review and edit key topics.
8. Check work with your client.

Training Flow—Macrodesign

1. Research existing activities.
2. Brainstorm activities.
3. Select possible activities.
4. Estimate time for possible activities.
5. Outline training design.
6. Articulate objectives for segments.
7. Sketch out transitions.
8. Review your macrodesign.
9. Check macrodesign with your client.

Training Flow—Microdesign

1. Identify specific objective for each activity.
2. Define the universe of acceptable responses.
3. Develop the steps and the processes for each activity.
4. Refine time estimates.
5. Develop initiators.
6. Develop transitions.
7. Check time estimates one final time.
8. Review microdesign.
9. Complete outline of the training design.
10. Determine whether to check the microdesign with your client.

Training Materials

1. Establish requirements for materials.
2. Identify what training materials are required and what materials are optional.
3. Draft required materials.
4. Review drafts of required materials.
5. Select, draft, and review optional materials.
6. Have others review the materials.
7. Finalize the materials.

Running Example: Materials

Simone, working from her microdesign and other sources, is now ready to begin developing training materials. Her Materials file already contains some notes from previous stages of the design process:

Sample Appraisals. Both well-written and poorly written appraisals from her research. She will want to use pieces of them for the learning activity in which participants will translate gut feelings into behavioral descriptors of performance.

Visual Model of Content Categories. Simone needs to create a wall chart or a three-dimensional model of the key topics in this training—something for the trainer to refer to while making transitions during the training. There are four key topic areas:

- First-Class Appraisals
- WIIFM
- Looking Back
- Looking Forward

Coaching Tool. Simone needs to create a tool for participants' managers to use to assist with transfer of learning.

Prizes. Simone will want to remind the trainers to buy fun prizes for the translation game.

Prereading. In creating this piece for the segment on performance improvement, Simone will need to include the following:

- One or more samples of ineffective performance expectations
- Instructions on how to improve/clarify expectations
- Comments on how and why to address the impact of performance on the work and the work group
- Ways to handle suggestions for improvement in the appraisal

Simone will be creating the trainer's materials herself. A colleague in the Reprographics Department will offer design advice and handle the technical work of creating and reproducing participant materials and learning aids. Because this training is targeted for a select and rather small audience, Simone will not include any computer-assisted learning aids, such as CD-ROM application exercises; so she will not need any assistance from the Multimedia Department for this design.

1. Establish Requirements for Materials

Having worked at Jexon for several years, Simone is familiar with the standard requirements for materials. Beyond that, she has met with the key client as well as a focus group to determine any additional requirements for participant materials. She works closely with the trainers who will be facilitating this training, so she is easily able to find out what they need.

Here's what she learns about requirements:

Participant Materials

- Workbook format, so that participants can easily retrieve material when they are writing appraisals.
- Minimum number of handouts; must be easy to insert into workbook to consolidate take-away materials.
- Numbered pages.
- Allow room for notes on each page.
- Pages containing basic how-to information (job aids) should be reproduced on bright-colored paper for ready reference after the training.
- Balance verbal and graphic presentations.
- Incorporate all major learning aids (such as models and objectives) into participant materials—for reference and so that participants do not waste time copying learning aids from charts.

Trainer's Materials

- Prepare in two layers, per trainers' request.
    - Layer 1: an overview that describes objectives, times, and brief process directions
    - Layer 2: more detailed for use in preparation
- Put resources (articles, suggested lecturettes, and so on) at the back of the trainer's guide.
- Use three-ring binder so that trainers can insert additional resources.
- Leave space for trainer notes on each page.

Learning Aids

- Model (three-dimensional or wall chart) of key points for reference during training.
- Post agenda for reference.
- Post goal and objectives for reference.

- Use mostly flip charts and wall charts; important to keep costs down, as this training program will be offered only to a small audience.

NOTE TO READER

The steps of the Running Example again address only Segment 4, Part C: the game on translating gut language. You will find illustrations—designer's drafts, finished products, or both—for some of the materials.

2. Identify What Training Materials Are Required and What Materials Are Optional

Simone marks up a copy of her microdesign to show where she thinks participant materials and learning aids are required (an *R* in a box) and where they are optional (an *O* in a box). Trainer's materials are needed for the entire microdesign, of course, so she makes notes only where particular reference materials might be especially useful for the trainer.

Simone's "Materials" Notes on Microdesign

C. Game: translating gut language. (25 min.)

(1) Small-group game: fix gut language from above activities—as many as possible in limited time. (10 min.)

a. Setup. (5 min.)

- Put participants into triads (some random method—count off by 3s, birthdays, colors, and so forth).
- Overhead transparency remains visible to highlight vague/judgmental statements. Overhead [R]

Initiator Points

- *5 minutes to fix as many of the statements as possible.* FC: Directions [R]
- *"Fixing" means translating into descriptive and behavioral language, as we did earlier.*
- *Record translations on flip chart; there's one for each team.*
- *If you finish all the statements, go back and develop additional translations.*
- *Team receives 1 point for each correct translation.*
- *Prize for winning team or teams.* Prizes [R]
- *Solicit questions about directions.*

continued

b. Small-group game. (5 min.) *Worksheet* R

- Trainer circulates and helps correct statements as appropriate. *Wall chart:* O
- Remind when there are 2 minutes and 1 minute remaining. *(Def. of behavioral language)*

(2) Large group compares and refines results (prizes for each group in some category). (15 min.)

- Review point system for game.
- For each group, review each translated statement.
- Determine whether behavioral; if not, lead a brief discussion on what it would take to make it behavioral. *FC: Debrief* R
- Assign points on groups' flip charts.
- Award prizes (different categories—most points, most creative, most humorous—a prize to each group). *Prizes* R

Transition Points

- *Have come up with ways to fix appraisal language.*
- *Now practice on real-life situation, receive feedback.*

3. Draft Required Materials

Using the information in her microdesign, Simone drafts all the required materials.

Participant Materials. She decides to create a worksheet for the game to meet the needs of a variety of learning styles. Some learners will not use it, as they will prefer to process the information verbally in their small groups. Others will need to write the information out in order to deal with it; the worksheet will help support their learning process. Simone also knows that some learners will want to make note of others' reactions and suggestions.

She drafts the worksheet—with a sketch of an applause meter, which she would like the artist to include.

Simone's Draft of Game Worksheet

Worksheet: "Translating" Game

Note: This worksheet is optional. Use it if it helps you. Your group will have five minutes to fix as many of the "gut language" statements as possible. This worksheet will help you through the process and serve as a reminder after the training. There is space to record the reactions of other participants to your group's work.

Good luck!

Gut Language Statement

Underline the problems within the statement.

Translation into Behavioral Language

Reactions to Translation: Applause Meter

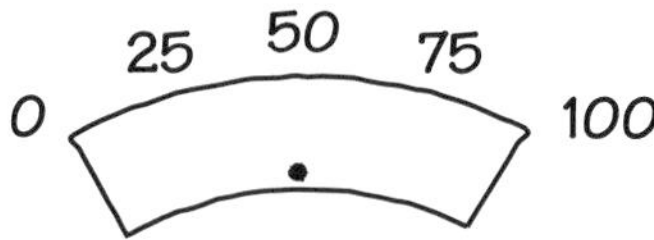

Trainer's Materials. Simone starts with her microdesign to create the trainer's materials, but she does not stop there. She reworks it a bit—adding or deleting details, rewording process descriptions, renumbering sequences, inserting notes about participant materials and learning activities—to make it a useful document for the trainers, who are not as intimately familiar with the training design as she is. As requested, she drafts two layers, starting with the simpler one.

Layer 1 of the trainer's guide is more detailed than the macrodesign, less detailed than the microdesign; the trainers will probably use it as they deliver the training.

Layer 1 (Overview): Trainer's Guide for Game

Time	Activity/Content	Participant Materials	Learning Aid	Notes
	Segment Objective. Participants will demonstrate their ability to identify vague language and translate it into behavioral language.		• Debrief FC	
25 min.	C. Game: translating gut language			
	(1) Group participants into triads. (2 min.)			
	(2) Directions. (3 min.)		• FC: Game Dirs.	
	a. Review directions.			
	• Refer to overhead.		•Overhead	
	• Refer to worksheet.	• Worksheet X		
	b. Solicit questions.			
	(3) Game. (5 min.)			
	a. Circulate; refine work when appropriate.			
	b. Remind: 1 min./2 min. remaining.			
	(4) Debrief discussion. (15 min.)		• FC: Debrief	
	a. Review point system.			
	b. Each group reads statements.			
	c. Large group: determine whether behavioral.			
	• If not, refine.			
	Transition Points			
	• *Have come up with ways to fix appraisal language.*			
	• *Now practice on real-life situation, receive feedback.*			

Layer 2 gives more direction on both process and content; trainers will probably use it as they prepare for the training.

Layer 2 (Detail): Trainer's Guide for Game

Time	Activity/Content	Participant Materials	Learning Aid	Notes
	Segment Objective. Participants will demonstrate their ability to identify vague language and translate it into behavioral language.		• Debrief FC	
25 min.	C. Game: translating gut language			
	(1) Group participants into triads. (2 min.) (random method—count off by 3s, birthdays, colors,and so on).			
	(2) Directions. (3 min.)		• FC: Game Dirs.	
	a. Review directions. (on FC)			
	• 5 min. to fix as many statements as possible.			
	• "Fixing" means translating into descriptive and behav-ioral language, as earlier.			
	• Record on FC.			
	• If finished, go back and do more.			
	• 1 point for each correct translation.			
	• Prize for winning team(s).			
	b. Refer to gut language highlightedon trans-parency.		•Overhead	
	c. Refer participants to worksheet to think through translations.	• Worksheet X		
	d. Solicit questions about directions.			

continued

Time	Activity/Content	Participant Materials	Learning Aid	Notes
	(3) Game. (5 min.) a. Circulate; correct work when appropriate. b. Remind: 1 min./2 min. remaining. (4) Debrief discussion. (15 min.) a. Review point system. b. Each group reads statements. c. Remind: There will be opinions. d. Large group: determine whether behavioral. • If not, refine. *Note:* Remind group that point is whether statement is objective and descriptive, not whether they like the way it is said. Because there will be opinions on whether a translation is behavioral, refine only those that a majority of participants find unacceptable or that you determine need refinement. Where there is disagreement, you can say, "We have a variety of opinions on this one. What changes could we make that would make the statement more objective and descriptive?" In this way, you don't have to make an arbitrary decision on something when there is no clear distincition.		• FC: Debrief	
	(5) Award prizes—one for each team. *Transition Points* • *Have come up with ways to fix appraisal language.* • *Now practice on real-life situation, receive feedback.*		• Prizes	

Learning Aids. Of the learning aids required for the workshop overall, one is particularly intriguing—the visual model for the entire workshop. Simone knows she will need a lot of help, so she sketches out her rough ideas as a draft for the artist.

Simone's Draft: Visual Model

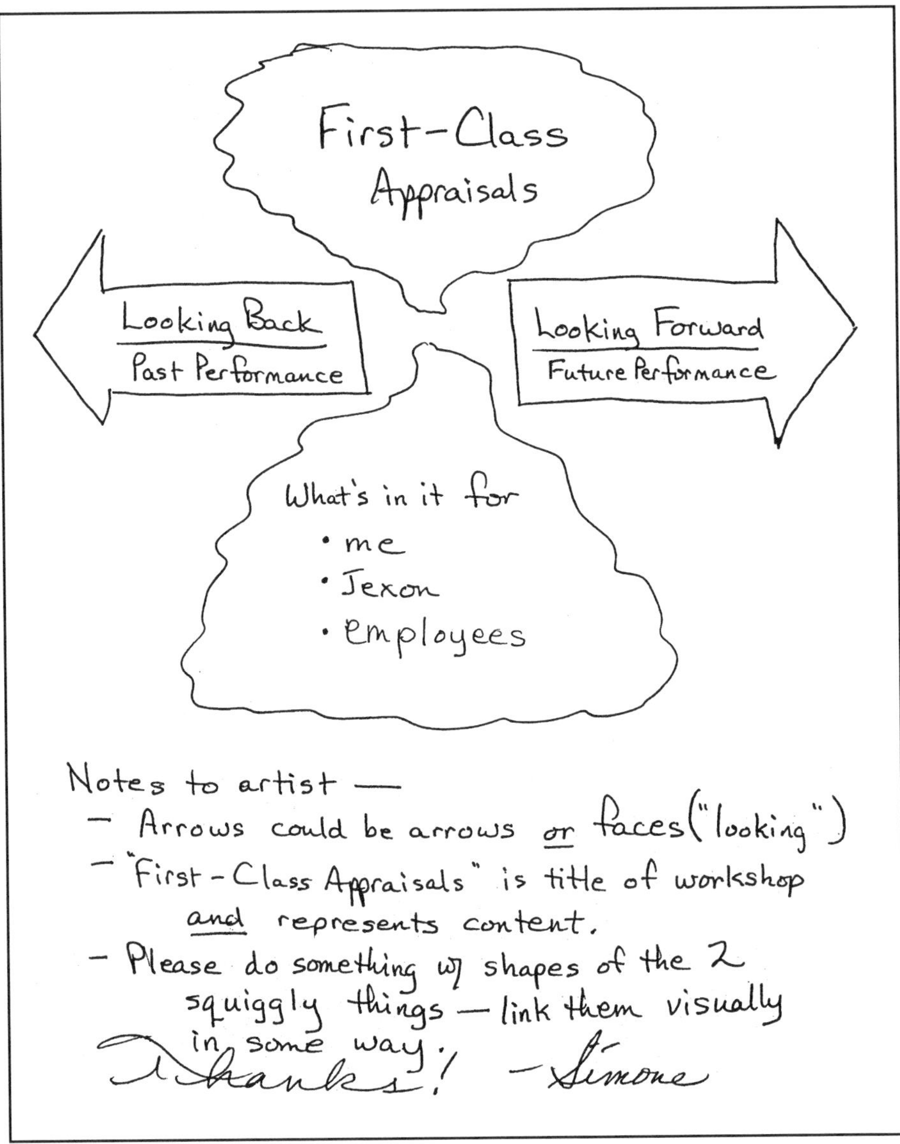

Within the game segment, four learning aids are required:

- *Overhead transparency:* Used first in the preceding activity to identify gut language that needs to be translated. It will contain segments from three performance appraisals and will be an exact replica of the handout that participants will use individually during that activity. The trainer will, in the preceding activity, highlight those phrases that the group agrees are gut language. This overhead will remain up during the game and the debrief as a point of reference for group work. Simone pulls these passages from the appraisals.
- *Directions flip chart:* The trainer will use it to review the directions and then leave it up during the game as a point of reference. Simone drafts the words and adds her ideas for art, grateful that she has someone to help with illustration.

Simone's Draft: Directions Flip Chart

- 1 point for each "fix" (correct translation)
- Record translations on flip chart

- If you finish all, go back and do alternate translations.
- Prizes!!

- *Debrief flip chart:* Used to guide the large-group comparison of data. Simone is particularly concerned that this debrief discussion stay focused on whether the translation is behavioral. She knows that this segment deals with opinions and a large universe of acceptable responses; still, she wants to help the trainer focus participants on whether the language is behavioral, rather than on whether it is said as they would say it. Her draft is like an illustrated flow chart, incorporating graphics as well as words.

Simone's Draft: Debrief Flip Chart

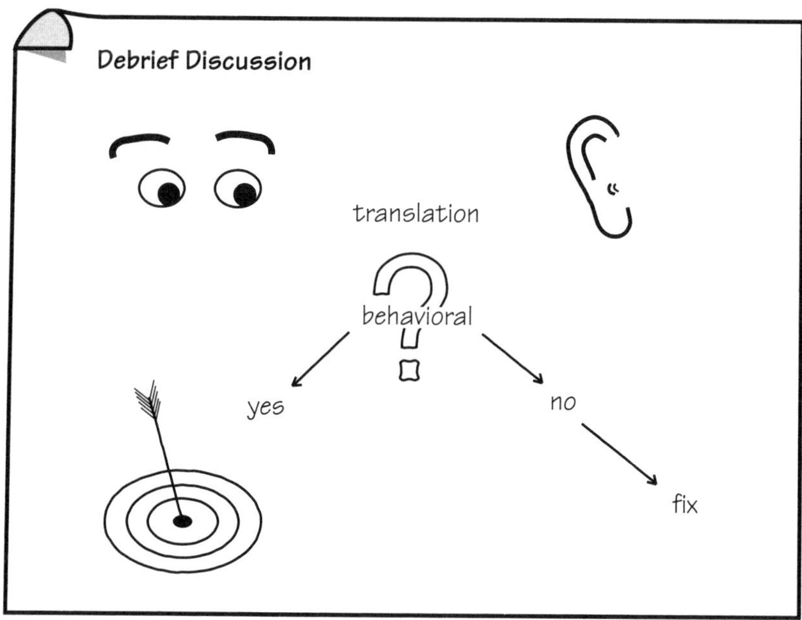

- *Prizes:* To be awarded for the game. The trainers will be purchasing these prizes, so she has provided some guidance in a list of materials provided for the workshop.

Simone goes through this drafting process for each of the required materials. She does most of the drafting alone, some of it with the graphic artist, until she has drafts of all of the required materials. Some of them are still a bit rough, and that's fine. Simone does not want to put too much time into them until she receives some feedback.

4. Review Drafts of Required Materials

She reviews the draft materials against the requirements she established for each category of materials.

Participant Materials. The drafts look pretty good. There is a nice balance between verbal and graphic presentation—the artist has agreed to include at least one graphic (a border, an icon, or an illustration) on every other page of participant materials. There is adequate room for notes, and the participant materials include the visual model that will be used throughout the training. The pages that will serve as job aids will have a special border and are to be copied on bright-colored paper.

There is one area on which Simone will do some more work: she has some separate handouts that she thinks could be incorporated in the workbook instead, in keeping with the requirements.

Trainer's Materials. Simone has prepared the materials in two layers, as requested. For additional resources, she has secured permission to reprint two articles that she thinks will give solid content background, and she has prepared resource pages on key topic areas such as legal requirements. Simone asked both trainers to take a quick look at a portion of her draft trainer's guide for the first two segments of the training; she did not want to go too far without some feedback, because the trainer's guide requires so much time and effort. The trainers were pleased with what they saw, so Simone has used the same format in developing the rest of the trainer's guide.

Learning Aids. Simone has created learning aids that will reinforce key points and serve as reference points for transitions during the training. To keep costs down, she has decided to present the overall model on a beautiful wall chart, not in three-dimensional format. There are other learning aids she would like to create if there is time. For example, the focus groups yielded some powerful quotes about the effects of well-done and poorly done appraisals, and Simone would like to post those quotes on the walls during the training if possible; she will wait to see whether there is time to develop the quotes as posters.

Overall, Simone concludes, her draft materials certainly highlight and reinforce the learning objectives. Each page of the workbook includes either a title or an icon that links it to one of the objectives for the training. The learning aids are simple and include many graphic elements. The trainer's guides use language and acronyms that are very familiar to Jexon trainers.

The learners will leave with a variety of practical job aids. There is very little theory in the materials, and that approach is a good fit with the Jexon culture. Nonetheless, Simone has included a bibliography for those who are interested. She has also ensured that some of the key articles and books are available in the Human Resource Department library for those who might want to consult them. In all the materials, Simone has made certain to include examples that will appeal to a variety of learning styles.

5. Select, Draft, and Review Optional Materials

From her identified optional materials, Simone selects two optional participant materials and one optional learning aid that she has time to draft. The participant materials are worksheets—one for the WIIFM segment and one for the discussion of the prereading. The learning aid is a wall chart that will reinforce the definition of behavioral language: "Behavioral language is objective and descriptive," perhaps with an attractive border. She adds a reference in the trainer's guide.

Even though she would like to be able to develop additional optional materials, such as the posters with quotes, Simone knows that she still has to attend to her evaluation strategy and tools; she also wants to allow plenty of time for the artwork and reproduction. She may come back and do a few more optional materials later if there is still time.

At this point, Simone reviews the drafts of optional materials and is satisfied that they are well done. It is now time for her to put all her materials into the hands of reviewers who are not as close to them, in order to hear how the materials look to the people who will use them.

6. Have Others Review the Materials

For participant materials, Simone asks five supervisors who will actually take part in the training to take a look at the materials. She explains that, because the materials are meant to be used in the training, some of them will not stand on their own. She also gives the reviewers the following instructions:

Please note:

- Words or phrases that are confusing
- Language that feels overly complex
- Directions that are hard to follow
- Graphics that you do not understand

Also, please make any other suggestions you would like.

She asks the trainers to review the sample portions of the trainer's guide, using the following instructions:

Please note:

- Language that is unclear
- Places where you need additional information or resources
- Activities that need clarification

Also, please make any other suggestions you would like.

Simone asks both groups to review the learning aids. For the sake of efficiency, they will meet with her briefly to review the aids and make comments; that way, she will be able to explain what each one is and how it fits into the training.

7. Finalize the Materials

The reviewers are very pleased with the materials. There are a few suggestions for simplifying language and directions, and Simone incorporates these ideas into the participant materials and learning aids. The trainers are very complimentary and grateful for the two levels. They request that the first page or two of the trainer's guide show an overview of the names and times of the segments, plus all the materials needed for facilitating the training. Simone includes this page at the front of the trainer's guide.

Artist's Version: Visual Model

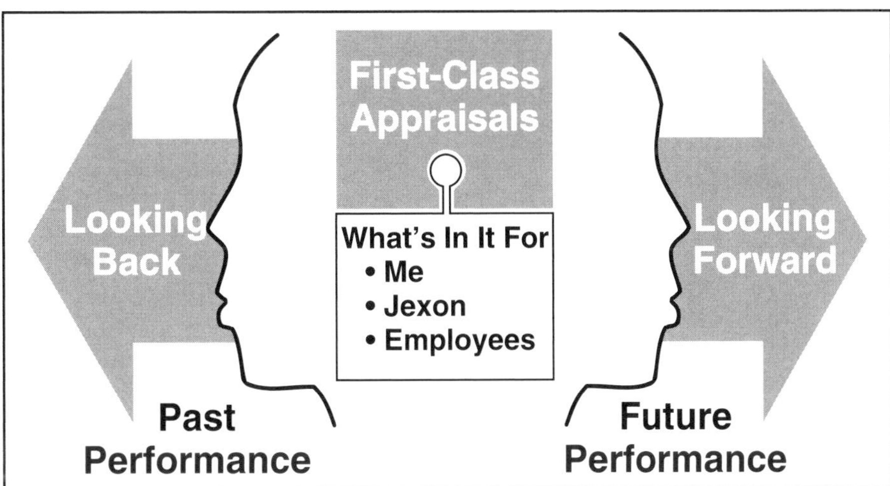

Simone sends the drafts of participant materials and learning aids to the graphic artist so that he can convert them into works of art. Simone has allowed time in the schedule in case any changes in materials are needed during the next stage of the SIM.

Simone is now ready to focus on evaluation.

11 The SIM

Evaluation Tools

At last you have arrived at the final stage of the SIM. During the earlier stages, you assessed the needs of your learners and your organization and determined appropriate training objectives on the basis of those needs. Building on those objectives, you examined what learners will need to know in order to perform the desired behaviors, and you microdesigned a learning event that will achieve the objectives in an effective, efficient, and engaging manner. With all that accomplished, you developed materials for the participants, the trainer, and the learning environment.

It is time to look at ways to find out how successful you, the trainer, and your learners are. During this stage of the SIM, you will finalize a strategy for evaluation and then develop the tools to achieve that strategy. Quite likely, some of your tools have already been designed—those that were necessary for helping ensure that participants reach objectives. The Evaluation Tools stage of the SIM is where you fit them all together and fill in any remaining holes.

PRODUCTS OF THE EVALUATION TOOLS STAGE

By the time you complete this stage of the SIM, you will have a pair of final products:

- *Evaluation Strategy:* A plan for evaluating the success of your training design.
- *Evaluation Tools:* The instruments for gathering the required data.

You and your client have been talking all along about how you will measure success—whether you used the term "evaluation" or not. At this stage, you help the client by identifying an overall strategy for evaluation, and you design the necessary tools to support the parts of evaluation for which you are responsible; in most instances, the designer's evaluation responsibility is primarily at the levels of reaction and learning.

For example, in the evaluation strategy for the training on listening skills for medical professionals, there might be a number of considerations: assume that the session is a one-time training event, but that the client is hoping to introduce more regular training for the staff. Client and designer have been discussing evaluation since the beginning of the process, and it is clear that the client wants the evaluation to be simple. The client has two specific needs: the relationship between improved listening skills and better diagnosis and reactions that may guide later thinking about introducing additional training.

Here is how the evaluation strategy might look:

- *Before Training:* No need for new data. Data already available on diagnostic errors attributable to listening errors.
- *During Training:* Practice of skills, but no formal evaluation of participants.
- *During and After Training:* Participants' perceptions of training event.
- *After Training:* Tools with activities that supervisors can use individually and at team meetings to reinforce and measure mastery of skills. Data comparison on diagnostic errors attributable to listening errors.

EVALUATION TOOLS: WHY? AND WHY NOW?

After all your work, you are eager to know whether the training design you have worked so hard to create is successful! That is reason enough to evaluate. Your client, too, is eager to evaluate. The organization is investing time and money in the training program, and of course the purpose of that investment is to empower employees to perform the desired behaviors—behaviors that are linked with organizational objectives. Evaluation is a way for everyone involved with the design and delivery of training to measure its effects.

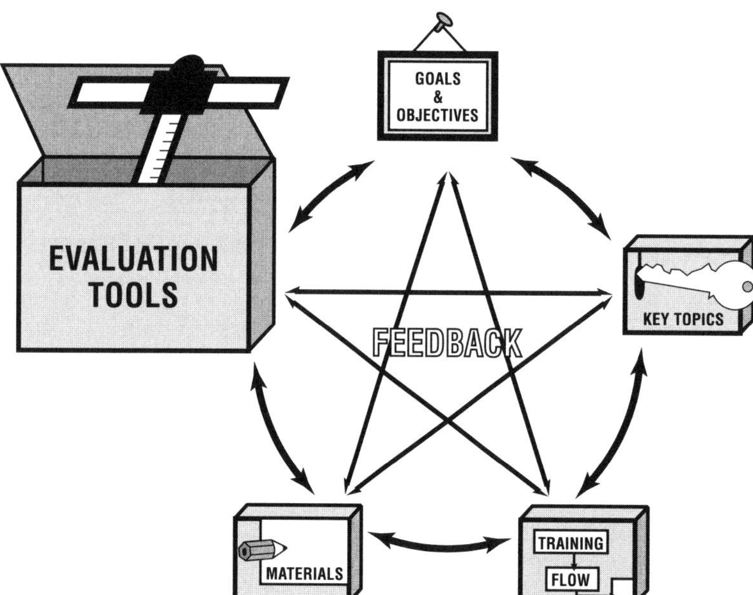

Some other design approaches recommend constructing evaluation tools immediately after objectives have been agreed upon for the training—as soon as the designer knows what is to be measured. The SIM, in contrast, has you wait until this stage because we are not talking just about tools. We are talking about a strategy. With the SIM, you and your client have been discussing possibilities for evaluation all along; the constant attention to desired behaviors and training objectives has demanded that you think about evaluation the whole time you are designing.

Now, as you finalize your strategy and prepare to design evaluation tools, you will find that using the SIM has helped you in four ways:

- You have been in close touch with your objectives all the way through the design process; you know, because training design is iterative and sometimes messy, that your objectives may have changed since the Goals and Objectives stage. By following the SIM, you have avoided wasting time on evaluation tools that might have turned out to be irrelevant. You have also been able to refine your objectives as necessary, because you did not have to worry about whether doing so might undermine already-prepared evaluation tools.
- Your work in the Training Flow stage of the SIM involved selecting learning activities; in making the selections, one of your major criteria was how well the activities fit with the objectives. If you matched your activities carefully with your objectives, then some of the activities are tools that will evaluate what the participants are learning.
- Now that your design for the learning event is complete, you know what factors you have designed into the learning environment about which you want feedback. For example, you may have consciously tried to build more interaction into the training than participants are accustomed to, and you may want to solicit feedback on that approach. Or you may have introduced a new type of job aid and may want initial perceptions of its usefulness.
- Because you have developed a detailed training flow, you are now in a position to identify some key times during the training when the trainer might benefit from checking out participants' reactions.

APPROACHING EVALUATION STRATEGICALLY

In far too many organizations, the evaluation of training is something of an afterthought, perhaps some questions to be answered on a quick end-of-training form. At the other extreme, there may be reams of data distributed to half the people on the organizational chart. We recommend a more thoroughgoing strategy that will help link the training event to the organizational objectives and to the entire training process, by means of information that is targeted and directly useful. Developing a strategy for evaluation is important for three reasons:

- A strategy allows you to identify and obtain the specific data that are needed to assess your training program: Is it effective in meeting objectives? Is the design as efficient and engaging as possible? Is it having a positive impact on the organization?
- A strategic approach implies finding out not only what evaluation data will be required but also what data are not desired or useful. For example, do not ask for participants' assessments of the training space if there is no other space available. The simple act of asking questions raises expectations; people assume that you intend to do something with their responses. If participants realize that many of them have requested a change and they never see that change, they may well have negative feelings about the training department and about future evaluations.
- A strategic approach to evaluation obtains the most useful data in the least painful way; it helps ensure that the evaluation process will be effective, efficient, and engaging. Evaluation is *effective* if it brings the most useful data to the people who really need it. It is *efficient* if it wisely manages the time, energy, and resources of the people who will provide, gather, analyze, and use the data. Finally, evaluation is *engaging* if it helps people to approach the task purposefully, in a way that will yield the highest-quality data.

EVALUATION LEVELS

Donald Kirkpatrick has given the training profession a great gift by describing four levels of evaluation in language that is easy to grasp and work with (1994, p. 21): Level 1, "Reaction"; Level 2, "Learning"; Level 3, "Behavior"; and Level 4, "Results."

At Level 1, Reaction, you are evaluating your participants' and clients' feelings, thoughts, and perceptions about the learning event itself. These people are your customers, and you want to know how they have responded to what you created. You can solicit reactions about any number of factors:

- Perceived usefulness of what was learned
- The physical environment
- Participant materials
- Learning aids
- Learning activities
- The trainer
- The learning environment
- Training times
- Content

At Level 2, Learning, you are measuring what participants have actually learned during the training. Because you have written objectives that BAG 'M, you have already identified behaviors that you will use as measures of learning. Many of the learning activities you have already created will give participants an opportunity to apply and measure learning during the training event.

Level 3, Behavior, focuses on the application of what is learned. At this level, you are measuring whether and how the learning has been translated to behaviors on the job or in one's life. For example, if participants demonstrated certain conflict-resolution skills during the training, you and the client might want to know whether those skills have been translated into behaviors on the job. Remember, you started the SIM process by identifying desired behaviors. Now you are asking, "To what extent has the training actually resulted in those behaviors?" Surely you know already that there are many other variables—aside from the effectiveness of the training design—that influence performance on the job: training delivery, supervision, reinforcement, reward and compensation systems, clarity of performance expectations, personal motivation, and resources and systems, to name a few. The critical challenge of a Level 3 evaluation is to isolate the relationship between training and on-the-job performance.

Level 4, Results, asks, "What is the impact of the training on organizational objectives?" It measures, for example, whether the training has resulted in increased sales, fewer quality problems, decreased customer complaints, decreased production time, or increased profits. Level 4 is an evaluation of the return on investment. It is a critical question to ask about training, as the investment of time and money in training is significant. Like Level 3, it can be difficult to plan and manage; there are many variables besides training that influence organizational objectives. For example, a very successful sales training program could lead to dramatic behavioral changes in a sales force (Level 3); those changes would ordinarily lead to dramatic positive changes in sales figures (Level 4), but a competitor's new product or campaign could hurt sales and wash out the effects of new sales skills. Carefully constructed and analyzed Level 4 evaluations would ferret out or at least raise questions about relevant variables.

Responsibility for Evaluation Levels

All training designers are responsible for Level 2 evaluations, as many of the learning activities that the designer develops are themselves measures of behavior. For example, if you design a game in which participants earn points by answering questions correctly, the game uses behaviors that indicate the group's mastery of content.

Many designers also design evaluation forms that are used during or at the end of training; these forms generally focus on Level 1, the participants' reactions to the learning event. In some organizational settings, Level 3 and Level 4 evaluations are done with input from training designers; in some, they are planned and implemented by others in the organization.

The SIM will help you to plan a strategy and to design tools for evaluation in relation to your responsibilities.

Incorporating Level 1 and 2 Evaluations in the Design

As the designer, you have the chance to determine when and how to do Level 1 and Level 2 evaluations. We recommend that you design them right into the training event whenever possible; doing so will provide both the trainer and the participants with opportunities to make adjustments as necessary.

Level 1 Evaluations. There is a tendency to think of Level 1 evaluations as "smile sheets" completed by participants at the end of training. We have two major concerns about this tendency.

First, the term "smile sheets" implies that the data being gathered are of little value. True, it is a challenging task to construct evaluations so as to obtain useful data, but a Level 1 evaluation is not a throwaway. It is a rich opportunity to obtain immediate feedback from your key clients—the learners. If the perception of the learning event is negative, even if the objectives have been met, the impact is bound to be felt. Future participants may come to training with negative expectations, which might diminish the effectiveness of the training program. Also, whether or not trainers and designers like it, part of their job is to market training services in an organization. The perceptions of the end users (the participants) will largely determine whether and how the services are used.

Our second concern has to do with timing. If learners are displeased with some aspect of training that is under the control of the trainer, what good is it to find out only at the end of the event? Of course, if the event is to be replicated, then changes can be made for the future offerings. But why wait? As the designer, you can include evaluation points that the trainer can use to make adjustments during the learning event, both to increase its effectiveness and to send a clear message that learners are valued customers. For example, you can include a spot check during a break in the training, asking participants to identify what is going well and what they would like more of or less of. Participants might share their reactions in a large group, write them on index cards, or jot them on a flip chart on the way out of the room for a break.

Level 2 Evaluations. Aside from learning activities that are themselves Level 2 evaluation tools, other tools can be used to measure learning. Tests given during or after training are one example. In addition, during or at the end of training, you can ask participants about their perceptions of what they have learned. After the training, you can use focus groups or interviews to evaluate what participants learned. Naturally, the longer you wait to evaluate learning after the training, the more you will have to account for forgetting—especially if the learning has not been reinforced through some transfer mechanisms. Planning for this type of Level 2 evaluation is clearly a part of the designer's task.

THE DESIGNER AND THE CATERER

Imagine the caterer preparing for the party. At this point, she will have an overall plan for how to evaluate success, as well as some specific ways to conduct the evaluation. She will have some checkpoints established during the preparation process—times when she can assess whether she is on target. She will have some ideas about what she needs to assess after the party—probably including how much food came back (an observation that may need some further probing in order to determine the causes) and to what extent the party ran on schedule. She may also have planned some questions that she will ask the client during a post-party interview.

HOW TO DESIGN EVALUATION TOOLS

When you have completed the steps for this stage of the SIM, you will have created a strategy for evaluating the success of your training design and the tools to implement your evaluation strategy.

RECOMMENDED RESOURCES FOR EVALUATION

If you are interested in learning more about the specific techniques of designing evaluation tools, here are some excellent resources:

American Society for Training and Development. *Info-Line* series. Alexandria, VA: Author. ("Essentials of evaluation" [1986] [#8601]; "Measuring attitudinal and behavioral change" [1991] [#9110]; "Testing for learning outcomes" [1989] [#8907].)

American Society for Training and Development. (1992). Evaluating the results of training. In *ASTD Trainer's Toolkit.* Alexandria, VA: Author.

Mager, R. F. (1997). *Measuring instructional results.* Atlanta, GA: Center for Effective Performance.

Phillips, J. J. (1997). *Return on investment.* Houston, TX: Gulf.

Phillips, J. J. (ed.). (1994). *In action: Measuring return on investment.* Alexandria, VA: American Society for Training and Development.

Before plunging into the steps below, clarify your responsibilities regarding evaluation: Are you expected to evaluate at all four levels? At Levels 1, 2, and 3 only? Or just at Levels 1 and 2? After you are clear on the expectations, then you can apply the steps within the scope of your responsibility.

THE SEVEN STEPS IN EVALUATION TOOLS

1. Determine who needs evaluation data.
2. Establish data requirements for each client.
3. Develop the evaluation strategy.
4. Draft evaluation tools.
5. Review and edit evaluation tools.
6. Solicit feedback on evaluation tools.
7. Finalize the evaluation tools.

1. Determine Who Needs Evaluation Data. The first step in developing an evaluation strategy and evaluation tools is to identify your clients. Who needs information concerning the success of this training event? The key word here is *needs.* Many designers are so accustomed to providing certain types of evaluation summaries to certain people in the organization that they no longer question why. This first step is meant to help you focus your evaluation strategy by starting with your clients. Here is how to approach the task:

______ Identify key people who have been involved with the request for and development of the training.

______ Consider the typical recipients of training-evaluation data, and identify those who need data about this particular training event. Recipients may include any or all of the following:

- ______ Participants
- ______ Trainers
- ______ Other designers
- ______ Supervisors and managers
- ______ Senior management
- ______ Training/Human Resource Department
- ______ Training committees
- ______ Union representatives

_____ With many of your potential recipients, it may be fairly easy to determine whether they really need the information. With others, you may want to initiate a conversation to clarify their needs.

During this process, you may well identify some people who do not really need data but want them, and there may be organizational or political reasons for satisfying their wishes. In fact, unless there is some compelling argument against it (for example, your direct client has asked you not to), you will most likely provide them the evaluation data.

2. Establish Data Requirements for Each Client. To avoid overwhelming people with data and to manage time, resources, and energy, do your best to provide only the data that a particular client needs. For example, trainers may be most interested in data related to their performance and the perceived usefulness of the training; operational managers may care more about test results. At the same time, be realistic about how you and your organization can manipulate data; first, define requirements so you will be able to edit out the data that clients do not want. Here is how:

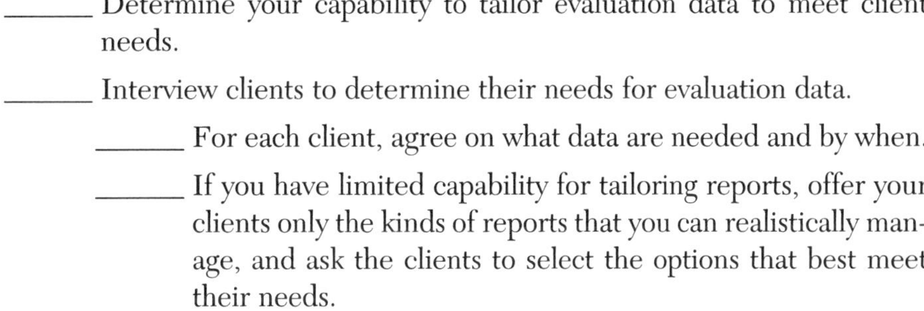

_____ Determine your capability to tailor evaluation data to meet client needs.

_____ Interview clients to determine their needs for evaluation data.

- _____ For each client, agree on what data are needed and by when.
- _____ If you have limited capability for tailoring reports, offer your clients only the kinds of reports that you can realistically manage, and ask the clients to select the options that best meet their needs.

Be prepared to use your best interpersonal and negotiating skills during these interviews. A client may well want data that you cannot reasonably provide. Negotiate requirements so that your client obtains the data she needs and so that you can be confident that you can supply the data in the agreed-on time frame.

3. Develop the Evaluation Strategy. You know by this time what you or your organization is capable of gathering, and you know what your clients need. Now you develop the strategy to identify when you will gather data, from whom, and how.

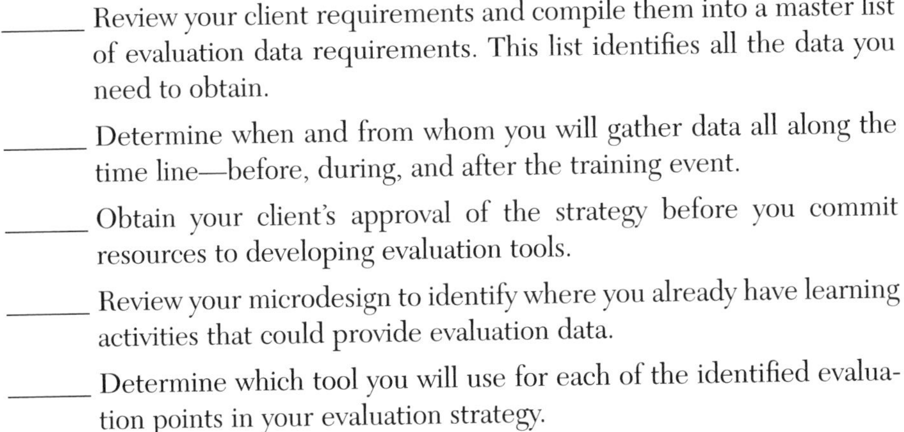

_____ Review your client requirements and compile them into a master list of evaluation data requirements. This list identifies all the data you need to obtain.

_____ Determine when and from whom you will gather data all along the time line—before, during, and after the training event.

_____ Obtain your client's approval of the strategy before you commit resources to developing evaluation tools.

_____ Review your microdesign to identify where you already have learning activities that could provide evaluation data.

_____ Determine which tool you will use for each of the identified evaluation points in your evaluation strategy.

Remember, the point of having a strategy is to be able to gather, analyze, and distribute the necessary data to help make sure the training is meeting organizational objectives. Keep sight of that purpose.

4. Draft Evaluation Tools. For each of the evaluation tools that you identified in your evaluation strategy, you or someone else must design a tool that will gather the required data. For example, if you need supervisory feedback on changed behaviors three weeks after the training, then design an evaluation tool that will obtain the information from supervisors. To prepare for drafting each of the evaluation tools:

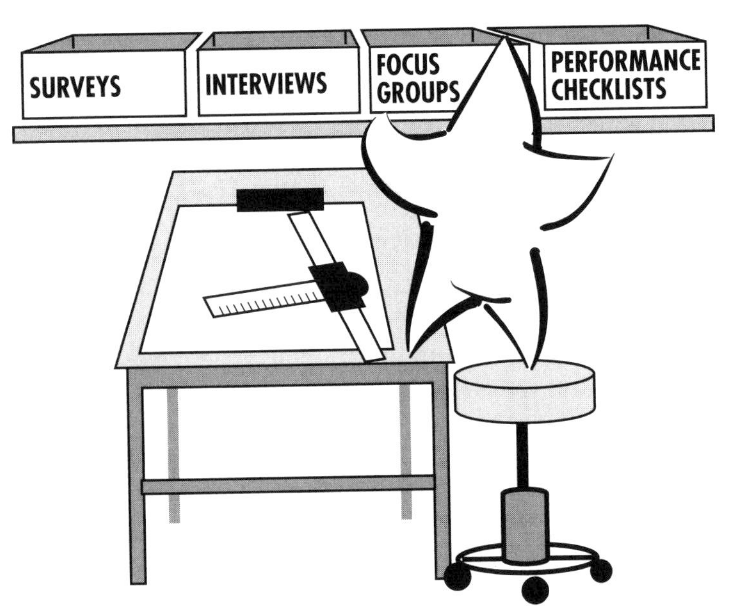

_____ Articulate clearly what data you must collect in this particular part of your evaluation strategy. Ask yourself, "What am I trying to find out here?"

_____ Consider the needs and abilities of those who will provide the data. You do not want to place unreasonable demands on people, lest you adversely affect the data you collect. Also, you do not want to use language or ask people to provide feedback on areas beyond their expertise. For example, it is probably not a good idea to ask participants what they thought of the organizational structure in the training design, although that language would have meaning for designers. Instead, you might ask, "How easy was it to follow the training as it moved from point to point?"

_______ Consult resources, as needed, to help you draft tools. (Also see the "Recommended Resources" listed earlier in this chapter.)

EVALUATION TOOLS

Tools for evaluating training come in a wide range of varieties. Here are some of the types most commonly employed:

- Tests
- Performance observation
- Interviews
- Focus groups
- Surveys and questionnaires
- Learning activities wherein participants demonstrate competencies

---

5. Review and Edit Evaluation Tools. Be certain that the tools you have designed will, in fact, obtain the data your clients require. Also ensure that the tools are as efficient as possible and that they fit both your organization and those who will be using them. Here is how to do that:

_______ Review each tool, asking yourself the following questions:

_______ Does the tool probe for the evaluation information that is required for this particular need?

_______ Are there any questions or requests for information that can be deleted from the tool?

_______ Is the tool written in language that will be familiar to the user?

_______ Is the tool compatible with any organizational standards for evaluation?

_______ Modify the evaluation tools as necessary.

Basically, you are checking to make sure that your evaluation tools will be *effective*—will obtain the required data; *efficient*—will do so in the easiest, most direct way possible; and *engaging*—will be designed in such a way that people will actually use them.

6. Solicit Feedback on Evaluation Tools. Evaluation tools, like participant materials, will be going into the hands of your clients. Make certain that they are as easy as possible to use; the best way to find out is to ask for feedback. Questions that may seem perfectly direct and straightforward to you may seem vague or complicated to clients. Here is how to obtain feedback that will be useful:

______ For reviewers, select representative clients from all relevant sectors.

______ Give reviewers some guidance about the kind of feedback you want—on language, ease of use, or content, for example.

After you have the feedback, you can decide which changes you wish to incorporate.

7. Finalize the Evaluation Tools. Using the feedback and your own judgment, decide which of the reviewers' comments to incorporate in your final evaluation tools. Then make the changes; some of them may take you back into the materials you prepared in the previous step of the SIM, and that is okay. As you did when finalizing your materials, bear several considerations in mind:

______ Look especially for patterns in the feedback.

______ Proofread and check materials carefully, asking for help if you can.

______ Allow a little extra time, just in case anything goes wrong.

After you have finished your evaluation tools, you can send your materials to be duplicated, because now you really are finished with the SIM design process. You have a training event that is ready to be tried out. Congratulations!

COMMON QUESTIONS

Question: Do I need to use an evaluation form at the end of every training session?

Answer: We don't think so. The key is what data your clients need. If your clients need to know about every offering of a particular workshop, then you need to do an evaluation at the end of every offering. If they need data about the perceived usefulness of a new process that is being introduced in the training, then you might be able to use a random sample.

Do keep asking the question. There seems to be an unwritten law that says, "Use an evaluation form at the end of every workshop." But why? Evaluation forms take time to design, administer, and analyze. They are a means to an end, not an end in themselves. We recommend that you use them only when they are needed for gathering the required data. If your design incorporates Level 1 and Level 2 evaluations as part of the learning event, you may not need any evaluation at the end.

One of the most common purposes of evaluation forms is to check out whether the training is working well or whether it needs modification. For this purpose, there are alternatives to having every participant complete an end-of-workshop evaluation—such as random-sample surveys, focus groups, and informal interviews.

Question: Can you give me at least a few tips on constructing evaluation forms, especially for Level 1 evaluations?

Answer: Here are three key considerations we use in constructing evaluation forms.

The first is the issue of *standard* versus *tailored* forms. If you use a standard form for all workshops, then comparing data is quite simple; the drawback is that you are limited to general questions. If you tailor the form with specific questions about content, objectives, and learning activities for the particular learning event, you will obtain more focused data, but comparing them with evaluations of other learning events will be more complicated. To strike a balance, you can combine standard and tailored questions.

Second is the issue of *narrative* versus *numerical* evaluation. Obviously, both gathering and comparing data are easier with numerical than with narrative evaluation formats. However, numbers alone do not tell enough about what was positive or problematic about a particular learning event. Here, too, many designers use a combination of evaluation items. To make the most of narrative items, limit their number and focus the questions on the required information. For example, if your supervisory or management clients are looking for data about transfer of learning, then instead of asking, "What can management do to reinforce what you have learned in here?" it might be better to ask, "What are three concrete, practical, and realistic things your supervisor or manager could do to ensure that you will transfer what you learned in here back to your job?"

A final consideration is how to construct the *evaluation scales.* Deciding whether to use a four-point or five-point evaluation scale may seem like an insignificant issue, but it is not. In general, we recommend using a four-point scale wherever possible, with the choices equally divided between positive and negative options. If you provide an even number of choices, participants pretty much have to express an opinion; they cannot just pick the middle of the scale. It is also important to avoid using an evaluation scale that mirrors other scales in your organization (such as performance appraisal ratings or quality ratings), so that the evaluation data will not be influenced by the other scales.

Question: You talked about using spot checks during the workshop to do evaluations. But isn't this setting the trainer up for failure?

Answer: This can be a significant concern. If the trainer has no control over something, why ask participants whether they like it? For example, if your organization requires that new employees take tests to measure their product knowledge during their initial training, then why ask for feedback on whether participants like the tests? Everyone has to take them, no matter what. However, it might be very useful to both the participants and the trainer to ask, "What are we doing in the training that is helping you prepare for the tests? What else could we do that would help you?"

So your question is particularly important to the designer as he microdesigns Level 1 spot-check evaluations for the training. If, on the one hand, he is designing an evaluation to help the trainer modify the training as she goes forward, he wants to make sure that the product of the evaluation, as well as the initiator he prepares, will focus on obtaining information the trainer can do something about.

On the other hand, there may be times when the designer wants to encourage participants to make judgments—to evaluate—simply because assigning personal value to what is being learned is an important part of adult learning. With such evaluations, the designer will want to make it clear to trainers that they are to acknowledge judgments but not try to change them. For example, in the debriefing after a major segment of learning in our work, we often ask participants to consider what we have just covered in three categories: what confirmed something they already knew or believed before the training; new insights, or "light bulbs," gained; and things they want to think about because they are not quite comfortable yet with how they would use them. This is a key evaluation point; the discussion that it engenders provides the trainer with plenty of data about participant comprehension, insights, and comfort levels. There may be subtle ways, later in the training, in which the trainer will attend to what is uncomfortable; but the designer wants to give the trainer clear directions that this is not the time to try to talk participants out of their discomfort. To do so would send the message that it is not okay to pass personal judgment on what is being learned.

The key to designing evaluation points within the training is to do what you can to ensure that the trainer can respond appropriately, whatever the evaluation feedback.

Question: I'm discouraged. You've been saying that the SIM is an iterative process, but it still seems to me that by this stage I shouldn't have to do any major modifications in my design. I just realized, as I was designing evaluation tools for my training, that I can't measure the behaviors that my training objectives specified. I said that participants would be able to demonstrate their ability to manage difficult customers, and there is no way I can evaluate that competency in a three-hour training. Iterative or not, I feel that I should have caught this problem much earlier. What did I do wrong?

Answer: It can be discouraging to find that you have to go back to an early design stage at this point, but it is far better than pretending that everything is okay and then going forward with objectives you cannot meet. Probably this painful awareness will make you much more realistic next time you are designing and trying to make your objectives BAG 'M.

Take heart. This probably is not a major change in your design. You have just realized that it is not attainable to have participants demonstrate the skill during the training. You can adjust the objective down from the how-to level to the about-how-to level and have participants describe how they would use what they have learned to manage difficult customers. You could have them select specific techniques from the training that they wish to practice on the job and identify what types of difficult customers these techniques would help them manage.

After you adjust your objectives so that they BAG 'M, you have two tasks: first, review the rest of your design and make adjustments to support the new objectives. This adjustment is usually in the area of training flow, specifically in learning activities. Second, you may wish to talk with your client about transfer systems that can be put into place to ensure that the competency (managing difficult customers) will be demonstrated, coached, and reinforced soon after the training.

Question: I find it very difficult to persuade participants to write much on workshop evaluation forms. They will fill in the numbers, but the comment spaces are generally left blank.

Answer: We experience the same challenge. It seems that participants have become so accustomed to end-of-training evaluation forms that it is difficult to change their perceptions simply by the way the form is constructed. Nevertheless, we have found some techniques that help:

- Limit requests for narrative comments to those places where the data are truly required.

- Have the trainer spend a moment before the evaluation highlighting why the feedback is important and what will be done with it.
- When the evaluation data are especially important (as in the pilot of a program), do not rely on the written evaluation form as the primary source for the data; consider adding a Level 1 evaluation discussion at the end of training. Sometimes we ask participants to individually write their answers to two or three key evaluation questions and then have a large-group discussion of their responses. If necessary, we can quantify their responses as part of the discussion, and we can also collect their written responses. Participants seem more likely to think through their written comments when they know there will be a discussion. If you include such an evaluation discussion in your training design, think about whether to have the trainer or someone else facilitate the discussion. Participants may find it difficult to provide feedback when the person who delivered the training is facilitating the evaluation discussion.

Question: Frequently, I use how-to objectives because I want to focus on having participants demonstrate competencies. However, realistically I know that the trainer will not be able to observe and evaluate every participant demonstrating this skill. Does this mean that I have to change the objective?

Answer: Not necessarily. If there is an organizational reason why the trainer absolutely must evaluate every participant's competency in a specific area, then design a tool to meet that need. However, for most training it is perfectly acceptable for participants to demonstrate a particular skill (described in the training objectives) and receive some form of feedback on their performance—not necessarily formal evaluation. Such feedback can come from individual participants themselves, from success on the task, from other participants, or from the trainer. The participants are still demonstrating success at the behavior identified in the objective, so there is no need to change the objective.

Question: I find Level 3 evaluations almost impossible to design and implement. I do not want to set the evaluation up in a way that training is held accountable for things beyond its control. Often, the reason an employee is not using a skill mastered in training has nothing to do with the training.

Answer: You are absolutely right on both counts. Level 3 evaluations are difficult to design, and the lack of application of a learned skill may have nothing to do with the effectiveness of the training design or delivery.

Evaluation data should raise questions, not point fingers. If performance data suggest that behaviors demonstrated in training are not being applied on the job, then raise the questions about why. Perhaps the simulations in the training were not close enough to the work situation to make the skill transferable; that would be a design issue. There may be a host of other reasons—such as lack of a system or of management support for the new behavior—that have nothing to do with the training design.

Another way to address the accountability issue has to do with the training process; design and delivery are just two components of that process (Chapter Five). As long as an organization considers only design and delivery in its assumptions about training, then Level 3 evaluations are dangerous—because, no matter what goes wrong, it will be interpreted as the fault of the training design or delivery. When the organization makes the transition to thinking of the entire training process, then Level 3 evaluations really can raise questions about where to make improvements that will help increase the application of desired behaviors on the job. The areas for improvement can be in the assessment of needs, the design of training, the delivery of training, transfer systems and structures, evaluation strategies and tools, or the alignment of the entire process with the organizational objectives. In fact, the problem may stem from unarticulated or poorly developed organizational objectives. A full appreciation for the training process shifts the ownership for learning to all individuals, groups, systems, and structures that facilitate learning within the organization.

BEFORE YOU MOVE ON

"What?" you ask. "I'm done?" You are. And if all has gone well, you have come from the identification of training needs to the completed design of a training event that addresses those training needs. It is time to move on to the next project or to the ten other design projects you have been juggling during your work on this particular design.

We would like you to take a moment to reflect on two things at this point. First, look in your imaginary computer files to marvel at what you have created. Second, look at yourself in relation to the SIM and see how it fits for you.

Let's look back at those computer files, now that you have completed the SIM design process. In the Goals and Objectives file, the umbrella with your goal for the training and the objectives with related skills under the umbrella are now solid and fixed. You are quite comfortable that your design supports the goals and objectives and that, by meeting these objectives, participants will be enabled to be more successful at their jobs or life tasks. The second file, Key Topics, is empty. In the third file, Training Flow—Macrodesign, is the big-picture outline. The fourth file, Training Flow—Microdesign, is a detailed outline of the learning event. The outline contains sequenced learning activities, objectives for each activity, process directions, key initiators and transitions, and time estimates. The Materials file contains three subfiles. The first subfile, Participant Materials, has all the materials that participants will use before, during, and after the training; it may include worksheets, job aids, a workbook, articles, and other resources. The second, Trainer's Materials, has the trainer's guide and any resource materials you have prepared for the trainer. The third, Learning Aids, has all the audio and visual materials you have selected or designed to establish the learning environment; it may contain models, videos, flip charts, wall charts, electronic tools, or music.

The final file is your newest addition: Evaluation Tools. It contains two things: your evaluation strategy, which identifies when and how you will eval-

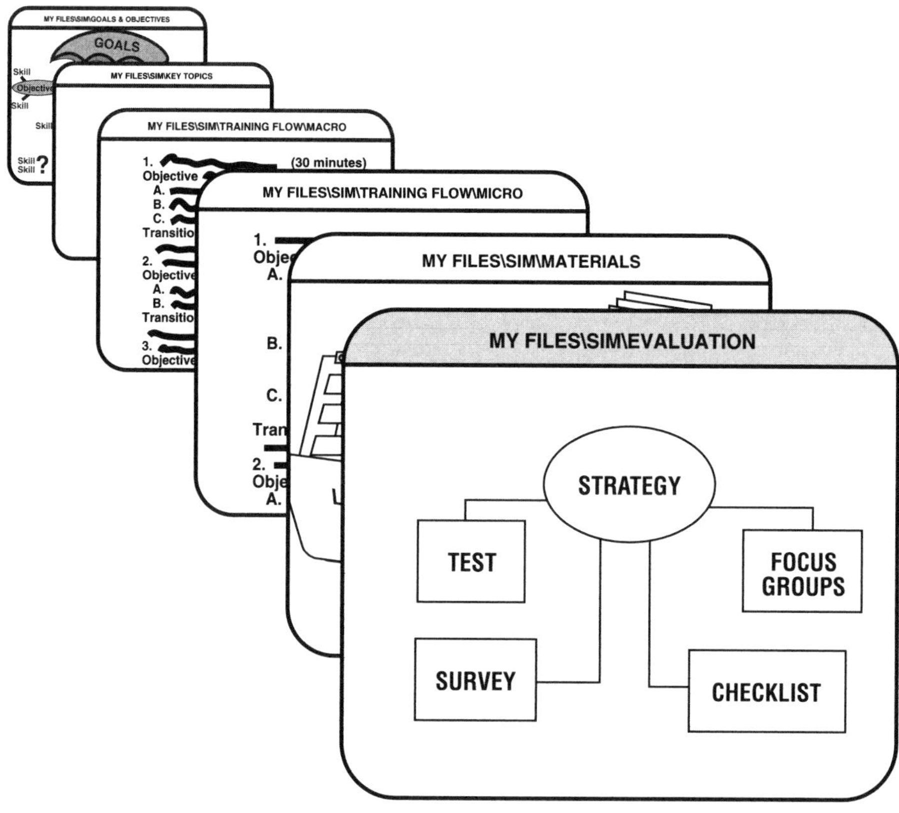

uate and from whom you will obtain data; and the evaluation tools you have designed to support your strategy, such as tests, surveys, directions for facilitating focus groups, and checklists for performance observations.

You have created everything it will take to help learners to master the training objectives that will enable them to perform the desired behaviors and to measure their success.

How about you and the SIM? You are an adult learner, and you have just gone through a comprehensive design process. We offer you the following questions to support your learning:

- What parts of the SIM are already parts of your design process (even though you may have called them by other names)?
- What parts are new to you?
- What parts feel comfortable or uncomfortable to you?
- What parts do you think will improve your design process?
- Next time you design, what are two or three things from the SIM that you definitely want to work on?
- What picture comes to mind that expresses what you would most like to remember about the SIM?
- What analogies work for you? The SIM is like a . . . , because . . .

OUR HOPE

We trust that you will find the SIM a powerful and practical process for design. It is the result of many years of designing training and coaching others to do so. We know that it works. We know that it can help you capitalize on what you do well and stretch into the areas that do not come naturally. The stretch may sometimes feel painful, but we believe it is ultimately rewarding.

We suggest that you follow the SIM several times to become comfortable with the entire process and then make it your own. Adapt it to fit your design style and your design situation. It is a tool—a very powerful tool. Experience tells us that we work best with any new tool—an electric drill, a communication skill, a meditation practice, a software package—when we spend time becoming used to it and letting it become our own. Do spend the time with the SIM.

We hope that the SIM will feel ever more comfortable, reliable, and useful as you design training events that are effective, efficient, and engaging.

Looking Back

Here is the SIM process up to this point:

Goals and Objectives

1. Review design requirements.
2. Establish a goal statement.
3. Brainstorm the skills for reaching the desired behaviors.
4. Edit: determine essential versus nonessential skills for reaching the desired behaviors.
5. Consolidate: cluster related skills together.
6. Draft objectives.
7. Review and edit the proposed goals and objectives.
8. Review the goals and objectives with your client.

Key Topics

1. Research the subject.
2. Brainstorm possible key points.
3. Determine essential versus nonessential points.
4. Group key points into key topics.
5. Identify additional points for key topics.
6. Consider possible organizational structures.
7. Review and edit key topics.
8. Check work with your client.

Training Flow—Macrodesign

1. Research existing activities.
2. Brainstorm activities.
3. Select possible activities.
4. Estimate time for possible activities.
5. Outline training design.
6. Articulate objectives for segments.
7. Sketch out transitions.
8. Review your macrodesign.
9. Check macrodesign with your client.

Training Flow—Microdesign

1. Identify specific objective for each activity.
2. Define the universe of acceptable responses.
3. Develop the steps and the processes for each activity.
4. Refine time estimates.
5. Develop initiators.
6. Develop transitions.
7. Check time estimates one final time.
8. Review microdesign.
9. Complete outline of the training design.
10. Determine whether to check the microdesign with your client.

Training Materials

1. Establish requirements for materials.
2. Identify what training materials are required and what materials are optional.
3. Draft required materials.
4. Review drafts of required materials.
5. Select, draft, and review optional materials.
6. Have others review the materials.
7. Finalize the materials.

Evaluation Tools

1. Determine who needs evaluation data.
2. Establish data requirements for each client.
3. Develop the evaluation strategy.
4. Draft evaluation tools.
5. Review and edit evaluation tools.
6. Solicit feedback on evaluation tools.
7. Finalize the evaluation tools.

Running Example: Evaluation Tools

Simone, having put her training materials into good shape, turns to finalizing the evaluation strategy and tools. All along, she has been having discussions with her key client on the senior management team about what is important to evaluate. The request for this training came about because there has been a steady increase in employee complaints about written appraisals in the past sixteen months, and senior management is eager to reduce the complaints. Simone and the client are clear that the training Simone is designing will be only one part of the organizational intervention to address the problem.

On this project, Simone is responsible for the strategy and for the selection or design of all tools for evaluation at Level 1 (Reaction) and Level 2 (Learning). She will also be a member of an evaluation team that will develop the strategy and tools for evaluation at Level 3 (Behavior) and Level 4 (Results). Here is how Simone goes about her work on this part of the design:

1. Determine Who Needs Evaluation Data

Three key client groups require evaluation data for this project:

- The senior management team, which requested the training
- The training team, which includes the two trainers and Simone
- The director of employee relations

Simone is glad to be part of the team that is responsible for the Level 3 and 4 evaluations. The client groups that she has identified are interested in better written appraisals (Behavior, Level 3) and a decrease in employee complaints (Results, Level 4). Much of what Simone will learn in the next step, when she interviews clients to determine their data needs, will be useful to the evaluation team.

2. Establish Data Requirements for Each Client

In terms of capability to tailor evaluation data, Jexon is a very interesting place. It is highly sophisticated in its ability to gather, analyze, and disseminate data; at the same time, it is a culture in which great pains are taken to keep things simple—that is, keep the data to what is absolutely required so that people are not overwhelmed with the unimportant and miss the truly important. For that reason, every client group has told Simone to keep the evaluation process as simple as possible.

Here are the results of her client interviews:

Senior Management Team

Level 1

What:

- Would like summary of perceptions of learning event.
- Mainly concerned with perceptions of relevance and usefulness of what is presented.

When: Would like summary data every two weeks during training cycle.

Level 2

What:

- Not concerned that formal data be gathered during training. Comfortable with having trainer evaluate demonstrated group competencies.
- Because there will be a time lag between when some participants take this training and when they will write appraisals, senior management wants data to indicate retention between the training and the time of appraisal writing.

When: Every two weeks between start of training and time when appraisals must be written.

Level 3

What: Want evaluation data from the director of employee relations indicating changes in written appraisals.

When: Three times a week during two-week cycle when appraisals are due.

Level 4

What: Data comparing number of employee complaints in this appraisal year compared with previous two cycles.

When: Weekly for first month after appraisals are written, then monthly for remainder of year.

Training Team

Level 1

What: Perceptions of learning event; particularly

- Usefulness of content
- Trainer performance
- Ease of using new automated registration system
- Timeliness of receiving prereading materials
- Usefulness of participant materials (especially job aids)
- Effectiveness of learning activities

When: Day after each session.

Level 2

What:

- Want assurance during training that participants are meeting objectives.
- Like senior managers, also want some data between end of training and start of writing appraisals.

When: First, during event; second, flexible after event.

Level 3

What and when: Same as senior managers.

Level 4

What and when: Same as senior managers.

Director of Employee Relations

Level 1

What: Wants data indicating usefulness and relevance of what is presented.

When: At least every two weeks in training cycle.

Level 2

No request for data.

Level 3

What: Wants to see random samples of evaluations.

When: Every two to three days during two-week period when appraisals are to be written.

Level 4

What: Data concerning employee complaints regarding appraisals.

When: Weekly for three months after appraisals are written, then monthly for remainder of year.

3. Develop the Evaluation Strategy

Simone forwards the requests for Level 3 and Level 4 data to the other members of the evaluation team. She will focus her evaluation strategy on Levels 1 and 2 data. The remainder of the evaluation strategy will be worked out by the evaluation team.

As she compiles the requirements from the three client groups for Level 1 and Level 2 evaluation data, Simone comes up with the following list:

Level 1

- Perceptions of relevance and usefulness of content
- Trainer performance
- Registration system
- Timeliness of receiving prereading material
- Usefulness of participant materials (especially job aids)
- Effectiveness of learning activities

Level 2

- Meeting objectives during training
- Retention of learning after training but before writing of appraisals

Simone's strategy involves six critical evaluation points:

- The training pilot
- During training
- Immediately after training
- Between the training and the writing of appraisals

- During the writing of actual appraisals
- After employees receive appraisals

All the data Simone needs for evaluations at Levels 1 and 2 will be obtained from the supervisors and managers who go through the training. Data for Levels 3 and 4 will come from the employee relations team. There is no need to gather any additional baseline data before the training because there already are data about skills (existing appraisals on file) and complaints (employee relations data).

Here is the strategy Simone presents to her clients:

Pilot

Tool. Debrief (written and oral). Immediately after the pilot, a trainer (the one not delivering the pilot) will facilitate an hour-long discussion focusing on perceived usefulness and relevance of content, usefulness of participant materials (especially job aids), and effectiveness of learning activities.

Process. Data will be summarized, tailored to meet client requests, and distributed at a joint meeting the day after the pilot. Any recommendations for modifications will be presented at that meeting.

During Training

Tool. Learning activities. Simone has reviewed the microdesign, and she is confident that the activities provide ample opportunity for participants to demonstrate the behaviors described in the training objectives. She will highlight in the trainer's guide where these checkpoints occur in the training.

Process. The trainers and Simone have agreed to meet twice a week during the training cycle to review their observations regarding demonstration of competencies during the training.

Immediately After Training

Tool. E-mail evaluation form. The form will focus on participants' perceptions of usefulness and relevance of content, usefulness of participant materials (especially job aids), trainer performance, the registration system, and timeliness of prereading materials.

Process. Data will be summarized, and tailored reports will be distributed to appropriate clients weekly during training cycle.

Between Training and Writing Appraisals

Tools. E-mail activities; application activities. Quick exercises, distributed regularly by e-mail, can serve as a transfer mechanism; assuming that the activities are short and anonymous, they can also provide data on skill mastery and retention. The application activities can be part of the coaching tool that Simone has developed to serve as an additional transfer mechanism.

Process. The data from the e-mail activities will be summarized weekly. The data from the application activities in the coaching tool will be summarized in managers' weekly reports, to indicate any patterns observed in appraisal-writing skills. Trends from the two tools will point out any interventions that will be needed before the beginning of the appraisal writing.

During Appraisal-Writing Cycle

Tools. Survey by e-mail or phone. A random sample of participants will be asked to complete a brief survey by e-mail or phone, focusing on how often they are using job aids and perceived usefulness of job aids.

Process. Data will be summarized, and tailored reports will be distributed to appropriate clients every two days during two-week appraisal writing cycle.

After Employees Receive Appraisals

Tools. Complaints received in employee relations. The employee relations team will summarize the data and forward the summary to the senior management team and the training team.

The clients approve Simone's strategy, commenting that it is very much in line with Jexon's culture. The demands on participants will be reasonable, and the information about learning activities will be available quickly enough that modifications can be made if necessary.

Senior managers are particularly enthusiastic about the evaluation point during the appraisal-writing cycle; that survey should yield important data and will also help reinforce management's concern about the quality of the appraisals. They make one recommendation: even though only a random sample will actually be surveyed, all supervisors and managers should be notified by e-mail that they may be asked to participate in a brief survey about using the job aids for writing appraisals. Just receiving the notification will remind supervisors and managers about the job aids and help reinforce the importance of well-written appraisals. Simone thinks that this is a great idea, and it will be easy to do with the Jexon e-mail system. She readily agrees.

4. Draft Evaluation Tools

Simone is fortunate to have excellent resources within Jexon to help with the design and construction of evaluation tools. The experts wholeheartedly support the "keep it simple" philosophy. Piece by piece, Simone drafts all the evaluation tools.

Simone's Draft: Debrief of Pilot

Facilitator's Outline

1. Thank participants for taking part in pilot.
2. Reinforce importance of evaluation data and how they will be used.
3. Ask participants to complete evaluation form; tell them that it will be discussed.
4. Individual work on evaluation form (attached).
5. *Discussion:* Go through each question; solicit and record feedback. Tell participants that they may change ratings during discussion if they wish. Evaluation forms will be collected at end of debrief.

Simone's Draft: Evaluation Form for Pilot

Evaluation, "First-Class Appraisals" Pilot

Key Content	*Very Useful*	*Useful*	*Somewhat Useful*	*Not Useful*
~~	____	____	____	____
~~	____	____	____	____
~~	____	____	____	____
Learning Activities	*Very Effective*	*Effective*	*Somewhat Effective*	*Not Effective*
~~	____	____	____	____
~~	____	____	____	____
~~	____	____	____	____
Participant Materials	*Very Useful*	*Useful*	*Somewhat Useful*	*Not Useful*
~~	____	____	____	____
~~	____	____	____	____
~~	____	____	____	____

Simone's Draft: E-Mail Evaluation

Training Evaluation, "First-Class Appraisals"

Thank you for participating in the First-Class Appraisals workshop. To help us ensure that the training we provide continues to meet your needs, please complete this brief survey and use the automatic return feature. Please return it within two days.

Thank you for your time! We hope the workshop and materials will make your job easier and more satisfying.

Usefulness of Content

The key content covered in the training was

Overall, I found the content to be

___ very useful ___ useful ___ somewhat useful ___ not useful

The content I found most useful was

The content I found least useful was

Usefulness of Materials

The materials you received as part of the workshop included

Overall, I found the materials to be

___ very useful ___ useful ___ somewhat useful ___ not useful

The materials I found most useful were

The materials I found least useful were

continued

E-Mail Registration System

Jexon has introduced a new e-mail registration system that you used for this workshop. We are very interested in your reaction to this new system.

What I like best about the registration system

What I like least about the system

Suggestions for the system

Workshop Prereading Materials

You received prereading materials for this workshop. How long before the workshop did you receive the materials?

From your point of view, was the timing of the materials

_____ too early _____ just right _____ too late

Trainer's Performance

Your trainer, [system inserts name], would like feedback on management of the training. Please rate your trainer, using the scale provided, with 4 being the highest and 1 being the lowest rating.

	4	3	2	1
Treating learners with respect	_____	_____	_____	_____
Knowledge of subject	_____	_____	_____	_____
Ability to involve participants	_____	_____	_____	_____

Comments/suggestions to the trainer

General comments/suggestions

Simone's Draft: E-Mail/Telephone Survey

Job Aids, "First-Class Appraisals"

Thank you for taking the time to respond to this survey. It will take under ninety seconds, we promise!

When you participated in the "First-Class Appraisals" workshop, you received some resources to help you write performance appraisals, and now is the time for those appraisals!

How often are you using the job aids to help you write appraisals?

_____ very often _____ regularly _____ rarely _____ not at all

If you are using the job aids, how useful are they to you?

___ very useful ___ useful ___ somewhat useful ___ not useful

Any comments or suggestions related to the job aids?

Thanks again!

5. Review and Edit Evaluation Tools

To review her materials, Simone asks herself four critical questions about each one:

- *Does the tool probe for the evaluation information that is required for this particular need?* Yes. Each of the tools clearly solicits the required evaluation data.
- *Are there any questions or requests for information that can be deleted from the tool?* There do not seem to be, but the e-mail post-training evaluation may be too long. Will ask for feedback from reviewers to see if it can be cut down without sacrificing the required data.
- *Is the tool written in language that will be familiar to the user?* Yes. In particular, the key content and learning activities are listed wherever feedback about them is solicited—both to remind participants of what they were and to allow for the possibility that the terms "key content" and "learning activities" might not be familiar to them.

- *Is the tool compatible with any organizational standards for evaluation?* Absolutely. Jexon consistently uses e-mail evaluations successfully; the people coming to the pilot have already agreed to stay for a one-hour debrief; and the random-sample survey on job aids is brief and to the point.

One possibility for shortening the e-mail post-training evaluation might be to do two versions: a version including just the numerical items, another including the narrative items as well. The automated system could send the longer form to a random sample of participants, the short form to the remaining participants. If this approach is chosen, the evaluation experts can help Simone determine what size sample she will need for statistically significant results. She decides to wait for feedback before acting on this idea.

6. Solicit Feedback on Evaluation Tools

Simone selects six representative reviewers, and for each of the written evaluation tools, she asks them to provide the same kind of information.

Simone's Draft: Request for Feedback

Dear ________________:

Thank you for agreeing to give me feedback on this tool for evaluating the "First-Class Appraisals" workshop. Please answer the following questions, and feel free to make any other comments that come to mind.

Thanks again!

Simone

Estimate how long it would take you to complete the tool. __________
Do you consider that amount of time to be

_____ acceptable _____ unacceptable

What suggestions or recommendations do you have to make the tool easier to complete?

Please circle any language on the tool that you think could be confusing.

7. Finalize the Evaluation Tools

On all of the evaluation tools, the feedback is basically positive. In response to a few suggestions, Simone decides to do the following:

- Make minor language changes.
- Provide two versions of the e-mail evaluation, because three of the reviewers agreed it was too long.
- Conduct the job-aids survey only by e-mail. Reviewers were concerned that results might be skewed in a phone survey; people might be uncomfortable admitting that they are not using the job aids or that they have not yet started writing the appraisals.

The pilot of "First-Class Appraisals" is scheduled for next week. Using feedback from the pilot, Simone will make her recommendations for changes and then execute them as needed in the training design—not more than a few, she fervently hopes. Simone will also keep in touch with the trainers and with the other members of the evaluation team responsible for evaluations at Levels 3 and 4.

In the meantime, Simone congratulates herself on a job well done. Then the telephone rings. Could it signal the beginning of her next design project? She takes a deep breath, smiles, and picks up the phone.

12 Making the Training Design Shine

After having worked your way through the SIM process, you may be asking, "What else can there be to training design?" In this chapter, we would like to address three particular types of learning activities, often overlooked or tacked on as afterthoughts, that deserve more focused attention than they usually receive. Thoughtfully and creatively integrated with your design, these activities can lend your work a smooth, professional luster, can turn an ordinary training design into one that really shines. We are talking about introductory activities, transitions, and summaries.

The creation of sparkling introductory activities, transitions, and summaries is not really separate from the SIM; it is not something you address anew when your design is finished. Rather, it is an enhancement. With the basic SIM process (Chapters Six through Eleven), you will be able to create perfectly solid training designs. Then, when you are confident with the basics of the SIM, you can apply the principles and tips in this chapter throughout your design work to polish your training designs. Think of this chapter as Advanced Training Design.

In any training design, a good *introductory activity* is a powerful way to engage participants and help them open up to learning while focusing on the topic. Well-designed *transitions* can do much more than merely link learning activities; they can relate segments of the learning to the core reference points. Powerful *summaries* can serve as checkpoints for the trainer and the participants; they can also engage learners in thinking about the value of what has been covered as well as about the application of the learning.

In this chapter, we will help you improve your ability to create shining introductory activities, transitions, and summaries—to make them into powerful elements that will enhance the integrity of your design and make it more polished.

INTRODUCTORY ACTIVITIES

How many times have you participated in a training event that opened with a fun icebreaker that apparently had little or nothing to do with the topic? You may have engaged in a game that was energizing and helped you meet people, and then you were invited (or told) to "settle down to the topic at hand."

We believe that the best introductory activities relate directly to the training topic and support the training objectives. They do more than break the ice. Certainly, there are plenty of predesigned introductory activities that are engaging and fun. But if they are disconnected from the rest of the training, they are not effective or efficient. We prefer introductory activities that grab the participants and begin moving them toward the desired objectives—and that do so without undue cost in time or energy.

Notice that we are phrasing all this in terms of *introductory activities*, not *icebreakers*. Here's why:

- The term *icebreaker* suggests a game that builds energy but is not really a part of the training. Often the disconnect seems to suggest that, although the icebreaker may be fun, the "real" training will not be.
- Thinking in terms of *introductory activities* impels the designer to ask, "Introductory to what?" The "what" is the focus of the training, which is exactly where the designer's attention belongs.

Incidentally, introductory activities that support the topic and objectives are not just for training; they can be used successfully to open meetings, conferences, and retreats as well.

Before we delve into how to make introductory activities powerful parts of training, let's be clear: we have nothing against enjoyable activities that create energy. Certainly there are times in training, particularly during long training events, when the sole purpose of an activity is to create energy or simply to refresh participants. In the afternoon especially, you may need an activity that involves movement, simply to energize participants; you may even choose to give participants some mental as well as kinesthetic relief at that time and just let them play a game. That's fine. We are definitely not saying that these are bad activities; they have a legitimate place in good design. Here, we are talking about introductory activities, which can and should support the training objectives—introductory activities that add value.

Thoroughly integrated introductory activities can create a need to know, assess participants' existing knowledge, or determine participants' comfort level with the topic. They can start participants thinking about content, skills, or what's in it for them to participate in this training or to use the skills presented in the training. The key to integrating an introductory activity successfully is to be very clear about its purpose. As a designer, ask yourself, "What result do I want from this introductory activity?" and "How does that result or outcome relate to the rest of the training?"

A Process for Designing Introductory Activities

The process for designing introductory activities is a focused and reduced version of the SIM. You will establish requirements for the introductory activity, and then you will design it. Although the process is similar to the SIM process, it has a very specialized focus. Because you are designing the first activity of the learning event, you especially want to establish a safe and engaging learning environment and to draw participants' attention quickly to the topic at hand.

OVERVIEW: PROCESS FOR INTRODUCTORY ACTIVITIES

Here is how to create introductory activities:

Establish Requirements

- Key characteristics of participants
- Time
- Purpose
- Content

Design the Activity

- Macrodesign
- Microdesign
- Develop materials

Establish Requirements. As with any design task, start by determining what the requirements are. While you are designing the activity, the requirements are your touchstone.

Key Characteristics of Participants. Before beginning the SIM, you converted needs assessment data into design requirements. Now, using your design requirements, review your participant analysis; identify any of the key characteristics that seem particularly significant for the introductory activity of the training. Such characteristics will probably include number of participants, whether they know one another, any issues that might get in the way of creating a safe learning environment, and the participants' expectations.

Time. If you have a specific time requirement, of course you will work within it. The appropriate time allocations for introductory activities can vary widely, depending on how long the whole training event will be and how the activity will be integrated with the rest of the event.

Purpose. Determine what you want to have happen in the introductory activity. Some introductory activities have a general statement of purpose, such as, "Participants will learn a bit about one another and share insights related to the topic." Others have as their purpose a very specific objective or product, such as, "Participants will create a list of their hopes and concerns regarding this learning event." In order to design the activity, consider whether it will yield a product that will support some other part of the learning event.

Content. Consider what specific content must be included. Content for an introductory activity may include demographic information about participants (name, job, and so on); participants' reflections on the topic (such as objectives, expectations, hopes, or concerns); or essential key content you have identified for the training (participants' reactions to a model or principle, for example).

Design the Activity. After the requirements are clear, you are ready to select, tailor, or design the introductory activity. The process is similar to the Training Flow stage of the SIM—first you macrodesign, then you microdesign.

Begin by generating some possible activities to meet your requirements. Select a likely possibility, and then macrodesign it so that you have enough detail to determine whether it will match your requirements and be an effective, efficient, and engaging way to begin the training. If you are satisfied, then microdesign the activity so that you can make a refined time estimate and describe it in sufficient detail to guide your development of materials. If not, try another one. After the activity is designed, develop any materials you will need for the activity.

Introductory Activity: An Example

As an example, let's look at the requirements and the design for an introductory activity we often use in our workshop on training design.

The Requirements. For any introductory activity, the requirements include pertinent group characteristics, time allotment, purpose, and content desired.

Key Characteristics of Group. There are typically ten to twelve participants, who have varying degrees of experience and who design different kinds of training. People usually have some anxiety; in particular, those who are new to design may fear that they will not be able to do it.

Time. We allow sixty minutes. The training is four days long, so the time is not out of line for an introductory activity that is thoroughly integrated with the training. The activity establishes an environment that is creative and challenging, yet supportive of experimentation; it fosters the sense of a learning community that already has many relevant resources.

Purpose. Participants will share introductory information, create a list of skills they bring to this learning event and those they wish to walk away with, and recognize one another as resources.

Content. In terms of personal information, we want participants' names, where they work, job title, what types of training they design, and how long they have been designing training. In addition, we want to know one tool (a skill or talent) that each of them brings to the task of training design and one thing they would like to improve or develop during the workshop.

Design for the Activity. With those requirements in mind, here is the design for this introductory activity.

In Advance

- Two large wall charts are put up before the training begins. One shows a graphic of a designer's toolbox, the other a designer's wish list.
- At each participant's seat are two large, colored index cards: one headed "Designer's Toolbox," one headed "Designer's Wish List."

TEXT FOR TWO SAMPLE CARDS

Training Designer's Toolbox. Each of us brings gifts to every task we tackle. Think of the gifts as tools you bring to the task of training design. Regardless of your experience, imagine yourself in the role of training designer. Identify one tool you bring to that task, and draw a picture of it (no words, please!) on the other side of this card. Also, print your first name (what you would like to be called) on this card.

Training Designers' Wish List. Each of us brings some areas for development to whatever task we tackle. You bring both your gifts and your limitations to the role of training designer. Regardless of your experience, imagine yourself in the role of training designer. Identify one "tool" you would like to develop or improve during this workshop and draw a picture of that tool (no words, please!) on the other side of this card. Also, print your first name (what you would like to be called) on this card.

- Directions are posted on a "Welcome" flip chart at the front of the room.

As Participants Enter

- Trainer greets everyone, tells each that there are two cards at each seat.
- Trainer asks participants to complete the cards before the training begins.

For the Activity

- Trainer introduces self, posting own two cards and modeling the introduction formula.
- Trainer explains formula for introductions.
- As participants introduce themselves, they post their cards on the appropriate wall chart, to be referred to throughout the three-day training.
- Quick large-group discussion: themes, observations.

This activity yields wonderful results. In the discussion, participants—especially those who are relatively new to design—typically say how good it feels to realize that they do bring gifts to the design process and how reassuring it is to see that others have similar wishes for development. Often, some participants remark on the balance in the group: the particular skills that some participants bring are the very skills that others are looking for. The trainer always suggests that participants consider one another as resources, and participants do use the list of skills as they choose peer consulting groups to review their designs during the workshop. The list also serves as a powerful core reference point for the remainder of the training, allowing the trainer to refer to specific skills as they relate to various stages in the design process.

Introductory Activity: A Critical Factor

Design your introductory activity with care, because it will communicate a great deal to participants about the learning event. The situation in training is much like the challenge to our friend the caterer. She knows that what people see and hear when they enter the room, as well as the first food that is served to them, will go a long way toward making or breaking the event. Those first moments can be awkward or captivating. If your introductory activity is good, the event will begin to sparkle for your participants.

Many wonderful books and other resources are filled with suggestions and plans for introductory activities. Before you begin looking at any of them, be sure to define your requirements—including a clear purpose for the introductory activity. That way, you can analyze potential activities to determine which ones simply are not a good match and which ones could be tailored to fit your requirements.

TRANSITIONS

In the SIM design process, transitions are addressed during the macrodesign and microdesign stages. As the designer, you use transitions to verify the integrity of your design by assessing how one activity flows into the next. You use them to clarify for the trainer the connections you see. In those senses, transitions enable both the designer and the trainer to assist learners in joining one learning activity smoothly to the next. But they can do even more. Well-designed transitions, in addition to linking one learning activity to another, can connect learning activities with core reference points to integrate the training as a whole.

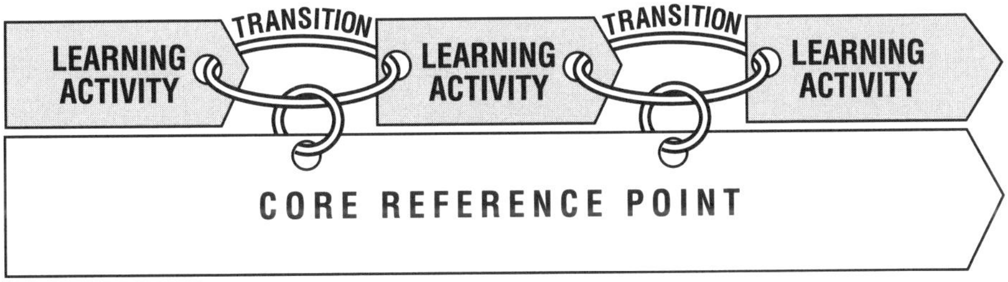

What is a core reference point? It is as simple as the words imply: something that learners can keep going back to, that can connect the various points of the training. For example, a workshop on project management might use the metaphor of a journey into space as its core reference point. Or, in a workshop on supervisory skills, the core reference point might be a case study. During your design process using the SIM, one or more possibilities for core reference points will probably emerge. Your list of objectives is sure to be one of them. You might very well have others, too: desired performance, a conceptual model, the organizational structure you have selected. The core reference points are the source for transitions that make your training shine.

The designer's challenge is to create transitions that increase the effectiveness and efficiency of the training design—and that enhance the participants' ability to engage in the learning as well. Transitions make training more *effective* if they reinforce key learning points and clarify relationships among parts of the training. They make training more *efficient* if they quickly orient participants to the relationships among what they have accomplished so far, what they will do next, and the core reference points—so that participants do not waste time trying to figure out what is going on. Transitions make training especially *engaging* if they are interactive.

Yes, transitions can be interactive—and without taking much training time. As the designer, you can make that happen. Remember that the trainer, under the pressure of the moment, is more likely to use interactive transitions if they are already part of the design. Here are some possibilities for very quick interactive transitions:

- Simply have the trainer ask participants how they think the next topic is related to what they have just covered.
- To relate the learning activities to a core reference point, have the trainer ask participants to reflect on the relationships among what has just been covered, what is next on the agenda, and the core reference point.

To manage time efficiently in training, designers often combine a transition with a summary, to forecast the next segment of learning as they bring closure to the one being completed. For example, at the end of a learning activity, you might have the trainer first ask participants how they might apply their learning on the job; then, after a brief discussion, the trainer would introduce the next segment of the training and ask participants how it might relate to the application examples just generated.

SUMMARIES

In most designs, summaries—whether at the end of a learning segment or at the end of the whole event—are either ignored or left entirely to the trainer's on-the-spot ingenuity. As a result, most trainers are likely to deliver a lecturette reiterating what has just been covered. If the lecturette is done well, it at least highlights some key points related to the objectives, so it has some potential for reinforcing learning. However, because it is a one-way trans-

mission of information, it may fall far short of being effective, efficient, or engaging. In addition, such a summary offers no opportunity for either the trainer or the participants to check for comprehension. If the trainer conducts the summary as a lecturette, all anyone can verify is that the *trainer* knows what has just been covered.

Ways to Focus Summaries

A summary offers a wonderful opportunity not only to check for comprehension but also to engage participants in analyzing how they will apply what they have learned and in otherwise reacting to what has been covered. Such interaction also facilitates comprehension and retention, thereby making the training more effective. Summaries can focus in different ways:

- Key learning points
- Objectives
- Application
- Values, feelings, or beliefs related to what has just been covered
- Core reference points
- Some combination of the above

Key Learning Points. A summary focusing on key learning points might seem to be possible only through lecture. Not necessarily. There are a few different approaches to designing such a summary to make it interactive:

- If you must verify that particular key learning points have actually been conveyed—for example, in a summary following the presentation of a new policy—your design can combine participant input and trainer input.
    - Have participants identify key learning points that they want to remember, and then have the trainer add only the ones not mentioned by participants.
    - Have the trainer list key learning points and ask participants what they remember about each of them.
    - Have the trainer list key learning points and invite participants, individually or in small groups, to create something—an acronym, a song, or a poster—to help them remember the key learning points.

- If the designer and the organization will be comfortable with whatever learning points the participants identify as key to them, then the design can call for the trainer to solicit key learnings from participants. The question can be as simple as "What will you take away with you from this workshop?" or "What seems really important to you from our work here?"

Objectives. Summaries that focus on objectives ask participants to reflect on what they have learned in light of the training objectives. A trainer, left to her own devices, may just review the objectives at the end of the training or the end of a training segment and ask a closed question, such as, "Did we meet the objectives?" Worse, the trainer may simply announce that the participants have met the stated objectives. These approaches do not tell the trainer or the participants much about accomplishing objectives, nor do they reinforce learning in relation to objectives. They are not what we would call effective, efficient, or engaging—but you already knew that!

To take an interactive approach to summarizing by objectives, have the designer refer participants to the objectives and ask some focused questions. Here are some ideas:

- Ask participants to think about and then share one learning related to each objective.
- For each objective, ask participants to identify a specific skill necessary for meeting it.
- Ask participants to describe a performance-related use for each of the objectives.

Application. Summaries focusing on application can readily facilitate the transfer of learning. Sample designs for application-focused summaries include the following:

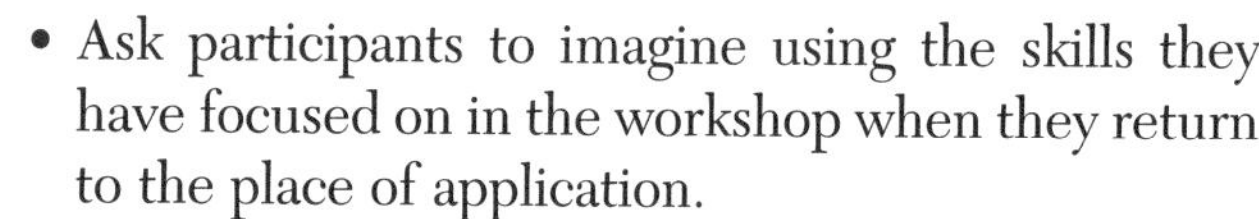

- Ask participants to imagine using the skills they have focused on in the workshop when they return to the place of application.
- Have participants write down some specific advice they want to remember about application.
- Ask participants to create an acronym that will help them remember what they want to apply.
- Have participants create their own job aids to assist them in application.

Values, Feelings, or Beliefs. Consider addressing the affective domain (Chapter Six) in your summaries. Most training does not seem to use it, but we believe it can be very powerful. First, the affective domain can help tap into personal motivation, which is a critical factor in transfer and application. Second, adult learners are independent; they are passing judgment all the time (Chapter Three). You can tap into their judgments to help facilitate comprehension and retention.

Any summary that focuses on values, feelings, or beliefs has an infinite universe of acceptable responses (Chapter Nine) and must be designed so that it does not seem to imply "right answers." One design approach is to supply affective categories and ask participants to record what they remember in those categories, such as the following:

- Things that felt comfortable/uncomfortable to me
- Ideas I am excited about
- What fits easily with what I already do/what will be a stretch for me
- Things I need some more time to think about before I am sure how I feel
- Things that have real meaning for me

Core Reference Points. Often you will be using core reference points throughout your training design in addition to your objectives. Summaries can ask participants to relate specific learnings to a reference point. There are two general approaches:

- Ask participants to name concrete key learnings related to a core reference point.
- Invite participants to develop their own summaries, either individually or in small groups, that articulate how the key learnings relate to a core reference point.

Combination Summaries. Of course, summaries can easily be designed to focus on more than one of the categories. For example, you can ask participants to develop a motto they would like to put on their desks to capture what they want to remember about the workshop or the segment just completed. One participant may choose to focus on application, another on a core reference point, a third on values.

Summaries and the Adult Learner

Taking advantage of how adults learn is a key factor in creating summaries that clarify the training and unite it into a gleaming whole.

Learning Styles. Summaries are a wonderful way to engage your participants by tapping into their natural variety of learning styles. For example, you might design a summary worksheet to include optional categories, so that participants can work with whatever category or categories appeal to them:

- A drawing that will help me remember the key points from this section
- Three things I want to do with what I have learned
- An acronym that helps me remember the learning so that I can apply it
- A word or phrase that captures what this content means to me

Passing Judgment. One of our favorite techniques for creating a basic summary is to post a flip chart with a simple graphic. We invite participants to share something that they knew or believed before the workshop that has been confirmed in the workshop ("Oh Yeah"), something new they learned from the workshop ("Wow"), and one thing from the workshop that they want some time to think about—in terms of either how they feel about it or how they would apply it ("?"). This summary, perfectly simple to design and facilitate, taps into both the cognitive and the affective domains (Chapter Six). It respects the adult learners' need to pass judgment on the material. It also provides the trainer with a wealth of information about what learners remember, what they perceive to be important, and how they feel about the information.

A FEW LAST WORDS

We hope that this chapter stimulates you to think about introductory activities, transitions, and summaries as opportunities to make your good, solid designs really shine.

You can have opening activities that merely break the ice at the beginning of the session, prosaic transitions that laboriously link learning activities, summaries that are dull lecturettes telling participants what they have just done. Or you can have gleaming, seamless training designs that immediately captivate and engage the learners, efficiently and smoothly move them through the learning event, and help them focus effectively on what they have learned. You are the designer. The choice is up to you.

For a moment now, imagine yourself a participant in one of our workshops on training design. We often end by putting up two or three giant wall charts (each made of eight pages of flip-chart paper taped together). In the center of each giant chart we write "Training Request," and then we ask people to work in groups to create mind-maps of everything they remember about the SIM process, moving from the training request to a completed design for the training event. Beyond that, there is only one rule: "no words, only pictures." We play music, and we make lots of colored markers available. After each group has finished, we conduct "museum visits." The full group goes from one exhibit to the next, and everyone tries to figure out each mind-map, asking questions of the creators as they wish.

Not only is the activity a highly interactive way to summarize the workshop, but it also gives participants an opportunity to see what they have learned and to create symbols that once again embed the learning in personally meaningful ways. We are always amazed at what participants create. The graphics are wonderfully colorful and original. More than that, the amount of information that participants are able to remember, the relationships they see among topics, the visual symbols that metaphorically illustrate what the key topics mean to them, and the sheer fun—all make us step back and appreciate the learning that has taken place in the workshop.

This summary brings forth not only the learning that we planned when we designed the learning event; even more exciting is the learning that happens spontaneously whenever adult learners are brought together in a safe and inquiring environment. We wish the same for you.

Appendix: Common Organizational Structures

Many organizational structures are used in training design, and the lines between them are sometimes quite fuzzy. Some of the common organizational structures are outlined below.

Structure	Description	Examples	Advantage	Challenge
Chronological & reverse chronological	Organizes data in terms of time.	Orientation session; training to introduce a new policy in an organization.	Clarifies history and background.	History may not be of much interest to participants.
Process to product & product to process	Highlights the steps one takes in order to produce a product.	Sales, writing, or manufacturing skills.	Reinforces a sequence used when actually performing a task.	Learners may resist a clearly defined process, especially if they have experienced other ways to produce the same product or reach the same end.
Categorical	Organizes the training into categories that are logical and related to the topic.	Systems overviews (why, components of system, how to make requests); communication	Divides the training into components that are easily comprehended and retained.	May not adequately reinforce the relationships among components.

Structure	Description	Examples	Advantage	Challenge
		skills (active listening, initiating, feedback); product training for sales and customer service people (features and benefits).		
Parts to whole & whole to parts	A subtype of categorical organization; relates the component categories to the whole.	Supervisory or management skills (hiring, coaching, delegating); public speaking skills (voice, eye contact, posture, and movement).	Continually relates each component part to the whole behavior being focused on in the training.	A relationship may seem forced if it does not naturally resonate with learners.
Problem to resolution & resolution to problem	Links what is being learned with what problems are being addressed.	New policies; communication skills; stress and time management; technical skills development or enhancement.	Can be used to engage learners by explicitly focusing on problems they experience and feel a need to manage.	For complex skills, such as interpersonal relations, may be difficult to draw a one-to-one relationship between any particular skill and the resolution of a problem. Also, the problem being addressed in the training may be one identified by management but not perceived as a problem by participants.

Structure	Description	Examples	Advantage	Challenge
General to specific & specific to general	Begins with the big picture and then moves to detail, or the reverse.	Strategic planning (from general organizational implications to specific components of the plan); writing skills (specific grammatical rules to general writing tone).	Engages both the concrete and the abstract thinking preferences of participants.	Learners with one preference may be frustrated until the training addresses their interests.
Known to unknown & unknown to known	Explicitly acknowledges the experience participants bring to training and adds to that experience. May begin with an acknowledgment of what is known and introduce new content/skills, or may begin with what is new and fold that into what is already known.	Any type of review; new products for seasoned sales people; interpersonal skills.	Explicit acknowledgment of participants' experiences.	It may highlight discrepancies in participants' experiences.
Theoretical to practical & practical to theoretical	First treats theoretical underpinnings and then moves to application, or vice versa.	Diversity workshop (understand and agree on principles/benefits of proactive diversity management, then move to specific steps	Provides a balance between "how" and "why" in training.	Many participants have clear preferences for theory or practical application. It is difficult to engage both learning preferences for

Structure	Description	Examples	Advantage	Challenge
		for increasing and managing diversity); parenting skills (consideration and practice of skills, followed by analysis of expert theory).		any length of time without continually integrating theory and application.
Simple to complex & complex to simple	Acknowledges that some parts of the training are easier to comprehend or actualize than others. May begin with simpler parts to establish early learner successes, then move to the complex, or may start with the most challenging and move to the simpler components.	Math, computer, interpersonal, analytical skills.	Can either give participants comfort by beginning with early success or create a strong need to know because of the initial challenge.	Keeping the momentum can be difficult. Training may be perceived as too elementary if it begins with the simple.

References and Recommended Reading

American Society for Training and Development. (1990). *ASTD trainer's toolkit: Needs assessment instruments.* Alexandria, VA: Author.

American Society for Training and Development. (1992). *ASTD trainer's toolkit: Evaluating the results of training.* Alexandria, VA: Author.

American Society for Training and Development. (1994). *In action: Measuring return on investment.* Alexandria, VA: Author.

American Society for Training and Development. (1995). *In action: Conducting needs assessment.* Alexandria, VA: Author.

American Society for Training and Development. (1996). *In action: Designing training programs.* Alexandria, VA: Author.

American Society for Training and Development. (1997). *In action: Transferring learning to the workplace.* Alexandria, VA: Author.

Block, P. (1981). *Flawless consulting.* San Francisco: Jossey-Bass/Pfeiffer.

De Bono, E. (1985). *Six thinking hats.* Boston: Little, Brown.

Dhority, L. (1991). *The ACT approach* (2nd ed.). West Germany: PLS.

Gardner, H. (1993). *Multiple intelligences: The theory in practice.* New York: Basic Books.

Gottesman, B. L., & Jennings, J. O. (1994). *Peer coaching for educators.* Lancaster, PA: Technomic.

Herrmann, N. (1995). *The creative brain.* Lake Lure, NC: Ned Herrmann Group.

Kirkpatrick, D. L. (1994). *Evaluating training programs: The four levels.* San Francisco: Berrett-Koehler.

Knowles, M. (1990). *The adult learner: A neglected species* (4th ed.). Houston, TX: Gulf.

Kolb, D. A. (1984). *Experiential learning.* Upper Saddle River, NJ: Prentice Hall.

Merriam, S. B., & Caffarella, R. S. (1991). *Learning in adulthood.* San Francisco: Jossey-Bass.

Nadler, L. (1983). *Designing training programs: The critical events model.* Reading, MA: Addison-Wesley.

Newstrom, J., & Scannell, E. (1989). *Games trainers play.* New York: McGraw-Hill.

Robinson, D. G., & Robinson, J. C. (1995). *Performance consulting: Moving beyond training.* San Francisco: Berrett-Koehler.

Rogers, C. (1969). *Freedom to learn.* Columbus, OH: Merrill.

Rose, C. (1989). *Accelerated learning.* New York: Dell.

Rothwell, W. J., & Kazanas, H. C. (1992). *Mastering the instructional design process: A systematic approach.* San Francisco: Jossey-Bass.

Rylatt, A., & Lohan, K. (1997). *Creating training miracles.* San Francisco: Jossey-Bass/Pfeiffer.

Silberman, M. (1990). *Active training.* San Francisco: Jossey-Bass/Pfeiffer.

Silberman, M. (1992, 1993, 1997). *Twenty active training programs* (Vols. 1–3). San Francisco: Jossey-Bass/Pfeiffer.

Silver, H. F., & Hanson, J. R. (1980, rev. 1994). *A learning style inventory for adults.* Princeton, NJ: Hanson Silver Strong & Associates.

About the Authors

Michael Milano is passionate about training design and facilitation, about creating learning events that help people learn while being affirmed in their competence. Since 1986, he has been president of Murphy & Milano, Inc., a training and organization development company in Alexandria, Virginia; he has been designing and facilitating adult learning events since 1971. Among his clients are large international organizations, such as the United Nations and the World Bank; federal government organizations, including the Department of Commerce and the Library of Congress; companies as well known as W. R. Grace Company and MCI Telecommunications; and not-for-profit groups, ranging from United Way of America to the Gay Men's Chorus of Washington. In the late 1980s, Michael was invited to design courses in training design and in presentation skills for the Training Specialist Certificate Program at Georgetown University, and he is still teaching both courses. He is a member of the American Society for Training and Development and the Association for Psychological Type.

Diane Ullius is principal of Word Tamers, a consulting firm in Arlington, Virginia, that focuses on training and coaching in writing and speaking. Her clients range from Time-Life Inc. and the National Institutes of Health to the Sexual Minority Youth Assistance League. She is also an adjunct professor at Georgetown University. She has previously been published in *Training & Development, The Editorial Eye,* and *The Bookwoman.* She is a member of the Washington, D.C., chapter of the American Society for Training and Development and since 1990 has been a national board member of WNBA, the Women's National Book Association. Diane believes that words are power—that you can take charge of your words and make them do what you want them to do.

Index

D

E

F

G

M

N

O

M

N

O

S

T

U

V

W

Z